PENGUIN BOOKS

INNER WORKINGS

J. M. Coetzee's work includes *Dusklands, In the Heart of the Country, Waiting for the Barbarians, Life & Times of Michael K, Foe, Age of Iron, The Master of Petersburg, Boyhood, Disgrace, Youth, Elizabeth Costello, Slow Man,* and *Diary of a Bad Year.* Coetzee has won many literary awards, including the CNA Prize, South Africa's premier literary award (three times); the Booker Prize (twice); the Prix Etranger Femina; the Jerusalem Prize; the Lannan Literary Award; the *Irish Times* International Fiction Prize; and the Commonwealth Writer's Prize. In 2003, he was awarded the Nobel Prize in Literature. He lives in Australia.

Inner Workings

Literary Essays 2000–2005

J. M. Coetzee

with an Introduction by
Derek Attridge

PENGUIN BOOKS

PENGUIN BOOKS

Published by the Penguin Group
Penguin Group (USA) Inc., 375 Hudson Street, New York, New York 10014, U.S.A.
Penguin Group (Canada), 90 Eglinton Avenue East, Suite 700, Toronto,
Ontario, Canada M4P 2Y3 (a division of Pearson Penguin Canada Inc.)
Penguin Books Ltd, 80 Strand, London WC2R 0RL, England
Penguin Ireland, 25 St Stephen's Green, Dublin 2, Ireland (a division of Penguin Books Ltd)
Penguin Group (Australia), 250 Camberwell Road, Camberwell,
Victoria 3124, Australia (a division of Pearson Australia Group Pty Ltd)
Penguin Books India Pvt Ltd, 11 Community Centre,
Panchsheel Park, New Delhi – 110 017, India
Penguin Group (NZ), 67 Apollo Drive, Rosedale, North Shore 0632,
New Zealand (a division of Pearson New Zealand Ltd)
Penguin Books (South Africa) (Pty) Ltd, 24 Sturdee Avenue,
Rosebank, Johannesburg 2196, South Africa

Penguin Books Ltd, Registered Offices:
80 Strand, London WC2R 0RL, England

First published in the United States of America by Viking Penguin,
a member of Penguin Group (USA) Inc. 2007
Published in Penguin Books 2008

10 9 8 7 6 5 4 3 2 1

Copyright © J. M. Coetzee, 2007
All rights reserved

Page vii constitutes an extension of this copyright page.

Derek Attridge's introduction is published by arrangement with Harvill Secker,
an imprint of The Random House Group, publisher of *Inner Workings* in Great Britain.

THE LIBRARY OF CONGRESS HAS CATALOGED THE HARDCOVER EDITION AS FOLLOWS:
Coetzee, J. M., 1940–
Inner workings : literary essays, 2000–2005 / J. M. Coetzee ; with
an introduction by Derek Attridge.
p.   cm.
Includes bibliographical references (p. 292).
ISBN 978-0-670-03865-7 (hc.)
ISBN 978-0-14-311378-2 (pbk.)
1. Literature—History and criticism.   I. Title.
PR9369.3.C58I66   2007
809—dc22   2006036954

Printed in the United States of America

Contents

Acknowledgements

The essay on Arthur Miller first appeared in *Writers at the Movies*, ed. Jim Shepard (New York: HarperCollins, 2000).

The essay on Robert Musil first appeared as an introduction to *The Confusions of Young Törless*, trans. Shaun Whiteside (London: Penguin, 2001).

The essay on Graham Greene first appeared as an introduction to *Brighton Rock* (New York: Penguin, 2004).

The essay on Samuel Beckett is excerpted from the introduction to volume 4 of *Samuel Beckett: The Grove Centenary Edition* (New York: Grove, 2006).

The essay on Hugo Claus first appeared as an introduction to the paperbound edition of Hugo Claus, *Greetings: Selected Poems*, trans. John Irons (New York: Harcourt, 2006).

All other essays first appeared, in earlier form, in the *New York Review of Books*.

Introduction

Why might one be drawn to read a collection of the book reviews and literary introductions of a writer known above all for his fiction? J. M. Coetzee's novels have won acclaim across the globe; two have been awarded Booker Prizes, and it was for his fiction that he gained the Nobel Prize for Literature in 2003. Some of his books blend fiction and non-fiction, and he has often used a fictional persona – notably an Australian author named Elizabeth Costello – to address issues of current importance. In *Inner Workings*, however, he speaks in his own voice, continuing a prolific career as reviewer and critic that has already seen the publication of three collections of essays.

There are two obvious incentives for turning from the fiction to the critical prose: in the hope that these more direct compositions will throw light on the often oblique novels, and in the belief that a writer who in his imaginative works can penetrate to the heart of so many pressing concerns is bound to have much to offer when writing, so to speak, with the left hand. In particular, there is always an interest in seeing how an author at the forefront of his profession engages with his peers, commenting not as a critic from the outside but as one who works with the same raw materials. There is plenty of evidence that the second expectation is likely to be fulfilled. Coetzee's non-fictional and semi-fictional writing taken as a whole represents a substantial and significant contribution to the continuing discussion of literature's place in the lives of individuals and cultures. The interviews and essays published in *Doubling the Point*, the studies of South African literature and of censorship in *White Writing* and *Giving Offense*, and the 'lessons' of *Elizabeth Costello* explore, among many other topics, the relation of art and politics, the continuity between the aesthetic and the erotic, the responsibilities of the author, and the ethical potential of fiction. That Coetzee's novels and memoirs stage similar issues is testimony to the wholeness and persistence of his understanding of the artist's vocation.

In 2001 Coetzee published *Stranger Shores*, a collection of essays dating from 1986 to 1999, the majority of which were first published in the *New York Review of Books*. He has continued to write regularly for that organ, and the present volume is again largely made up of reviews produced according to its standards, both generous and exacting, together with a selection of other essays, mostly written as introductions to reprinted literary works. Although the chapters in these two books wear the garb of the occasional piece, they continue in another mode Coetzee's investigation of the place and purpose of literature – and, it must be stressed, of its pleasures as well as its challenges. Where the reader of the original reviews was primarily invited to consider them in isolation, the reader of this volume is encouraged to view them in relation to one another.

Most of the chapters that follow offer a portrait of the artist as the context for the specific book or books being discussed, and taken together they illustrate vividly the variety and unpredictability of writers' lives in the twentieth century. (There is one nineteenth-century writer, Walt Whitman, a poet out of his time as well as very much of it.) The first seven – Italo Svevo, Robert Walser, Robert Musil, Walter Benjamin, Bruno Schulz, Joseph Roth, and

Introduction

Sándor Márai – form a closely interrelated cluster: all their subjects were born in Europe in the late 19th century and experienced as young or middle-aged men the upheavals of the First World War, many living through, or into, the Second World War as well. In spite of their different national and ethnic origins (Italian, Swiss, Austrian, German, Polish, Galician, and Hungarian), the different languages they wrote in, and the separate trajectories of their lives, there are discernible connections among them. All felt the need to explore in fiction the passing of the world into which they had been born; all registered the shock waves of the new world that was emerging. Their bourgeois backgrounds did not shield them from the trials of exile, dispossession, and sometimes personal violence. Four were Jews, two of whom died as a result of Nazi persecution. (Among the seven, the exception to this pattern is one of the Jews: Italo Svevo, who remained rooted in Trieste until his death. The different course of his life is to be explained partly by the fact that he died in 1928: as Coetzee tells us, Svevo's widow spent the war years in hiding, and their grandson, who hid with her, was shot by the Nazis in 1945.) What emerges from this group of essays is a Europe in painful transition, and a series of literary works whose originality is seen as the artist's necessary response to far-reaching change. One obvious figure is missing (though he is mentioned in connection with several of these writers): Franz Kafka, whose works seem to sum up in concentrated form many of the passions and plights explored at greater length by these seven authors.

In a second group of writers, we turn from Europe's mid-century crisis to its aftermath. In these studies of Paul Celan, Günter Grass, W. G. Sebald and Hugo Claus it becomes harder to discern a pattern, as both national and individual stories diverge more markedly, although Europe's dark recent history remains a constant reference point.

For the second half of the volume, Coetzee is primarily concerned with works in English. (As he relates in *Boyhood*, he was brought up speaking English as his first language, although his parents were Afrikaans speakers; he is also at home in both Dutch and German, as his comments on works in these languages suggest.) Coetzee's attention is captured by the moral intensities of Graham Greene, the existential intensities of Samuel Beckett, and the homoerotic intensities of Walt Whitman. And the study of Whitman introduces another group, this time of American writers, with a quite different set of creative barriers and opportunities from those of the Europeans. Faulkner's biography, and biographies of Faulkner, are the topic of one chapter, and the story of wasted years spent writing hack Hollywood screenplays seems a far cry from the struggle to write against a background of contending nations. In Saul Bellow's early novels, Henry Miller's and John Huston's film *The Misfits*, and Philip Roth's historical fantasy *The Plot Against America*, we have three more versions of twentieth-century America, warts and all. One senses Coetzee's commitment both to art and to ethics when he offers, at the end of the chapter on *The Misfits*, a telling comment on the difference between the photographic image and the literary representation: the wild horses being rounded up in the movie were *really* traumatized.

Coetzee himself is usually thought of as neither a European nor an American writer: for most of his writing life he has lived in South Africa, and half of his novels take place in that country. He now lives in Australia, and his most recent novel, *Slow Man*, is set in his adopted city, Adelaide. The last three writers in the collection share this non-metropolitan background, and they also share global recognition in the form of the Nobel Prize for Literature: Nadine Gordimer, Gabriel García Márquez, and V. S. Naipaul. Coetzee's focus is on particular novels, rather than the authors' lives: we read these essays not as retrospective appreciation but as an engagement with contemporaries. Coetzee expects his own fiction to be judged by the same exacting standards he applies here to others.

One would not have predicted it if one had read the novels alone, but Coetzee is an ideal reviewer. He seems to have read everything relevant to his subject, often obscure works in an author's oeuvre; he writes with easy familiarity of the historical, cultural, and political background, whether it be the Austro-Hungarian Empire or the American South; he patiently summarizes plots so that busy readers can find out 'what happens' in the most painless way. We have little sense of a moonlighting novelist: there are few literary flourishes, and no sign of that rather grumpy internal voice that has characterised much of Coetzee's recent fiction. (We do, however, sense a profound sympathy with the struggles of the writer to be true to his vocation against all odds.) He doesn't hesitate to make judgements, but he is a generous reader, open to a wide variety of styles and themes.

What of the second reason for reading these essays, for possible illumination of Coetzee's fiction? Is the reader of this book likely to turn back to the novels and find them in any way different? One effect might be a sense of the inadequacy of the label 'South African' (or now 'Australian') writer: Coetzee creates out of a rich dialogue with writers in a number of traditions. In particular, his evident fascination with the European novelists of the first half of the twentieth century suggests that, although he has never lived in continental Europe, he is, if looked at from one angle, a deeply European writer. Equally evident is his absorption in the minutest questions of language: the essays on writers who do not use English are studded with detailed examinations of the translator's art. And, to take an example of a more specific connection, readers of *Boyhood* will be intrigued by the comments on Roth's creation of an autobiographical alter ego in *The Plot Against America*.

However, many readers looking for clues about Coetzee's own practice will be tempted to turn to the only chapter on a South African writer, where they will find an account of Gordimer's 2001 novel *The Pickup*. The question Coetzee poses to Gordimer cannot but be read as a question he has posed to himself: 'What historical role is available to a writer like her born into a late colonial community?' Gordimer was the author of a notorious review of Coetzee's *Life & Times of Michael K* in which she castigated her fellow novelist for his failure to serve the ethical and political needs of the South Africa of that time. Coetzee, who has shown some severity himself in his earlier accounts of Gordimer's work, is generous in recognizing the quest for justice as her consistent overriding principle; and in noting that *The Pickup*, which he calls 'an astonishing book', introduces a new, spiritual note into her work there is a sense that he is welcoming her into a domain he has inhabited, not always comfortably, for some time. For if there are gleams of transcendence in Coetzee's novels, they are not only hints of a possible justice, but of justice animated, as well as tested, by a more obscure demand that the word 'spiritual' can only gesture towards – a demand already adumbrated, from Dostoevsky on, by his formidable European predecessors.

Derek Attridge

I   Italo Svevo

A MAN – A very big man beside whom you feel very small – invites you to meet his daughters with an eye to choosing one to marry. There are four of them, their names all beginning with A; your name begins with Z. You call on them at home and try to make polite conversation, but insults come tumbling out of your mouth. You find yourself telling risqué jokes; your jokes are met with frosty silence. In the dark you whisper seductive words to the prettiest A; when the lights come on you find you have been wooing the A with the squint. You lean nonchalantly on your umbrella; the umbrella snaps in two; everyone laughs.

It sounds, if not like a nightmare, then like one of those dreams that, in the hands of a skilled Viennese dream-interpreter, Sigmund Freud for instance, will reveal all kinds of embarrassing things about you. But it is not a dream. It is a day in the life of Zeno Cosini, hero of *La coscienza di Zeno*, a novel by Italo Svevo (1861–1928). If Svevo is a Freudian novelist, is he Freudian in the sense that he shows how the lives of ordinary people are filled with slips and parapraxes and symbols; or in the sense that, using *The Interpretation of Dreams* and *Jokes and their Relation to the Unconscious* and *The Psychopathology of Everyday Life* as sources, he concocts a character whose inner life runs on textbook Freudian lines? Or is it possible that both Freud and Svevo belong to an age when pipes and cigars and purses and umbrellas seemed pregnant with secret meaning, whereas to the present age a pipe is just a pipe?

'Italo Svevo' (Italo the Swabian) is of course a pseudonym. Svevo was born Aron Ettore Schmitz. His paternal grandfather was a Jew from Hungary who had settled in Trieste. His father began as a pedlar and ended as a successful glassware merchant; his mother was from a Triestine Jewish family. The Schmitzes were observant Jews, but of an easygoing kind. Aron Ettore married a Catholic convert, and under pressure from her converted too (half-heartedly, it must be said). The autobiographical sketch issued under his name late in life, when Trieste had become part of Italy and Italy had become Fascist, is evasive about his Jewish, non-Italian antecedents. His wife Livia's memoir of him – somewhat hagiographic in tendency, though thoroughly readable – is similarly discreet.[1] In his own writings there are no overtly Jewish characters or themes.

Svevo's father – a dominant influence on his life – sent his sons to a commercial boarding school in Germany, where in his spare hours Svevo immersed himself in the German Romantics. Whatever advantage his German schooling was to give him as man of affairs in Austro-Hungary, it deprived him of a training in literary Italian.

Back home in Trieste, aged seventeen, Svevo was enrolled at the Instituto Superiore Commerciale. Dreams of becoming an actor ended when he was turned down at an audition because of his faulty Italian elocution.

In 1880 Schmitz senior suffered financial reverses and his son had to break off his studies. He took a job with the Trieste branch of Unionbank of Vienna and for the next nineteen years worked there as a clerk. Outside office hours he read the Italian classics and the wider European avant-garde. Zola became his idol. He frequented artistic salons and wrote for a newspaper with Italian nationalist leanings.

In his mid-thirties, having tasted what it was like to publish a novel (*Una vita,* 1892) at his own expense and be ignored by the critics, and on the point of repeating the experience with *Senilità* (1898), Svevo married into the prominent Veneziani family, owners of a plant where ships' hulls were painted with a patented compound that slowed down corrosion and prevented the growth of barnacles. Svevo joined the firm, where he supervised the mixing of the paint from its secret recipe and took charge of the workforce.

The Venezianis already had contracts with a number of the world's navies. When the British Admiralty indicated its interest, they opened a branch in London, which Svevo oversaw. To improve his English he took lessons from an Irishman named James Joyce who taught at the Berlitz school in Trieste. With the failure of *Senilità* Svevo had given up serious writing. Now, in his teacher, he found someone who liked his books and understood what he was up to. Heartened, he pressed on with what he called his scribbling, though he did not publish again until the 1920s.

Overwhelmingly Italian in culture, the Trieste of Svevo's day was nevertheless part of the Habsburg Empire. It was a prosperous city, the principal seaport for Vienna, with an enlightened middle class running an economy based on shipping, insurance, and finance. Immigration had brought in Greeks, Germans, and Jews; menial work was done by Slovenes and Croats. In its heterogeneity Trieste was a microcosm of an ethnically various empire that was having more and more trouble keeping a lid on inter-ethnic resentments. When these burst out in 1914, the empire was plunged into war, and Europe along with it.

Though they looked to Florence for their lead in cultural matters, Triestine intellectuals tended to be more open to currents from the north than their Italian counterparts. In Svevo's case, first

Schopenhauer and Darwin, then later Freud stand out as philosophical influences.

Like any good bourgeois of his time, Svevo fretted about his health: what constituted good health, how was it to be acquired, how maintained? In his writings health comes to take on a range of meanings, from the physical and psychic to the social and ethical. Where does the discontented feeling come from, unique to mankind, that we are not well, and what is it that we desire to be cured of? Is cure possible? If cure entails making our peace with the way things are, is it necessarily a good thing to be cured?

In Svevo's eyes, Schopenhauer was the first philosopher to treat those afflicted with the handicap of reflective thought as a separate species, coexisting warily with healthy, unreflective types, who in Darwinian jargon might be called the fit. With Darwin – read through a Schopenhauerian lens – Svevo carried on a dogged life-long tussle. His first novel was to have carried a Darwinian allusion in its title: *Un inetto*, the inept or ill-adapted one. But his publisher baulked, and he settled for the rather colourless *Una vita*. In exemplary naturalistic fashion, the book follows the history of a young bank clerk who, when at last he has to face the fact that he is vacant of all drive, desire, or ambition, does the correct evolutionary thing and commits suicide.

In a later essay entitled 'Man and Darwinian Theory', Svevo gives Darwin a more optimistic slant, one that carries over into *Zeno*. Our sense of not being at home in the world, he suggests, results from a certain unfinishedness in human evolution. To escape this melancholy condition, some try to adapt to their environment. Others prefer not to adapt. The unadapted may look from the outside like nature's rejects, yet paradoxically they may prove better fitted than their well-adjusted neighbours to whatever the unpredictable future may bring.

*

Svevo's home language was Triestine, a variant of the Venetian dialect. To be a writer he needed to master literary Italian, which is based on Tuscan. He never achieved this hoped-for mastery. To compound his problems, he had little feel for the aesthetic qualities of language and in particular no ear for poetry. To his friend the young poet Eugenio Montale he joked that it seemed a pity to use only part of the blank page when you had paid for the whole of it. P. N. Furbank, one of Svevo's better translators, labels his prose 'a kind of "business" Italian, almost an esperanto – a bastard and graceless language totally without poetry or resonance.'[2] When it first came out, *Una vita* was criticised for its grammatical errors, for its unwitting dialectal usages, and for the general poverty of its prose. Much the same was said of *Senilità*. When he had become famous and *Senilità* was to be reissued, Svevo agreed to check the text and fix up the Italian, but did so in only a desultory way. Privately he seems to have doubted mere editing would achieve anything.

To a degree the controversy about Svevo's command of Italian can be ignored as a matter for Italians only, irrelevant to outsiders who read him in translation. For the translator, however, Svevo's Italian raises a substantial question of principle. Should its defects, which run the gamut from wrong prepositions to archaic or bookish turns of phrase to a general labouredness of style, be reproduced or silently improved? Or, to put the question in converse form, how, without writing a deliberately clotted prose, does the translator get across what Montale calls the sclerosis of Svevo's world, seeping up from his very language?

Svevo was not unaware of the problem. His advice to the German translator of *Zeno* was to translate his Italian into grammatically correct German but not beautify or improve it.

Svevo disparaged Triestine as a *dialettaccio*, a petty dialect, or a *linguetta*, a sub-language, but he was not being sincere. Much more from the heart is Zeno's lament that outsiders 'don't know what it entails for those of us who speak dialect [*il dialetto*] to write in Italian . . . With every Tuscan word of ours, we lie!'[3] Here Svevo treats the step from the one dialect to the other, from the Triestine in which he thought to the Italian in which he wrote, as inherently treacherous (*traditore traduttore*). Only in Triestine could he tell the truth. The question for non-Italians as well as Italians to ponder is whether there might have been Triestine truths that Svevo felt he could never get down on the Italian page.

Senilità grew out of an affair Svevo had in 1891–92 with a young woman of, as one of his commentators delicately puts it, indeterminate profession, later to become a circus equestrienne. In the book the girl is named Angiolina. Emilio Brentani has an idea of Angiolina as an innocent whom he will instruct in the finer aspects of life, while in return she will devote herself to his wellbeing. But it is Angiolina who in practice dishes out the lessons; and the induction she provides for Emilio into the evasions and squalors of erotic life would be well worth the money he forks out, were he not too wrapped up in self-deceiving fantasy to absorb it. Years after Angiolina has run off with a bank clerk, Emilio will look back on his time with her through a rosy haze (Joyce learned by heart the wonderful last pages of the book, bathed as they are in romantic cliché and ruthless irony, and recited them back to Svevo). The truth is that the affair has been senile through and through, in Svevo's unique sense of the word: not youthful and vital at all, but on the contrary lived from the beginning through the medium of the self-regarding lie.

In *Senilità*, self-deception is a willed yet unrecognised state of being. The fiction Emilio constructs for himself about who he is and who Angiolina is and what they are doing together is threatened by the fact that Angiolina sleeps promiscuously with other men and is too incompetent or too indifferent or perhaps too malicious to conceal it. Along with *The Kreutzer Sonata* and *Swann's Way*, *Senilità* is one of the great novels of male sexual jealousy, exploiting the technical repertoire bequeathed by Flaubert to his successors to enter and leave a character's consciousness with a minimum of obtrusiveness and to express judgements without seeming to do so. Svevo's exploration of Emilio's relations with his rivals is particularly keen-sighted. Emilio both wants and does not want his male friends to make a play for his mistress; the more clearly he is able to visualise Angiolina with another man, the more intensely he desires her, to the point that he desires her *because* she has been with another man. (The eddying of homosexual currents within the triangle of jealousy was of course pointed out by Freud, but only years after Tolstoy and Svevo had done so.)

The standard English translations of *Senilità* and *Zeno* hitherto have been by Beryl de Zoete, an Englishwoman of Dutch descent and Bloomsbury connections whose main claim to fame is as a pioneering student of Balinese dance. In the introduction to his new translation of *Zeno*, William Weaver discusses De Zoete's versions and suggests, as gently as can be, that the time may have come to retire them.

De Zoete's 1932 translation of *Senilità* under the title *As a Man Grows Older* is particularly dated. *Senilità* is very much about sex: sex as a weapon in the battle between the sexes, sex as a commodity to be traded. Though his language is never improper, Svevo does not pussyfoot around this subject. De Zoete's rendering is too decorous. For instance, Emilio broods on the sexual doings of Angiolina, imagining her leaving the bed of the rich but repulsive Volpini and, in order to rid herself of the *infamia* (disgrace, but also horror) of his touch, plunging straight into bed with someone else. Svevo's phrasing is barely metaphorical: by a second act of sex Angiolina will be trying to wash (*nettarsi*) traces of Volpini off herself. De Zoete delicately passes over the self-cleansing: Angiolina goes 'in search of a refuge from such an infamous embrace'.[4]

Elsewhere De Zoete simply elides or synopsises passages that – rightly or wrongly – she decides do not contribute to the sense, or are too colloquial to get across in English. She also overinterprets, filling in what she *thinks* is going on between the characters where the text itself is silent. The commercial metaphors that characterise Emilio's relations with women are sometimes missed. On one occasion De Zoete gets the sense calamitously wrong, attributing to Emilio a decision to force himself sexually on Angiolina (possess her), whereas all he intends is to clear up the question of who owns her (possesses her).

The new translation of *Senilità* by Beth Archer Brombert is a marked improvement. Unerringly she picks up the submerged metaphors that De Zoete passes over. Her English, though firmly of the late twentieth century, has a formality that reflects an earlier era. If there is one criticism to be made, it is that in an effort to be up to date she uses expressions that are likely to age quite rapidly: 'the bottom line'; to 'be there for someone'; to be 'all excited'.[5]

Svevo's titles have always been a headache for his translators and publishers. As a title, *A Life* (*Una vita*) is simply dull. On Joyce's recommendation, *Senilità* first appeared in English under the title *As a Man Grows Older*, though it is not at all about growing older. Brombert reverts to an earlier working title, *Emilio's Carnival*, despite the fact that for the revised Italian edition Svevo refused to let go of *Senilità*: 'I would feel I were mutilating the book . . . That title was my guide and I lived by it.'[6]

Svevo's writing career stretches over four turbulent decades in Trieste's history, yet strikingly little of this history is reflected, whether directly or indirectly, in his fiction. From the first two books, set in the Trieste of the 1890s, one would never guess that Trieste's Italian middle class was in the grip of Risorgimento-like fervour for union with the motherland. And though Zeno's confession purports to be a document written during the 1914–18 war, the war casts no shadow over it until the last pages.

Through contracts with the government in Vienna, the Veneziani family made a great deal of money out of the war. At the same time they presented themselves at home as passionate Italian irredentists. John Gatt-Rutter, Svevo's biographer, calls this 'a hypocritical sham' and finds that Svevo himself at the very least played along with the sham. Gatt-Rutter is highly critical of Svevo's politics during the war and after the Fascist takeover of 1922. Like many upper-class Triestines, the Venezianis supported Mussolini. Svevo himself seems to have accommodated the new regime in what Gatt-Rutter calls 'perfect bad faith', on the grounds that Fascism was a lesser evil than Bolshevism. In 1925, in the person of Ettore Schmitz, he accepted a minor award from the state for his services to industry. While he never became a card-carrying Fascist, he did as an industrialist belong to the Fascist Confederation of Industrialists. His wife was an active member of the women's Fascio.[7]

If he was morally compromised by his association with the Venezianis, Svevo/Schmitz at least did not, to judge from his writing, hide this from himself. Consider the old man in the story 'The Nice Old Man and the Pretty Girl', written in 1926 but set during the war: 'Every sign of the war that struck [him] reminded him, with a pang, that, thanks to it, he was making so much money. The war brought him wealth and humiliation . . . He had long grown accustomed to the remorse caused by his business success and he went on making money in spite of his remorse.'[8]

The moral atmosphere in this late piece may be darker, and

the self-criticism more mordant, than we get in the essentially comic *Zeno*, but it is only a matter of degrees of darkness or mordancy. From Socrates to Freud, Western ethical philosophy has subscribed to the Delphic *Know yourself*. But what good does it do to know yourself if, taking your lead from Schopenhauer, you believe that character is founded on a substratum of will, and doubt that the will wants to change?

Zeno Cosini, the hero of Svevo's third novel and the masterpiece of his maturity, is a middle-aged man, comfortably married, prosperous, idle, drawing an income from the business founded by his father. On a whim, to see if he can be cured of whatever it is that is wrong with him, he embarks on a course of psychoanalysis. As a preliminary his therapist, Dr S, asks him to write down his memories as these occur to him. Zeno obeys in five story-length chapters whose subjects are: smoking; the death of his father; his courtship; one of his love affairs; one of his business partnerships.

Disappointed in Dr S, whom he finds obtuse and dogmatic, Zeno stops keeping appointments. To compensate himself for lost fees, Dr S publishes Zeno's manuscript. Hence the book we have before us: Zeno's memoir plus the frame story of how it came to be, 'an autobiography, but not my own', as Svevo put it in a letter to Montale. Svevo goes on to explain how he dreamed up adventures for Zeno, planted them in his own past, then, deliberately eliding the line between fantasy and memory, 'remembered' them.[9]

Zeno is a chainsmoker who wants to give up smoking, though not strongly enough to actually do so. He does not doubt that smoking is bad for him, he longs for fresh air in his lungs – the three great death scenes in Svevo, one in each novel, feature people who gasp and strain terrifyingly for breath as they die – yet he rebels against the cure. To give up cigarettes, he knows at some instinctive level, is to concede victory to people like his wife and

Dr S, who, with the best of intentions, will turn him into an ordinary, healthy citizen and thereby rob him of cherished powers: the power of thinking, the power of writing. With a symbolism so crude that even Zeno has to laugh at it, cigarette, pen, and phallus come to stand for one another. The story 'The Nice Old Man and the Pretty Girl' ends with the old man dead at his writing-desk, a pen clenched between his teeth.

To say that Zeno is ambivalent about smoking and therefore about being cured of his undefined malady is barely to scratch the surface of Svevo's corrosive yet curiously gay scepticism about whether we can improve ourselves. Zeno is dubious about the therapeutic claims of psychoanalysis as he is dubious about the notion of cure itself; yet who would dare say that the paradox he comes to embrace by the end of his story – that so-called sickness is part of the human condition, that true health consists in embracing what you are ('Unlike other diseases, life . . . admits of no cure') – does not itself invite sceptical, Zenonian interrogation?[10]

Psychoanalysis was somewhat of a craze in Trieste at the time when Svevo was working on *Zeno*. Gatt-Rutter quotes a Triestine schoolteacher: 'Fanatical adherents of psychoanalysis . . . were continually swapping stories and interpretations of dreams and telltale slips, carrying out amateur diagnoses of their own.' (p. 306) Svevo himself collaborated on a translation of Freud's *On Dreams*. Despite appearances, he did not consider *Zeno* to be an attack on psychoanalysis as such, merely on its curative claims. In his view he was not a disciple of Freud's but a peer, a fellow researcher into the unconscious and the grip of the unconscious on conscious life; he took his book to be true to the sceptical spirit of psychoanalysis, as practised by Freud himself if not by his followers, and even sent Freud a copy (it was not acknowledged). And indeed, in the larger picture, *Zeno* is not just an application of psychoanalysis to a fictional life, or just a comic interrogation of psychoanalysis, but an exploration of the passions, including such meaner passions as greed and envy and jealousy, in the tradition of the European novel, passions to which psychoanalysis proves only a very partial guide. The sickness of which Zeno does and does not want to be cured is in the end no less than the *mal du siècle* of Europe itself, a civilisational crisis to which both Freudian theory and *La coscienza di Zeno* are responses.

La coscienza di Zeno is another of Svevo's difficult titles. *Coscienza* can mean modern English conscience; it can also mean self-consciousness, as in Hamlet's 'Conscience does make cowards of us all.' In the book Svevo glides continually from one sense to the other in a way that modern English cannot imitate. Evading the problem, De Zoete entitled her 1930 translation *Confessions of Zeno*. For his new translation, William Weaver gives up on ambiguity and settles for *Zeno's Conscience*.

Weaver has published translations of, among other Italian writers, Luigi Pirandello, Carlo Emilio Gadda, Elsa Morante, Italo Calvino, and Umberto Eco. His translation of *Zeno* into appropriately unobtrusive, low-key English prose is of the highest standard. In one detail, however, the English language lets him down. Zeno makes a great deal of play on the *malato immaginario* versus the *sano immaginario*, rendered by Weaver as the 'imaginary sick man' and the 'imaginary healthy man'. (pp. 171, 176; chapter 6 of the original) But *immaginario* here is not, strictly speaking, 'imaginary' but 'self-imaginedly', and a *malato immaginario* is not, strictly speaking, an imaginary sick man but a man who imagines himself sick.

Zeno's *malato immaginario* is from the same stable as Molière's *malade imaginaire*, and it is Molière whom Zeno's wife clearly has in mind when, having listened to him going on and on about his ailments, she bursts into laughter and tells him he is nothing but a *malato immaginario*. By invoking Molière rather than more up-to-date theorists of the psyche, she in effect attributes her husband's ailments to a predisposition of character. Her intervention sets off Zeno and his friends on a pages-long discussion of the phenomenon of the *malato immaginario* versus the *malato reale* or *malato vero*: may a sickness born of the imagination not be more serious than one that is 'real' or 'true', even though it is not genuine? Zeno takes the inquiry a step further when he asks whether, in our age, the sickest of all may not be the *sano immaginario*, the man who imagines himself healthy.

The entire disquisition is carried on with a great deal more point and wit in Svevo's Italian than is possible in circumlocutory English. De Zoete is a step ahead of Weaver here in giving up on English and resorting to French: *malade imaginaire* for *malato immaginario*.

Published at Svevo's own expense in 1923, when he was sixty-two, *Zeno* was reviewed here and there, but in no case by a leader of critical opinion. One Triestine reviewer said he was put under pressure to ignore the book, since whatever else it might or might not be, it was clearly an insult to the city.

For old times' sake, Svevo sent a copy to Joyce in Paris. Joyce showed it to Valery Larbaud and other influential figures on the French scene. Their response was enthusiastic. Gallimard commissioned a translation, though on condition that cuts were made; a literary journal ran a Svevo issue; PEN hosted a banquet for Svevo in Paris.

In Milan an appreciative overview of Svevo's work appeared, signed by Montale. *Senilità* was reissued in its revised form. Italians began to read Svevo widely; a younger generation of novelists adopted him as a godfather. The right reacted with hostility. 'In real life Italo Svevo bears a Semitic name – Ettore Schmitz,' wrote *La Sera*, and suggested the Svevo craze was part of an all-embracing Jewish plot.[11]

Buoyed by the unexpected success of *Zeno*, revelling in his newfound fame, Svevo set to work on a number of pieces whose common theme is the ageing self with its unquenched appetites. These may or may not have been intended to fit into a fourth novel, a sequel to *Zeno*. They can be found, in translations by P. N. Furbank and others, in volumes 4 and 5 of the five-volume uniform edition of Svevo's writings published in the 1960s by the University of California Press in the USA and by Secker & Warburg in the UK but now out of print. It is time for a reissue.

Volume 5 also contains a translation of the late play *Regeneration*. Svevo never lost his interest in the theatre and wrote numerous plays over the years, even when working for the Venezianis. Only one, *The Broken Triangle*, was staged during his lifetime.

Svevo died in 1928 from complications after a minor automobile accident. He was buried in the Catholic cemetery of Trieste under the name Aron Hector Schmitz. Livia Veneziani Svevo, reclassified as a Jew, spent the war years, along with the Svevos' daughter and the daughter's third son, hiding out from the purification squads. This third son was shot by the Germans during the Triestine uprising of 1945. The other two sons had by that time perished on the Russian front, fighting for Italy and the Axis.

(2002)

2 Robert Walser

ON CHRISTMAS DAY, 1956, police in the town of Herisau in eastern Switzerland received a call: children had stumbled upon the body of a man frozen to death in a snowy field. Arriving at the scene, the police first took photographs, then removed the body.

The deceased was soon identified: he was Robert Walser, aged seventy-eight, missing from a local mental hospital. In his earlier years Walser had won somewhat of a reputation, in Switzerland and in Germany too, as a writer. Certain of his books were still in print; someone had even published a book about him, a biography. During a quarter of a century spent in mental institutions, however, his own writing had dried up. Long country walks – like the one on which he had perished – had become his main recreation.

The police photographs showed an old man in overcoat and boots lying sprawled in the snow, his eyes wide open, his jaw slack. These photographs have been widely (and shamelessly) reproduced in the critical literature on Walser that has burgeoned since the 1960s.[1] Walser's so-called madness, his lonely death, and the posthumously discovered cache of secret writings became the pillars on which a legend of Walser as a scandalously neglected genius was erected. Even the sudden growth of interest in Walser became part of the scandal. 'I ask myself,' wrote Elias Canetti in 1973, 'whether, among those who build their leisurely, secure, dead regular academic life on that of a writer who had lived in misery and despair, there is a single one who is ashamed of himself.'[2]

Robert Walser was born in 1878 in the canton of Bern, the seventh of eight children. His father, trained as a bookbinder, ran a store selling stationery. At the age of fourteen Robert was taken out of school and apprenticed to a bank, where he performed his clerical functions in exemplary fashion until without warning, possessed by a dream of becoming an actor, he decamped and ran off to Stuttgart. There he did an audition, which proved a humiliating failure: he was rejected as too wooden, too expressionless. Abandoning his stage ambitions, he determined to become – 'God willing' – a poet.[3] He drifted from job to job, writing poems, prose sketches, and little verse plays ('dramolets') for the periodical press, not without success. Soon he was taken up by Insel Verlag, publisher of Rilke and Hofmannsthal, who put out his first book.

In 1905, with the aim of advancing his literary career, he followed his elder brother, a successful book illustrator and stage designer, to Berlin. As a prudent measure he also enrolled in a training school for servants and worked briefly as a butler in a country house, where he wore livery and answered to the name 'Monsieur Robert'. Before long, however, he found he could support himself on the proceeds of his writing. His work began to appear in prestigious literary magazines; he was welcomed in serious artistic circles. But the role of metropolitan intellectual was not one to which he found it easy to conform. After a few drinks he tended to become rude and aggressively provincial. Gradually he retreated from society to a solitary, frugal life in bedsitters. In these surroundings he wrote four novels, of which three have survived: *Geschwister Tanner* (The Tanner Children, 1906), *Der Gehülfe* (The Factotum, 1908), and *Jakob von Gunten* (1909). All draw for their material on his own experiences; but in the case of *Jakob von Gunten* – the best known of the three, and deservedly so – that experience is wondrously transmuted.

'One learns very little here,' observes young Jakob von Gunten after his first day at the Benjamenta Institute, where he has enrolled himself as a student. There is only one textbook, *What is the Aim of Benjamenta's Boys' School?*, and only one lesson, 'How Should a Boy Behave?' The teachers lie around like dead men. All the actual teaching is done by Fräulein Lisa Benjamenta, sister of the principal. Herr Benjamenta himself sits in his office counting his money, like an ogre in a fairy tale. In fact, the school seems a bit of a swindle.[4]

Nevertheless, having run away from what he calls 'a very very small metropolis' to the big city – not named but clearly Berlin – Jakob has no intention of retreating. He gets on with his fellow students; he does not mind wearing the Benjamenta uniform; and besides, going downtown to ride the elevators gives him a thrill, makes him feel thoroughly a child of the modern age. (p. 40)

Jakob von Gunten purports to be a diary that Jakob keeps during his stay at the Institute. It consists mainly of his reflections on the kind of education he receives there – an education in humility – and on the strange brother and sister who offer it. The humility taught by the Benjamentas is not of the religious variety. Most of their graduates aspire to be serving men or butlers, not saints. But Jakob is a special case, a pupil for whom lessons in humility have an added inner resonance. 'How fortunate I am,' he writes, 'not to be able to see in myself anything worth respecting and watching! To be small and to stay small.' (p. 155)

The Benjamentas are a mysterious and, on first acquaintance, forbidding pair. Jakob takes it as his task to penetrate their mystery. He treats them not with respect but with the cheeky self-assurance of a child who is used to having his mischief-making excused as cute. He mixes effrontery with patently insincere self-abasement, giggling at his own insincerity, confident that candour will disarm all criticism, and not really caring if it does not. The word he would like to apply to himself, the word he would like the world to apply to him, is *impish*. An imp is a mischievous sprite; but an imp is also a lesser devil.

Soon Jakob begins to gain ascendancy over the Benjamentas. Fräulein Benjamenta hints that she has become fond of him. He pretends not to understand. In fact, she discloses, what she feels for him is perhaps more than fondness, is perhaps love. Jakob replies with a long, evasive speech full of respectful sentiments. Thwarted, Fräulein Benjamenta pines away and dies.

As for Herr Benjamenta, once hostile to Jakob, he is soon manoeuvred to the point of pleading with the boy to be his friend, to leave the school behind and come wandering the world with him. Primly Jakob declines: 'But how shall I eat, Principal? . . . It's your duty to find me a decent job. All I want is a job.' Yet on the last page of his diary he announces he is changing his mind: he will throw away his pen and go off into the wilderness with Herr Benjamenta. To which one can only respond: With such a companion, God save Herr Benjamenta! (p. 172)

As a literary character, Jakob von Gunten is not without precedent. In the pleasure he takes in picking away at his own motives he reminds one of Dostoevsky's Underground Man and, behind him, of the Jean-Jacques Rousseau of the *Confessions*. But – as Walser's first French translator, Marthe Robert, pointed out – there is in Jakob too something of the hero of the traditional German folk tale, of the lad who confronts the giant in his castle and emerges victorious. Franz Kafka admired Walser's work (Max Brod records with what delight Kafka would read aloud Walser's humourous sketches). Barnabas and Jeremias, Surveyor K.'s demonically obstructive 'assistants' in *The Castle*, have Jakob as their prototype.

In Kafka one also catches echoes of Walser's prose, with its lucid syntactic layout, its casual juxtapositions of the elevated with the banal, and its eerily convincing logic of paradox. Here is Jakob in reflective mood:

> We wear uniforms. Now, the wearing of uniforms simultaneously humiliates and exalts us. We look like unfree people, and that is possibly a disgrace, but we also look nice in our uniforms, and that sets us apart from the deep disgrace of those people who walk around in their very own clothes but in torn and dirty ones. To me, for instance, wearing a uniform is very pleasant because I never did know, before, what clothes to put on. But in this, too, I am a mystery to myself for the time being. (p. 4)

What is the mystery in or about himself that Jakob finds so intriguing? In an essay on Walser that is all the more striking for being based on a very incomplete acquaintance with his writings, Walter Benjamin suggests that Walser's people are like characters from a fairy-tale that has come to an end, characters who must from now on live in the real world. They are marked by 'a consistently heartrending, inhuman superficiality', as if, having been rescued from madness (or from a spell), they must tread carefully for fear of being swallowed back into it.[5]

Jakob is such an odd being, and the air he breathes in the Benjamenta Institute is so rare, so near to the allegorical, that it is hard to think of him as representative of any element of society. Yet Jakob's cynicism about civilisation and about values in general, his contempt for the life of the mind, his simplistic beliefs about how the world really works (it is run by big business to exploit the little man), his elevation of obedience to the highest of virtues, his readiness to bide his time, awaiting the call of destiny, his claim to be of noble, martial descent (whereas the etymology he himself hints at for the name von Gunten – *von unten*, 'from below' – suggests otherwise), as well as his pleasure in the all-male ambience of the boarding school and his delight in malicious pranks – all of these features, taken together, point toward the type of petit-bourgeois male who, in a time of greater social confusion, would find Hitler's Brownshirts attractive. (p. 124)

Walser was never an overtly political writer. Nevertheless, his emotional involvement with the class from which he came, the class of shopkeepers and clerks and schoolteachers, ran deep. Berlin offered him a clear chance to escape his social origins, to defect, as his brother had done, to the *declassé* cosmopolitan intelligentsia. He tried that route and failed, or gave up on it, choosing instead to return to the embrace of provincial Switzerland. Yet he never lost sight of – indeed, was not allowed to lose sight of – the illiberal, conformist tendencies of his class, its intolerance of people like himself, dreamers and vagabonds.

In 1913 Walser left Berlin and returned to Switzerland 'a ridiculed and unsuccessful author' (his own self-disparaging words).[6] He took a room in a temperance hotel in the industrial town of Biel, near his sister, and for the next seven years earned a precarious living contributing sketches to the literary supplements. Otherwise he went on long country hikes and served out his obligations in the National Guard. In the collections of his poetry and short prose that continued to appear, he turned more and more to the Swiss social and natural landscape. Besides the three novels mentioned above, he wrote two more. The manuscript of the first, *Theodor*, was lost by his publishers; the second, *Tobold*, was destroyed by Walser himself.

After the World War, the taste among the public for the kind of writing Walser had relied on for an income, writing easily dismissed as whimsical and belletristic, waned. He was too cut off from wider German society to keep abreast of new currents of thought; as for Switzerland, the reading public there was too small to support a corps of writers. Though he prided himself on his frugality, he had to close down what he called his 'little prose-piece workshop'.[7] His precarious mental balance began to waver. He felt more and more oppressed by the censorious gaze of his neighbours, by their demand for respectability. He quit Biel in favour of Bern, where he took up a position in the national archives; but within months he was dismissed for insubordination. He moved from lodgings to lodgings. He drank heavily; he suffered from insomnia, heard imaginary voices, had nightmares and anxiety attacks. He attempted suicide, failing because, as he disarmingly admitted, 'I couldn't even make a proper noose.'[8]

It was clear that he could no longer live alone. He came from a family that was, in the terminology of the times, tainted: his mother had been a chronic depressive; one brother had committed suicide; another had died in a mental hospital. Pressure was put on a sister to take him in, but she was unwilling. So he allowed himself to be committed to the sanatorium in Waldau. 'Markedly depressed and severely inhibited,' ran the initial medical report. 'Responded evasively to questions about being sick of life.'[9]

In later evaluations Walser's doctors would disagree about what, if anything, was wrong with him, and would even urge him to try living outside again. However, the bedrock of institutional routine would appear to have become indispensable to him, and he chose to stay. In 1933 his family had him transferred to the asylum in Herisau, where he was entitled to welfare support. There he occupied his time in chores like gluing paper bags and sorting beans. He remained in full possession of his faculties; he continued to read newspapers and popular magazines; but, after 1932, he did not write. 'I'm not here to write, I'm here to be mad,' he told a visitor.[10] Besides, he said, the heyday of *littérateurs* was over.

(Years after Walser's death, one of the Herisau staff claimed that during his tenure he saw Walser at work writing. But even if this is true, no manuscript material dating from after 1932 has survived.)

Being a writer, someone who uses his hands to turn thoughts into marks on paper, was difficult for Walser at the most elementary of levels. In his earlier years he wrote a clear, well-formed script on which he prided himself. The manuscripts that survive from those days – fair copies – are models of fine handwriting. Handwriting was, however, one of the sites where disturbance in Walser's psyche first manifested itself. At some time in his thirties (he is vague about the date) he began to suffer from psychosomatic cramps of the right hand. He attributed these to unconscious animosity toward the pen as a tool; he was able to overcome them only by abandoning the pen in favour of the pencil.

Writing with a pencil was important enough for Walser to dub it his 'pencil system' or 'pencil method'.[11] The pencil method meant more than just use of a pencil. When he moved to pencil-writing Walser also radically changed his script. At his death he left behind some five hundred sheets of paper covered from edge to edge in rows of delicate, minute, pencilled calligraphic signs, a script so difficult to read that his executor at first took the papers to belong to a diary in secret code. But Walser kept no diary, nor is the script a code. The late manuscripts are in fact written in standard German script, but with so many idiosyncratic abbreviations that, even for editors familiar with it, unambiguous decipherment is not always possible. It is only in 'pencil-method' drafts that Walser's numerous late works, including his last novel *The Robber* (twenty-four sheets of microscript, some one hundred and fifty pages in print) have come down to us.

More interesting than the decipherment of the script itself is the question of what the pencil method made possible to Walser as a writer that the pen could no longer provide (he was still prepared to use a pen when merely transcribing, or for writing letters). The answer seems to be that, like an artist with a stick of charcoal between his fingers, Walser needed to get a steady, rhythmic hand movement going before he could slip into a frame of mind in which reverie, composition, and the flow of the writing tool became much the same thing. In a piece entitled 'Pencil Sketch' dating from 1926/7 he mentions the 'unique bliss' that the pencil method allowed him.[12] 'It calms me down and cheers me up,' he said elsewhere.[13] Walser's texts proceed neither by logic nor by narrative but by moods, fancies, and associations: by temperament he is less a thinker following an argument or even a story-teller following a narrative line than a belletrist. The pencil and the self-invented stenographic script allowed the purposeful, uninterrupted, introverted, dream-driven hand movement that had become indispensable to his creative mood.

The longest of Walser's late works is *Der Räuber* (The Robber), written in 1925–26 but deciphered and published only in 1972. The story is light to the point of being insubstantial. It concerns the sentimental entanglements of a middle-aged man known simply as the Robber, a man without employment who manages to subsist on the fringes of polite society in Berne on the basis of a modest legacy.

Among the women the Robber diffidently pursues is a wait-ress named Edith; among the women who somewhat less diffidently pursue him are assorted landladies who want him either for their daughters or for themselves. The action culminates in a scene in which the Robber ascends the pulpit and, before a large assembly, reproves Edith for preferring a mediocre rival to him. Incensed, Edith fires a revolver, wounding him slightly. There is a flurry of gleeful gossip. When the dust clears, the Robber is collaborating with a professional author to tell his side of the story.

Why 'the Robber' (*der Räuber*) as a name for this timid gallant? The word hints, of course, at Walser's first name. A painting by Karl Walser, Robert's brother, gives a further clue. In Karl's watercolour, Robert, aged fifteen, is dressed up as his favourite hero, Karl Moor in Schiller's early play *Die Räuber* (The Robbers; 1781). Robert the Robber of Walser's tale is, however, no brigand hero but a pilferer and plagiarist who steals no more than the affections of girls and the formulas of popular fiction.

Behind Robber(t) lurks a shadowy figure, the nominal author of the book, who treats Robber(t) now as a protégé, now as a rival, now as a mere puppet to be shifted around from situation to situation. This stage-master is critical of Robber(t) for handling his finances badly, for hanging around working-class girls, and generally for being a *Tagedieb*, a day-thief or idler, rather than a good Swiss burgher, even though, he confesses, he has to keep his wits about him lest he confuse himself with Robber(t). In character he is much like his rival, mocking himself even as he plays out his empty social routines. Every now and again he has a flutter of anxiety about the book he is writing before our eyes – about its slow progress, the triviality of its content, the vacuity of his hero.

Fundamentally *The Robber* is 'about' no more than the adventure of its own writing. Its charm lies in its surprising twists and turns of direction, its delicately ironic handling of the formulas of amatory play, and its supple and inventive exploitation of the resources of German. Its author figure, flustered by the multiplicity of narrative strands he suddenly has to manage now that the pencil in his hand is moving, is reminiscent above all of Laurence Sterne, the gentler, later Sterne, without the leering and the double entendres.

The distancing effects allowed by the splitting off of an author self from a Robber(t) self, and by a style in which sentiment can be indulged through a light veil of parody, allow Walser moments when he can write movingly about his own – that is, Robber(t)'s – defencelessness on the margins of Swiss society:

> He was always . . . lone as a little lost lamb. People perse-
> cuted him to help him learn how to live. He gave such a
> vulnerable impression. He resembled the leaf that a little boy
> strikes down from its branch with a stick, because its singu-
> larity makes it conspicuous. In other words, he invited perse-
> cution. (p. 40)

As Walser remarked, with equal irony but *in propria persona*, in a letter from the same period: 'At times I feel eaten up, that is to say half or wholly consumed, by the love, concern, and interest of my so excellent countrymen.'[14]

The Robber was not prepared for publication. In fact, in none of his many conversations with his friend and benefactor during his asylum years, Carl Seelig, did Walser so much as mention the work's existence. It draws on episodes from his life, barely disguised; yet one should be cautious about taking it as autobiographical. Robber(t) embodies only one aspect of Walser. Though there are references to persecuting voices, and though Robber(t) suffers from what in the psychoanalytic trade are called delusions of reference – he suspects hidden meaning, for example, in the way that men blow their noses in his presence – the more melancholic, more self-destructive side of the real Walser is kept firmly out of the picture.

In a major episode Robber(t) visits a doctor and with great candour describes his sexual problems. He has never felt the urge to spend nights with women, he says, yet has 'quite horrifying stockpiles of amorous potential', so much so that 'every time I go out on the street, I immediately start falling in love'. The stratagem he has devised to achieve happiness is to think up stories about his erotic object in which he becomes 'the subordinate, obedient, sacrificing, scrutinised, and chaperoned [one]'. In fact, he confesses, he sometimes feels he is really a girl. Yet at the same time there is also a boy inside him, a naughty boy (shades of *Jakob von Gunten*). The doctor's response is eminently sage. You seem to know yourself very well, he says – don't try to change. (pp. 105–6)

In another remarkable passage Walser simply lets the pencil flow (lets the censor doze) as it leads him from the pleasures of 'damselling' – experiencing a feminine life imaginatively from the inside – to a richly erotic participation in the experience of operatic lovers, to whom the bliss of pouring out one's love in song and the bliss of love itself are one and the same. (p. 101)

Christopher Middleton has been a pioneering student of Walser and one of the great mediators of modern German literature to the English-speaking world. His exemplary translation of *Jakob von Gunten* first came out in 1969. In her 2000 translation of *The Robber* Susan Bernofsky rises equally well to the challenge of late Walser, particularly to his play with the compound formations to which German is so hospitable.[15]

In an essay concerning some of the problems that Walser presents to the translator, Bernofsky offers the following illustrative passage:

He sat in the aforementioned garden, entwined by lianas, embutterflied by melodies, and rapt in the rapscallity of his love for the fairest young aristocrat ever to spring down from the heavens of parental shelter into the public eye so as, with her charms, to give the heart of a Robber a fatal stab.[16]

The ingenuity of the coinage 'embutterflied' (for *umschmetterlingelt*) is admirable, as is Bernofsky's resourcefulness in postponing the punch to the final word. But the sentence also happens to illustrate one of the vexing problems of Walser's microscript texts. The word translated here as 'aristocrat', *Herrentochter*, is deciphered by another of Walser's editors as *Saaltochter*, Swiss German for 'waitress'. (The woman in question, Edith, is certainly a waitress and no aristocrat.) If we cannot be sure of the text, can we trust the translation?

Now and again Walser sets a challenge to which Bernofsky fails to rise. I am not sure that 'scalawagging his way through [the] arcades' quite calls up the picture Walser intended, namely of a boy skipping school. One of the widows with whom Robber(t) flirts is characterised as *ein Dummchen*; and for two pages thereafter Walser proceeds to ring the changes on *Dummheit* in all its aspects. Bernofsky consistently employs 'ninny' for *Dummchen* and 'ninnihood' for *Dummheit*. But 'ninny' has connotations of mental incompetence, even of idiocy, absent from *Dumm-* words, and is anyhow rare in contemporary English. Neither 'ninny' nor any other single English word will consistently translate *Dummchen*, which carries senses sometimes of 'dummy' (a person who is dumb or stupid – the sense is stronger in American than in British English), sometimes of 'nitwit', and sometimes of emptyheadedness. (pp. 42, 26–27)

Walser wrote in High German (*Hochdeutsch*), the language that Swiss children learn in school. High German differs not only in a multitude of linguistic details but in its very temperament from the Swiss German that is the home language of three quarters of the Swiss populace. Writing in High German – which, if he wanted to earn a living from his pen, was the only choice open to Walser – entailed, unavoidably, adopting an educated, socially refined stance, a stance with which he was not comfortable. Though he had little time for a Swiss regional literature (*Heimatliteratur*) dedicated to reproducing Helvetic folklore and celebrating obsolescent folkways, Walser did, after his return to Switzerland, deliberately begin to introduce Swiss German into his writing, and generally try to sound Swiss.

The coexistence of two versions of the same language in the same social space is a phenomenon unfamiliar to the metropolitan English-speaking world, and one that creates intractable problems for the English translator. Bernofsky's response to so-called dialect in Walser – comprising not just the odd word or phrase but a Swiss colouring to his language that is hard to pinpoint – is, candidly, to ignore it, or at least to make no attempt to reproduce it. As she correctly says, translating Walser's more Swiss-German moments by evoking some or other regional or social dialect of English will yield nothing but cultural falsification.[17]

Both Middleton and Bernofsky write informative introductions to their translations, though Middleton's is by now out of date on Walser scholarship. Neither chooses to provide explanatory notes. The absence of notes will be felt particularly in *The Robber*, which is peppered with references to literature, including the obscurer reaches of Swiss literature.

The Robber is more or less contemporary in composition with Joyce's *Ulysses* and with the later volumes of Proust's *In Search of Lost Time*. Had it been published in 1926 it might have affected the course of modern German literature, opening up and even legitimating as a subject the adventures of the writing (or dreaming) self and of the meandering line of ink (or pencil) that emerges under the writing hand. But that was not to be. Although a project to bring together Walser's writings was initiated before his death, it was only after the first volumes of a more scholarly Collected Works began to appear in 1966, and after he had been noticed by readers in England and France, that Walser gained widespread attention in Germany.

Today Walser is judged on the basis of his novels, even though these form only a fifth of his output, and even though the novel proper was not his forte (the four long fictions he left behind really belong to the less ambitious tradition of the novella). He is more at home in shorter forms. Pieces like 'Helbling's Story' (1914) or 'Kleist in Thun' (1913), in which watercolour shades of sentiment are inspected with the lightest of irony and the prose responds to passing currents of feeling as sensitively as a butterfly's wing, show him at his best. His own uneventful yet, in its way, harrowing life was his only true subject. All of his prose pieces, he suggested in retrospect, might be read as chapters in 'a long, plotless, realistic story', a 'cut up or disjoined book of the self [*Ich-Buch*]'.[18]

Was Walser a great writer? If one finally hesitates to call him great, remarked Canetti, that is only because nothing could be more alien to him than greatness.[19] In a late poem Walser wrote:

> I would wish it on no one to be me.
> Only I am capable of bearing myself.
> To know so much, to have seen so much, and
> To say nothing, just about nothing.[20]

(2000)

3 Robert Musil, *The Confusions of Young Törless*

ROBERT MUSIL WAS born in 1880 in Klagenfurt in the Austrian province of Carinthia. His mother, who came from the upper bourgeoisie, was a highly strung woman with an interest in the arts, his father an engineer in the imperial administration who in his later years would be rewarded for his service with elevation to the minor nobility. The marriage was a 'progressive' one: Musil Senior accepted without protest a liaison between his wife and a younger man, Heinrich Reiter, initiated shortly after his son's birth. Reiter eventually settled in with the Musils in a *ménage à trois* that would last for a quarter of a century.

Musil himself was an only child. Younger and smaller than his classmates at school, he cultivated a physical toughness that he maintained throughout his life. The atmosphere at home seems to have been tempestuous; at the demand of his mother – and, it must be said, with the boy's enthusiastic consent – he was sent at the age of eleven to board at a military *Unterrealschule* outside Vienna. From there he moved in 1894 to the *Oberrealschule* in Mährisch-Weisskirchen near Brno, capital of Moravia, where he spent three years. This school became the model for 'W.' in *Young Törless*.

Deciding against a military career, Musil enrolled at the age of seventeen in the *Technische Hochschule* in Brno, where he flung himself into his engineering studies, disdaining the humanities and the kind of student attracted to the humanities. His diaries of the time reveal him as preoccupied with sex, but in unusually thoughtful ways. He found himself reluctant to accept the sexual role prescribed for him as a young man by the mores of his class, namely that he should sow his wild oats with prostitutes and working girls until it was time to make a proper marriage. He embarked on a relationship with a Czech girl named Herma Dietz who had worked in his grandmother's house; against the resistance of his mother, and at the risk of losing his friends, he lived with Herma in Brno and later in Berlin.

By linking himself with Herma, Musil took a major step in breaking the erotic spell that his mother held over him. For some years Herma remained the focus of his emotional life. Their relationship — straightforward on Herma's side, more complex and ambivalent on Robert's — became the basis of the later story 'Tonka', collected in *Three Women* (1924).

In intellectual content, the education Musil had received at his military schools was decidedly inferior to that offered in the classical *Gymnasia*. In Brno he began attending lectures on literature and going to concerts. What began as a project in catching up with his better educated contemporaries soon turned into an absorbing intellectual adventure. The years 1898 to 1902 mark a first phase of literary apprenticeship. The young Musil identified particularly with the writers and intellectuals of the generation that flowered in the 1890s and contributed so much to the Modernist movement. He fell under the spell of Mallarmé and Maeterlinck, rejected the naturalist credo that the artwork should faithfully ('objectively') reflect a pre-existing reality. For philosophic support he turned to Kant, Schopenhauer and (particularly) Nietzsche. In his diaries he developed for himself the artistic persona of 'Monsieur le vivisecteur', one who explored states of consciousness and emotional relations with an intellectual scalpel. He practised his vivisective skills impartially on himself, his family, and his friends.

Despite these new literary aspirations, Musil continued to prepare for a career in engineering. He passed his examinations with distinction and moved to Stuttgart as a research assistant at the prestigious *Technische Hochschule*. But his scientific work began to bore him. While still writing technical papers and working on an instrument he had invented for use in optical experiments (he would later patent the instrument, hoping rather unrealistically to be able to live on the royalties), he embarked on a first novel, *The Confusions of Young Törless*. He also began to lay the ground for a change in academic direction. In 1903 he formally abandoned engineering and departed for Berlin to study philosophy and psychology.

Young Törless was completed in early 1905. After it had been turned down by three publishers, Musil offered the manuscript for comment to the respected Berlin critic Alfred Kerr. Kerr lent Musil his support, suggested revisions, and reviewed the book in glowing terms when it appeared in print in 1906. Despite the success of *Young Törless*, however, and despite the mark he was beginning to make in Berlin artistic circles, Musil felt too unsure of his talent to commit himself to a life of writing. He continued with his philosophical studies, taking his doctorate in 1908.

By this time he had met Martha Marcovaldi, a woman of Jewish descent seven years his senior, separated from her second husband. With Martha – an artist and intellectual in her own right, *au courante* with contemporary feminism – Musil established an intimate and erotically intense relationship that lasted for the rest of his life. The two were married in 1911 and took up residence in Vienna, where Musil had accepted the position of archivist at the *Technische Hochschule*.

In the same year Musil published a second book, *Unions*,

consisting of the novellas 'The Perfecting of a Love' and 'The Temptation of Quiet Veronika'. These pieces were composed with an obsessiveness whose basis was obscure to their author; though short, their writing and revision occupied Musil day and night for two and a half years.

In the war of 1914–18 Musil served with distinction on the Italian front. After the war, troubled by a sense that the best years of his creative life were slipping away, he sketched out no fewer than twenty new works, including a series of satirical novels. A play, *The Visionaries* (1921), and the story collection *Three Women*, won awards. He was elected vice-president of the Austrian branch of the Organisation of German Writers. Though not widely read, he was on the literary map.

Before long the projected satirical novels had been abandoned or absorbed into a master-project: a novel in which the upper crust of Viennese society, oblivious of the dark clouds gathering on the horizon, reflects at length on what form its next festival of self-congratulation should take. The novel was intended to render a 'grotesque' (Musil's word) vision of Austria on the eve of the World War.[1] Supported financially by his publisher and by a society of admirers, he devoted all his energies to *The Man without Qualities*.

The first volume came out in 1930, to so enthusiastic a reception in both Austria and Germany that Musil – a modest man in other respects – thought he might win the Nobel Prize. The second volume proved harder to write. Cajoled by his publisher, yet full of misgivings, he allowed an extended fragment to appear in 1933. In secret he began to fear he would never complete the work.

A move back to the livelier intellectual environment of Berlin was cut short by the coming to power of the Nazis. Musil and his wife returned to Vienna, where the air was full of ill omen.

Musil began to suffer from depression and general poor health. Then in 1938 Austria was absorbed into the Third Reich, and the Musils removed themselves to Switzerland. Switzerland was meant to be a staging post en route to a haven offered by Martha's daughter in the United States, but the entry of the United States into the war put paid to that plan. Along with tens of thousands of other exiles, they found themselves trapped.

'Switzerland is renowned for the freedom you can enjoy there,' observed Bertholt Brecht. 'The catch is, you have to be a tourist.' The myth of Switzerland as a land of asylum was badly damaged by its treatment of refugees during World War Two, when its first priority, overriding all humanitarian considerations, was not to antagonise Germany. Pointing out that his writings were banned in Germany and Austria, Musil pleaded for asylum on the grounds that he could earn a living as a writer nowhere else in the German-speaking world. Though permitted to stay, he never felt at home in Switzerland. He was little known there; he had no talent for self-promotion; the Swiss patronage network disdained him. He and his wife survived on handouts. 'Today they ignore us. But once we are dead they will boast that they gave us asylum,' remarked Musil bitterly to Ignazio Silone. He was too depressed to make headway with the novel. In 1942, at the age of sixty-one, after a bout of vigorous exercise on the trampoline, he had a stroke and died.[2]

'He thought he had a long life before him,' said his widow. 'The worst is, an unbelievable body of material – sketches, notes, aphorisms, novel chapters, diaries – is left behind, of which only he could have made sense.' Turned away by commercial publishers, she privately published a third volume of the novel, consisting of fragments in no hard and fast order.[3]

Musil belonged to a generation of German-speaking intellectuals who experienced the successive phases of the breakdown of the

European order between 1890 and 1939 with particular immediacy: first, the premonitory crisis in the arts, embodied in the first wave of the Modernist movement; then the war of 1914–18 and the revolutions spawned by the war, which destroyed both traditional and liberal institutions; and finally the rudderless postwar years, culminating in the Fascist seizure of power. *The Man without Qualities* – a book to some extent overtaken by history during its writing – set out to diagnose this breakdown, which Musil more and more came to see as originating in the failure of Europe's liberal elite since the 1870s to recognise that the social and political doctrines inherited from the Enlightenment were not adequate to the new mass civilisation growing up in the cities.

To Musil, the most stubbornly retrogressive feature of German culture (of which Austrian culture was a part – he did not take seriously the idea of an autonomous Austrian culture) was its tendency to compartmentalise intellect from feeling, and then to relax into an unreflective stupidity of the emotions. He encountered this split most clearly among the scientists with whom he worked, men of intellect living what he considered to be coarse emotional lives. The education of the senses through a refining of erotic life seemed to him to hold some promise of lifting society to a higher ethical plane. He deplored the rigid roles, extending even into the realm of sexual intimacy, enforced by bourgeois mores on both women and men. 'Whole countries of the soul have been lost and submerged as a consequence,' he wrote.[4]

Because of the concentration he displays in his work, from *Young Törless* onwards, on the obscurer workings of sexual desire, Musil is often thought of as a Freudian. But he himself acknowledged no such debt. He disliked the cultishness of psychoanalysis, disapproved of its sweeping claims and its unscientific standards of proof. He preferred psychology of what he ironically called the 'shallow' – that is, empirical and experimental – variety.[5]

Both Musil and Freud were in fact part of a larger movement in European thought. Both were sceptical of the power of reason to guide human conduct; both were diagnosticians of *fin-de-siècle* Central European civilisation and its discontents; and both took on the dark continent of the feminine psyche as theirs to explore. To Musil, Freud was a rival rather than a source.

Musil's preferred guide in the realm of the unconscious was Nietzsche. In Nietzsche Musil found an approach to questions of morality that went beyond a simple polarity of good and evil; a recognition that art can in itself be a form of intellectual exploration; and a mode of philosophising, aphoristic rather than systematic, that suited his own sceptical temperament. The tradition of fictional realism had never been strong in Germany; as Musil developed as a writer, his fiction became increasingly essayistic in structure, with only perfunctory gestures in the direction of realistic narrative.

Die Verwirrungen des Zöglings Törless (*Verwirrungen* are perplexities, troubled states of mind; *Zögling* is a rather formal term, with upper-class overtones, for a boarder at a school) is built around a story of sadistic victimisation at an elite boys' academy. More specifically, it is an account of a crisis that one of the boys, Törless (his first name is never given), undergoes as a result of taking part in the deliberate humiliation and breaking down of a fellow student, Basini, who has the misfortune to be caught stealing. The exploration of Törless's inner crisis, moral, psychological, and ultimately epistemological, rendered largely from within the boy's own consciousness, makes up the substance of the novel.

In the end Törless has his own breakdown and is discreetly removed from the school. Looking back, Törless feels he has weathered the storm and come through. But it is not clear how far we should trust this self-assessment, since it seems to be based on a decision that the only way of getting along in the world is not to peer too closely into the abysses opened up in us by extreme experience, particularly sexual experience. The single glimpse we are allowed of Törless in later life suggests that he has become not necessarily a wiser or a better man, merely a more prudent one.

In later life Musil denied that *Young Törless* was about youthful experiences of his own or even about adolescence in general. Nevertheless, the originals of Basini and of his tormentors Beineberg and Reiting can easily be identified among the boys Musil knew at Mährisch-Weisskirchen, while one of Törless's deepest confusions – about the nature of his feelings toward his mother – is mirrored in Musil's own early diaries. The gap between Törless's outward sangfroid and the seething forces within him, between the well-regulated operation of the school by day and the eerie nocturnal floggings in the attic, has its parallel in the gap between the orderly bourgeois front presented by the Törless parents and what their son darkly knows must go on in private.

The master metaphor that Musil uses to capture these incommensurabilities (what Törless himself calls 'incomparabilities') comes from mathematics. Living in among the whole numbers and fractions of whole numbers – which together make up the so-called rational numbers – and somehow made to interlock with them by the operations of mathematical reasoning, are the infinitely more numerous irrational numbers, numbers that evade representation in terms of whole numbers. Adults, led by Törless's teachers, seem to have no trouble in making the rational and the irrational cohabit, but to Törless the latter are vertiginously beyond his grasp.

Concluding his testimony at the inquiry into the Basini affair, Törless claims to have resolved his mental confusion ('I know that

I was indeed mistaken') and to have emerged safely into young adulthood ('I'm not afraid of anything any more. I know: things are things and will remain so for ever'). The assembled teachers fail completely to understand the point of what he is saying: either they have never had experiences like his, or they have tightly repressed them. Törless is unusual in the thoroughness with which he has faced − or been driven to face − the darkness within; whether or not we regard as self-betrayal his later adoption of the pose of the self-absorbed aesthete, he is certainly, in his confused youth (confusion, *Verwirrung*, is a word Musil uses with continual irony), the figure of the artist in modern times, visiting the remoter shores of experience and bringing back report.[6]

Despite the amoralism that makes *Young Törless* so much a product of its age, the moral questions raised by the story will not go away. Beineberg, the more intellectually inclined of Törless's comrades, has a vulgar-Nietzschean, proto-Fascist justification for the punishment they inflict on Basini, which is that the three of them belong to a new generation to which the old rules no longer apply ('the soul has changed'); as for pity, pity is one of the lower impulses and its promptings must be overcome. Törless is not Beineberg. Nevertheless, his own particular perversity − making Basini talk about what has been done to him − is morally no better than the whippings the other two carry out; while in the homosexual acts he performs with Basini he is at pains to show the boy no tenderness.

In a world in which there are no more God-given rules, in which it has fallen to the philosopher-artist to give the lead, should the artist's explorations include acting out his own darker impulses, seeing where they will take him? Does art always trump morality? This early work of Musil's offers the question, but answers it in only in the most uncertain way.

Musil did not disown *Young Törless*. On the contrary, he

continued to look back with pleased surprise at what he had been able to achieve, even at a technical level, at so early an age. Its master metaphor, with its implication that our real, rational, everyday world has no real, rational foundation, is extended in *The Man without Qualities*, where Musil likens the spirit in which the brother and sister Ulrich and Agathe undertake their 'journey to the end of the possible', the perilous exploration of the limits of feeling that lies at the heart of the book, to 'the freedom with which mathematics sometimes resorts to the absurd in order to arrive at the truth'.[7] Musil's work, from beginning to end, is of a piece: the evolving record of a confrontation between a man of supremely intelligent sensibility and the times that gave birth to him, times he would bitterly but justly call 'accursed'.[8]

(2001)

4 Walter Benjamin, the Arcades Project

THE STORY IS by now so well known that it barely needs to be retold. The setting is the Franco-Spanish border, the time 1940. Walter Benjamin, fleeing occupied France, seeks out the wife of a certain Fittko he has met in an internment camp. He understands, he says, that Frau Fittko will be able to guide him and his companions across the Pyrenees to neutral Spain. Taking him on a trip to scout the best route, Frau Fittko notices that he has brought along a heavy briefcase. Is the briefcase really necessary, she asks? It contains a manuscript, he replies. 'I cannot risk losing it. It . . . *must* be saved. It is more important than I am.'[1]

The next day they cross the mountains, Benjamin pausing every few minutes because of his weak heart. At the border they are halted. Their papers are not in order, say the Spanish police; they must return to France. In despair, Benjamin takes an overdose of morphine. The police make an inventory of the deceased's belongings. The inventory shows no record of a manuscript.

What was in the briefcase, and where it disappeared to, we can only guess. Benjamin's friend Gershom Scholem suggested that the lost work was the latest revision of the as yet unfinished *Passagen-Werk*, known in English as the Arcades Project. ('To great writers,' wrote Benjamin, 'finished works weigh lighter than those fragments on which they work throughout their lives.') But by his heroic effort to save his manuscript from the fires of fascism and bear it to what he thought of as the safety of Spain and, further on, the United States, Benjamin became an icon of the scholar for our times.[2]

Of course the story has a happy twist. A copy of the Arcades manuscript left behind in Paris had been secreted in the Bibliothèque Nationale by Benjamin's friend Georges Bataille. Recovered after the war, it was published in 1982 as it stood, that is to say, in German with huge swathes of French. And now we have Benjamin's magnum opus in full English translation, by Howard Eiland and Kevin McLaughlin, and are at last in a position to ask the question: Why all the concern for a treatise on shopping in nineteenth-century Paris?

Walter Benjamin was born in 1892, in Berlin, into an assimilated Jewish family. His father was a successful art auctioneer who branched out into the property market; the Benjamins were, by most standards, wealthy. After a sickly, sheltered childhood, Benjamin was sent at the age of thirteen to a progressive boarding school in the countryside, where he fell under the influence of one of the directors, Gustav Wyneken. For some years after leaving school he would be active in Wyneken's anti-authoritarian, back-to-nature youth movement; he would break with it only in 1914, when Wyneken came out in support of the war.

In 1912 Benjamin enrolled as a student in philology at Freiburg University. Finding the intellectual environment not to his taste, he threw himself into activism for educational reform. When war broke out, he evaded military service first by feigning a medical condition, then by moving to neutral Switzerland. There he stayed until 1920, reading philosophy and working on a doctoral dissertation for the University of Berne. His wife complained that they had no social life.

Benjamin was drawn to universities, remarked his friend Theodor Adorno, as Franz Kafka was drawn to insurance companies. Despite misgivings, Benjamin went through the prescribed motions to acquire the *Habilitation* (higher doctorate) that would enable him to become a professor, submitting his dissertation, on German drama of the Baroque age, to the University of Frankfurt in 1925. Surprisingly, the dissertation was not accepted. It fell between the stools of literature and philosophy, and Benjamin lacked an academic patron prepared to urge his case. (When it was published in 1928, the dissertation received respectful attention from reviewers, despite Benjamin's morose claims to the contrary.)

His academic plans having failed, Benjamin launched himself on a career as translator, broadcaster, and freelance journalist. Among his commissions was a translation of Proust's *À la recherche*; three of the seven volumes were completed.

In 1924 Benjamin visited Capri, at the time a favourite resort of German intellectuals. There he met Asja Lacis, a theatre director from Latvia and a committed communist. The meeting was fateful. 'Every time I've experienced a great love, I've undergone a change so fundamental that I've amazed myself,' Benjamin wrote in retrospect. 'A genuine love makes me resemble the woman I love.'[3] In this case, the transformation entailed political reorientation. 'The path of thinking, progressive persons in their right senses leads to Moscow, not to Palestine,' Lacis told him sharply.[4] All traces of idealism in his thought, to say nothing of his flirtation with Zionism, had to be abandoned. His bosom friend Scholem had already emigrated to Palestine, expecting Benjamin to follow. Benjamin found an excuse not to come; he kept on making excuses to the end.

The first fruits of Benjamin's liaison with Lacis were an article co-written for the *Frankfurter Zeitung*. Nominally about the city of Naples, it is at a deeper level about an urban environment of an intriguing kind that the Berlin-bred intellectual is exploring for the first time, a labyrinth of streets where houses have no numbers and boundaries between private life and public life are porous.

In 1926 Benjamin travelled to Moscow for a rendezvous with Lacis. Lacis did not wholeheartedly welcome him (she was involved with another man); in his record of the visit, Benjamin probes his own unhappy state of mind, as well as the question of whether he should join the Communist Party and subject himself to the Party line. Two years later he and Lacis were briefly reunited in Berlin. They lived together and together attended meetings of the League of Proletarian-Revolutionary Writers. Their liaison precipitated divorce proceedings in which Benjamin behaved with remarkable meanness toward his wife.

On the Moscow trip Benjamin kept a diary which he later revised for publication. Benjamin spoke no Russian. Rather than fall back on interpreters, he followed what he would later call his physiognomic method, reading Moscow from the outside, refraining from abstraction or judgement, presenting the city in such a way that 'all factuality is already theory' (the phrase comes from Goethe).[5]

Some of Benjamin's claims for the 'world-historical' experiment he saw being conducted in the USSR – for instance, his claim that with a stroke of the pen the Party had severed the link between money and power – now seem naïve. Nevertheless, his eye remains acute. Many new Muscovites are still peasants, he observes, living village lives according to village rhythms; class distinctions may have been abolished but within the Party a new caste system is evolving. A scene from a street market captures the humbled status of religion: an icon for sale flanked by portraits of Lenin 'like a prisoner between two policemen'. (*V2*, pp. 32, 26)

Though Asja Lacis is a constant background presence in the 'Moscow Diary', and though Benjamin hints that their sexual relations were troubled, we get little sense of Lacis's physical self. As a writer Benjamin had no gift for evoking other people. In Lacis's own writings we get a much more lively impression of Benjamin: his glasses like little spotlights, his clumsy hands.

For the rest of his life Benjamin called himself either a communist or a fellow-traveller. How deep did his affair with communism run?

For years after meeting Lacis, Benjamin would repeat Marxist verities – 'the bourgeoisie . . . is condemned to decline due to internal contradictions that will become fatal as they develop' – without actually having read Marx.[6] 'Bourgeois' remained his cuss word for a mind-set – materialistic, incurious, selfish, prudish, and above all cosily self-satisfied – to which he was viscerally hostile. Proclaiming himself a communist was an act of choosing sides, morally and historically, against the bourgeoisie and his own bourgeois origins. 'One thing . . . can never be made good: having neglected to run away from one's parents,' he writes in *One-Way Street*, the collection of diary jottings, dream protocols, aphorisms, mini-essays, and satirical fragments, including mordant observations on Weimar Germany, with which he announced himself in 1928 as a freelance intellectual. (*V1*, p. 446) Not having run away early enough meant that he was condemned to run away from Emil and Paula Benjamin for the rest of his life: in reacting against his parents' eagerness to assimilate into the German middle class he resembled many German-speaking Jews of his generation, including Franz Kafka. What troubled Benjamin's friends about his Marxism was that there seemed to be something forced about it, something merely reactive.

Benjamin's first ventures into the discourse of the left are depressing to read. There is a slide into what one can only call willed stupidity as he rhapsodises about Lenin (whose letters have 'the sweetness of great epic,' he says in a piece not reprinted by the Harvard editors), or rehearses the ominous euphemisms of the Party: 'Communism is not radical. Therefore, it has no intention of simply abolishing family relations. It merely tests them to determine their capacity for change. It asks itself: Can the family be dismantled so that its components may be socially refunctioned?'[7]

These words come from a review of a play by Bertholt Brecht, whom Benjamin met through Lacis and whose 'crude thinking', thinking stripped of bourgeois niceties, attracted Benjamin for a while. 'This street is named Asja Lacis Street after her who, like an engineer, cut it through the author,' runs the dedication to *One-Way Street*. The comparison is intended as a compliment. The engineer is the man or woman of the future, the one who, impatient of palaver, armed with practical knowledge, acts and acts decisively to change the landscape. (Stalin too admired engineers. It was his view that writers should be engineers of human souls, meaning that they should take it upon themselves to 'refunction' humanity from the inside out.)

Of Benjamin's better-known writings, 'The Author as Producer', composed in 1934 as an address to the Institute for the Study of Fascism in Paris, shows the influence of Brecht most clearly. At issue is the old chestnut of Marxist aesthetics: which is more important, form or content? Benjamin's proposes that a literary work will be 'politically correct' only if it is also 'literarily correct'. 'Politically correct' is of course a shibboleth term; in practice it meant in accord with the Party line. 'The Author as Producer' is a defence of the left wing of the Modernist avant-garde, typified for Benjamin by the Surrealists, against the Party line on literature, with its bias toward easily comprehensible, realistic stories with a strong progressive message. To make his case Benjamin feels obliged to hold up the now forgotten Soviet novelist Sergei Tretiakov as exemplar of the union of 'correct political tendency' with 'progressive' technique, and to appeal once again to the glamour of engineering: the writer, like the engineer, is a technical specialist and should therefore have a say in literary-technical matters. (*V2*, pp. 769, 770)

Arguing at this crude level did not come easily to Benjamin. Did his decision to follow the Party line cause him no unease, at a time when Stalin's persecution of artists was in full swing? (Asja Lacis herself was to become one of Stalin's victims, spending years of her life in a labour camp.) A brief piece written in the same year, 1934, may give a clue. Here Benjamin mocks intellectuals who 'make it a point of honor to be wholly themselves on every issue', refusing to understand that to succeed they have to present different faces to different audiences. They are, he says, like a butcher who refuses to cut up a carcass, insisting on selling it whole. (*V2*, p. 743)

How is one to read this piece? Is Benjamin ironically praising old-fashioned intellectual integrity? Is he issuing a veiled confession that he, Walter Benjamin, is not what he seems to be? Is he making a practical, if bitter, point about the constraints faced by a hack writer? A letter to Scholem (to whom he did not always, however, tell the whole truth) suggests the last reading. Here Benjamin defends his communism as 'the obvious, reasoned attempt of a man who is completely or almost completely deprived of any means of production to proclaim his right to them'. In other words, he adheres to the Party for the same reason any proletarian should: because it is in his material interest. (*V2*, p. 853)

By the time the Nazis came to power, many of Benjamin's associates, including Brecht, had read the writing on the wall and taken flight. Benjamin, who had anyhow for years felt out of place in Germany, and spent time in France or on Ibiza whenever he could, soon followed. (His younger brother Georg was less prudent: arrested for political activities in 1934, he perished in Mauthausen in 1942.) He settled in Paris, where he scratched a precarious existence contributing to German newspapers under Aryan-sounding pseudonyms (Detlef Holz, K. A. Stempflinger), otherwise living on handouts. With the outbreak of war he found himself interned as an enemy alien. Released through the efforts of French PEN, he at once made arrangements to flee to the United States, then set off on his fatal journey to the Spanish border.

Benjamin's keenest insights into fascism, the enemy that deprived him of a home and a career and ultimately killed him, are into the means it used to sell itself to the German people: by turning itself into theatre. These insights are most fully expressed in (to use the title preferred by the Harvard translators) 'The Work of Art in the Age of its Technological Reproducibility' (1936) but were foreshadowed in 1930, in a review of a book edited by Ernst Jünger.

It is commonplace to observe that Hitler's Nuremberg rallies, with their combination of declamation, hypnotic music, mass choreography, and dramatic lighting, found their model in Wagner's Bayreuth productions. What is original in Benjamin is his claim that politics as grandiose theatre, rather than as discourse and debate, was not just the trappings of fascism but fascism in essence.

In the films of Leni Riefenstahl as well as in newsreels exhibited in every theatre in the land, the German masses were offered images of themselves as their leaders were calling upon them to be. Fascism used the power of great art of the past – what Benjamin calls auratic art – plus the multiplying power of the new post-auratic media, cinema above all, to create its new fascist citizens. For ordinary Germans, the only identity on show, the one looking back at them insistently from the screen, was a fascist identity in fascist costume and fascist postures of domination or obedience.

Benjamin's analysis of fascism as theatre raises many questions. Is politics as spectacle really the heart of German fascism, rather than *ressentiment* and dreams of historical retribution? If Nuremberg was aestheticised politics, why were Stalin's May Day extravaganzas and show trials not aestheticised politics too? If the genius of fascism was to erase the line between politics and media, where is the fascist element in the media-driven politics of Western democracies? Are there not different varieties of aesthetic politics?

Less questionable than his analysis of fascism is what Benjamin has to say about cinema. His sense of the potential of cinema to extend experience is prophetic: 'Film . . . burst [our] prison-world asunder by the dynamite of the tenth of a second, so that now, in the midst of its far-flung ruins and debris, we calmly and adventurously go travelling.'[8] His insight is all the more surprising because even by 1936 his film theory was out of date. He overvalued the practice of montage, where he followed Sergei Eisenstein and Eisenstein alone, underestimating the rapidity with which a more extensive grammar of film narrative would be mastered by cinema audiences. Nor had he any way of speaking about visual pleasure: to him cinema was about being jolted by startling montages into new ways of seeing (again Brecht's influence is manifest).

Benjamin's key concept (though in his diary he hints it was in fact the brainchild of the bookseller and publisher Adrienne Monnier) for describing what happens to the work of art in the age of its technological reproducibility (principally the age of the camera – Benjamin has little to say about printing) is *loss of aura*. Until about the middle of the nineteenth century, he says, an intersubjective relationship of a kind survived between an artwork and its viewer: the viewer looked and the artwork, so to speak, looked back. This mutuality defined aura: 'To perceive the aura of a phenomenon [means] to invest it with the capacity to look at us in turn.'[9] About aura there is thus something magical, derived from ancient links, now waning, between art and religious ritual.

Benjamin first speaks of aura in his 'Little History of Photography' (1931), where he tries to explain why it is that (in his eyes) the very earliest portrait photographs – the incunabula of photography, so to speak – have aura, whereas photographs of a generation later have lost it. One explanation he advances for this state of affairs is that, as photographic emulsions were improved and exposure times decreased, what was captured on film was no longer the inwardness of a subject collecting him- or herself for a portrait, but an instant excised from the continuity of the sitter's life. Another suggestion he makes is that the first generation of photographers were trained as artists, whereas the next generation were mere journeymen. Another is that something happened to the typical subject between the 1840s and the 1880s, something to do with the coarsening of the bourgeoisie.

In 'The Work of Art' the notion of aura is extended rather recklessly from old photographs to works of art in general. The end of aura, says Benjamin, will be more than compensated for by the emancipatory capacities of the new technologies of reproduction. Cinema will replace auratic art.

Even Benjamin's friends found it hard to get a grip on aura in its expanded version. Brecht, to whom Benjamin expounded the concept during lengthy visits to Brecht's home in Denmark, writes as follows in his diary. '[Benjamin] says: when you feel someone's gaze alight upon you, even on your back, you respond (!). the expectation that whatever you look at is looking at you creates the aura . . . all very mystical, despite his anti-mystical attitudes. this is the way in which the materialist approach is adapted! it is pretty horrifying.'[10] Other friends were no more encouraging.

Throughout the 1930s Benjamin struggles to develop a suitably materialist definition of aura and loss of aura. Film is postauratic, he says, because the camera, being an instrument, cannot see. (A questionable claim: actors certainly respond to the camera as if it were looking at them.) In a later revision Benjamin suggests that the end of aura can be dated to the moment in history when urban crowds grow so dense that people – *passers-by* – no longer return one another's gaze. In the Arcades Project he makes loss of aura part of a wider historical development: the spread of a disenchanted awareness that uniqueness, including the uniqueness of the traditional artwork, has become a commodity like any other commodity. The fashion industry, dedicated to the fabrication of unique handiworks – what it calls 'creations' – that are intended to be copied and reproduced on a mass scale, here points the way.

Before long, Benjamin tempered his optimism about the liberatory potential of technology. By 1939 he was likening the rhythm of the cinema projector to the rhythm of the conveyor belt. Even the 1936 essay 'The Storyteller' shows a change in his attitude. Memory is the chief preserver of tradition, he says, storytelling the chief transmitter; but the privatisation of life characteristic of modern culture is proving fatal to storytelling. Storytelling has become artificially confined to the novel, a creation of print technology and of the bourgeoisie.

Benjamin was not especially interested in the novel as a genre. On the evidence of his fiction in the Harvard *Selected Writings*, he had no talent as a storyteller. His autobiographical writings are instead built out of discontinuous, intense moments. His two essays on Kafka, which can usefully be supplemented with the long letter to Scholem of June 12, 1938, treat Kafka as a parabolist and teacher of wisdom rather than as a novelist. But Benjamin's most abiding hostility was reserved for narrative history. 'History decomposes into images, not into narratives,' he wrote. Narrative history imposes causality and motivation from the outside; things should be given a chance to speak for themselves.[11]

'A Berlin Childhood around 1900', Benjamin's most engaging work of autobiography, was unpublished during his lifetime. Despite its title, the earlier 'Berlin Chronicle' is built not chronologically but as a montage of fragments, interspersed with reflections on the nature of autobiography, and in the end is more about the vicissitudes of memory – the impress of Proust is strong – than about actual events in Benjamin's childhood. Benjamin uses an archaeological metaphor to explain his opposition to autobiography as the narrative of a life. The autobiographer should think of himself as an archaeologist, he says, digging deeper and deeper in the same few places in search of the buried ruins of the past.

Besides 'Moscow Diary' and 'A Berlin Chronicle', Volumes 1 and 2 contain a number of short autobiographical pieces: a rather literary account of being stood up by a lover; records of experiments with hashish; transcriptions of dreams; diary fragments (Benjamin was preoccupied with suicide in 1931 and 1932); and a Paris diary, worked up for publication, which includes a tour of a male brothel frequented by Proust. Among the more surprising revelations: an admiration for Hemingway ('an education in right thinking through correct writing'), a dislike of Flaubert (too architectonic). (*V2*, p. 472)

The groundwork for Benjamin's philosophy of language was laid early in his career. Although his ideas on language remained remarkably stable, his interest receded during his most political phase, re-emerging only in the late 1930s, when he again began to explore Jewish mystical thought. The key essay, 'On Language as Such and the Language of Man', dates from 1916. Here, following Schlegel and Novalis as well as what he had learned of Jewish mysticism from Scholem, Benjamin argues that a word is not a sign, a substitute for something else, but the name of an Idea. In 'The Task of the Translator' (1921) he tries to give body to his idea of the Idea, appealing to the example of Mallarmé and a poetic language set free of its communicative function.

How a Symbolist conception of language could ever be reconciled with Benjamin's later historical materialism is not clear, but Benjamin maintained that a bridge could be built, however 'strained and problematic' it might be.[12] In his literary essays of the 1930s he hints at what such a bridge might look like. In Proust, in Kafka, in the Surrealists, he says, the word retreats from signification in the 'bourgeois' sense and resumes its elementary, gestural power. Word as gesture is 'the supreme form in which truth can appear to us during an age deprived of theological doctrine'.[13]

In Adam's time, the word and the gesture of naming were the same thing. Since then language has undergone a long fall, of which Babel was only one stage. The task of theology is to recover the word, in all its originary, mimetic power, from the sacred texts in which it has been preserved. The task of criticism is substantially similar, for fallen languages can still, in the totality of their intentions, point us toward pure language. Hence the paradox of 'The Task of the Translator': that a translation becomes a higher thing than its original, in the sense that it gestures toward language before Babel.

Benjamin wrote a number of pieces on astrology, which are essential pendants to his writings on the philosophy of language. The astrological science we have today, he says, is a degenerate version of a body of ancient knowledge from times when the mimetic faculty, being far stronger, allowed real, imitative correspondences between the lives of human beings and the movements of the stars. Today only children preserve, and respond to the world with, a comparable mimetic power. As that mimetic faculty deteriorated through history, written language became its most important repository. Hence Benjamin's abiding interest in graphology, in handwriting as an 'expressive movement' of character. (*V2*, p. 399)

In essays dating from 1933, Benjamin sketches a theory of language based on mimesis. Adamic language was onomatopoeic, he says; synonyms in different languages, though they may not sound or look alike (the theory is meant to work for written as well as spoken language), have 'nonsensuous' similarities to what they signify, as 'mystical' or 'theological' theories of language have always recognised. (*V2*, p. 696) Thus the words *pain*, *Brot*, *xleb*, though superficially different, are alike at a profounder level in embodying the Idea of bread. (Persuading us that this claim is profound rather than vacuous demands Benjamin's utmost powers.) Language, the supreme development of the mimetic faculty, bears within itself an archive of these nonsensuous similarities. Reading has the potential of becoming a kind of dream experience giving access to a common human unconscious, the site of language and of Ideas.

Benjamin's approach to language is entirely out of step with that of twentieth-century linguistic science, but it gives him royal access to the world of myth and fable, particularly to the (as he conceives of it) primeval, almost prehuman 'swamp world' of Kafka. (*V2*, p. 808) An intensive reading of Kafka was to leave an indelible mark on Benjamin's own, pessimistic last writings.

The story of the Arcades Project is roughly as follows.

In the late 1920s Benjamin conceived of a work inspired by the arcades of Paris. It would deal with urban experience; it would be a version of the Sleeping Beauty story, a dialectical fairy tale told surrealistically by means of a montage of fragmentary texts. Like the prince's kiss, it would awake the European masses to the truth of their life under capitalism. It would be some fifty pages long; in preparation for its writing, Benjamin began to copy out quotations from his reading under such headings as Boredom, Fashion, Dust. But as he stitched a text together, it became overgrown each time with new quotations and notes. He discussed his problems with Adorno and Max Horkheimer, who convinced him he could not write about capitalism without a proper command of Marx. The Sleeping Beauty idea lost its lustre.

By 1934 Benjamin had a new and more philosophically ambitious plan: using the same method of montage, he would trace the cultural superstructure of nineteenth-century France back to commodities and their power to become fetishes, to which he had been alerted by Georg Lukács's *History and Class Consciousness*. As his notes grew in bulk, he slotted them into an elaborate filing system based on thirty-six convolutes (from German *Konvolut*, sheaf, dossier) with keywords and cross references. Under the title 'Paris, Capital of the Nineteenth Century' he wrote a resumé of the material he had thus far assembled, which he offered to Adorno (Benjamin was by then receiving a stipend from, and was thus in some measure beholden to, the Institute for Social Research, which had been relocated by Adorno and Horkheimer from Frankfurt to New York).

From Adorno Benjamin received such severe criticism that he decided to set aside the project for the time being and extract from his mass of materials a book about Baudelaire. Part of this book emerged in 1938 as 'The Paris of the Second Empire in Baudelaire', still built according to the method of montage. Again Adorno was critical: facts were being made to speak for themselves, he said; there was not enough theory. Benjamin produced a further revision, 'On Some Motifs in Baudelaire' (1939), which had a warmer reception.

Baudelaire was central to the Arcades plan because, in Benjamin's eyes, Baudelaire in *Les Fleurs du mal* first revealed the modern city as a subject for poetry. (Benjamin seems not to have read Wordsworth, who, fifty years before Baudelaire, wrote of what it was like to be part of a London street crowd, bombarded on all sides with glances, dazzled with advertisements.)

Yet Baudelaire expressed his experience of the city in allegory, a literary mode out of fashion since the Baroque. In 'Le Cygne', for instance, Baudelaire allegorised the poet as a noble bird, a swan, scrabbling about comically in the paved marketplace, unable to spread his wings and soar.

Why did Baudelaire use allegory? Benjamin calls upon Marx's *Capital* to answer the question. The elevation of market value into the sole measure of worth, says Marx, reduces a commodity to nothing but a sign – the sign of what it will sell for. Under the reign of the market, things relate to their actual worth as arbitrarily as, for instance, in Baroque emblematics a death's head relates to man's subjection to time. Emblems thus make an unexpected return to the historical stage in the form of commodities, which under capitalism are no longer what they seem, but, as Marx had warned, begin to '[abound] in metaphysical subtleties and theological niceties'. (*AP*, p. 196) Allegory, Benjamin argues, is exactly the right mode for an age of commodities.

While working on the Baudelaire book (which was never completed – the manuscript was published posthumously as *Charles Baudelaire: A Lyric Poet in the Era of High Capitalism*), Benjamin continued to take notes for the Arcades and add new convolutes. What was recovered after the war from its hiding place in the Bibliothèque Nationale amounted to some nine hundred pages of extracts, mainly from nineteenth-century writers but from contemporaries of Benjamin's as well, grouped under headings, with interspersed commentary, plus a variety of plans and synopses. These materials were published in 1982, in an edition by Rolf Tiedemann, as the *Passagen-Werk*. The Harvard *Arcades*

Project uses Tiedemann's text but omits much of his background material and editorial apparatus. It translates all the French into English and adds helpful notes as well as a wealth of pictorial illustrations. It is a handsome volume: its handling of Benjamin's complex cross-referencing is a triumph of typographical ingenuity.

The history of the Arcades Project, a history of procrastination and false starts, of wanderings in archival labyrinths in a quest for exhaustiveness all too typical of the collecting temperament, of shifting theoretical ground, of criticism too readily acted on, and generally speaking of Benjamin not knowing his own mind, means that the book that has come down to us is radically incomplete: incompletely conceived and hardly written in any conventional sense. Tiedemann compares it to the building materials of a house. In the hypothetical completed house these materials would be held together by Benjamin's thought. We possess much of that thought in the form of Benjamin's interpolations, but cannot always see how the thought fits or encompasses the materials.

In such a situation, says Tiedemann, it might seem better to publish only Benjamin's own words, leaving out the quotations. But Benjamin's intention, however utopian, was that at some point his commentary would be discreetly withdrawn, leaving the quoted material to bear the full weight of the structure.

The arcades of Paris, says an 1852 guidebook, are 'inner boulevards . . . , glass-roofed, marble-paneled corridors extending through whole blocks of buildings . . . Lining both sides . . . are the most elegant shops, so that such an arcade is a city, a world in miniature.' (*AP*, p. 31) Their airy glass and steel architecture was soon imitated in other cities of the West. The heyday of the arcades extended to the end of the century, when they were eclipsed by department stores. To Benjamin their decline was part of the unfolding logic of capitalist economics; he did not foresee their return, in the late twentieth century, in the form of urban malls.

The Arcades book was never intended to be an economic history (though part of its ambition was to act as a corrective to the entire discipline of economic history). An early sketch suggests something far more like 'A Berlin Childhood':

> One knew of places in ancient Greece where the way led down into the underworld. Our waking existence likewise is a land which, at certain hidden points, leads down into the underworld – a land full of inconspicuous places from which dreams arise. All day long, suspecting nothing, we pass them by, but no sooner has sleep come than we are eagerly groping our way back to lose ourselves in the dark corridors. By day, the labyrinth of urban dwellings resembles consciousness; the arcades . . . issue unremarked onto the streets. At night, however, under the tenebrous mass of the houses, their denser darkness protrudes like a threat, and the nocturnal pedestrian hurries past – unless, that is, we have emboldened him to turn into the narrow lane. (*AP*, p. 84)

Two books served Benjamin as models: Louis Aragon's *Un Paysan de Paris* (translated into English as *Nightwalker* in 1970 and as *Paris Peasant* in 1971), with its affectionate tribute to the Passage de l'Opéra, and Franz Hessel's *Spazieren in Berlin* (Strolling in Berlin), which focuses on the Kaisersgalerie and its power to summon up the feel of a bygone era. His own work would be informed by Proust's theory of involuntary memory, but dreaming and reverie would be more historically specific than in Proust. He would try to capture the 'phantasmagoric' experience of the Parisian wandering among displays of goods, an experience still recoverable in his own day, when 'arcades dot the metropolitan landscape like caves containing the fossil remains of a vanished monster: the consumer of the pre-imperial era of capitalism, the last dinosaur of Europe.' (*AP*, p. 540)

The great innovation of the Arcades Project would be its form. Like the Naples essay and the 'Moscow Diary', it would work on the principle of montage, juxtaposing textual fragments from past and present in the expectation that they would strike sparks from and illuminate each other. Thus, for instance, if item (2,1) of Convolute L, referring to the opening of an art museum at the palace of Versailles in 1837, is read in conjunction with item (2,4) of Convolute A, which traces the development of arcades into department stores, then ideally the analogy 'museum is to department store as artwork is to commodity' will flash into the reader's mind. (*AP*, pp. 37, 408)

According to Max Weber, what distinguishes modern times is loss of belief, disenchantment. Benjamin has a different angle: that capitalism has put people to sleep, that they will wake up from their collective enchantment only when they are made to understand what has happened to them. The inscription to Convolute N comes from Marx: 'The reform of consciousness consists *solely* in . . . the awakening of the world from its dream about itself.' (*AP*, p. 456)

The dreams of the capitalist era are embodied in commodities. In their ensemble these constitute a phantasmagoria, constantly changing shape according to the tides of fashion, and offered to crowds of enchanted worshippers as the embodiment of their deepest desires. The phantasmagoria always hides its origins (which lie in alienated labour). Phantasmagoria in Benjamin is thus a little like ideology in Marx – a tissue of public lies sustained by the power of capital – but more like Freudian dreamwork operating at a collective, social level.

★

'I needn't *say* anything. Merely show,' says Benjamin; and elsewhere: 'Ideas are to objects as constellations are to stars.' If the mosaic of quotations is built up correctly, a pattern should emerge, a pattern that is more than the sum of its parts but cannot exist independently of them: this is the essence of the new form of historical-materialist writing that Benjamin believed himself to be practising.[14]

What dismayed Adorno about the project in 1935 was Benjamin's faith that a mere assemblage of objects (in this case, decontextualised quotations) could speak for itself. Benjamin was, he wrote, 'on the crossroads between magic and positivism'. In 1948 Adorno had a chance to see the entire Arcades corpus, and again expressed doubts about the thinness of its theorisation.[15]

Benjamin's response to criticism of this kind depended on the notion of the dialectical image, for which he went back to Baroque emblematics – ideas represented by pictures – and Baudelairean allegory – the interaction of ideas replaced by the interaction of emblematic objects. Allegory, he suggested, could take over the role of abstract thought. The objects and figures that inhabit the arcades – gamblers, whores, mirrors, dust, wax figures, mechanical dolls – are (to Benjamin) emblems, and their interactions generate meanings, allegorical meanings that do not need the intrusion of theory. Along the same lines, fragments of text taken from the past and placed in the charged field of the historical present are capable of behaving much as the elements of a Surrealist image do, interacting spontaneously to give off political energy. ('The events surrounding the historian and in which he takes part,' Benjamin wrote, 'will underlie his presentation like a text written in invisible ink.')[16] In so doing the fragments constitute the dialectical image, dialectical movement frozen for a moment, open for inspection, 'dialectics at a standstill'. 'Only dialectical images are genuine images.' (*AP*, p. 462)

So much for the theory, ingenious as it is, to which Benjamin's deeply anti-theoretical book appeals. But to the reader unpersuaded by the theory, the reader to whom the dialectical images never quite come alive as they are supposed to, the reader perhaps unreceptive to the master narrative of the long sleep of capitalism followed by the dawn of socialism, what does *The Arcades Project* have to offer?

The briefest of lists would include the following:

(1) A treasure hoard of curious information about the Paris of the early nineteenth century (for instance, men with nothing better to do would go to the morgue and look at nude corpses).

(2) Thought-provoking quotations, the harvest of an acute and idiosyncratic mind trawling through thousands of books over the course of many years (Tiedemann lists some 850 titles actually cited). Some of these are from writers we thought we knew well (Marx, Victor Hugo), others from less known writers who, on the evidence here presented, deserve a revival – for instance, Hermann Lotze, author of *Mikrokosmos* (1864).

(3) A multitude of succinct observations, polished to a high aphoristic sheen, on a range of Benjamin's favourite subjects. 'Prostitution can lay claim to being considered "work" the moment work becomes prostitution.' 'What makes the first photographs so incomparable is perhaps this: that they present the earliest image of the encounter of machine and man.' (*AP*, pp. 348, 678)

(4) Glimpses of Benjamin toying with a new way of seeing himself: as collector of 'keywords in a secret dictionary', compiler of a 'magic encyclopedia'. Suddenly Benjamin, esoteric reader of an allegorical city, seems close to his contemporary Jorge Luis Borges, fabulist of a rewritten universe. (*AP* pp. 211, 207) What brings them together is, of course, the Kabbalah, over which Borges had long pored, and to which Benjamin turned his attention as his faith in the proletarian revolution waned.

From a distance, Benjamin's magnum opus is curiously reminiscent of another great ruin of twentieth-century literature, Ezra Pound's *Cantos*. Both works are the issue of years of jackdaw reading. Both are built out of fragments and quotations, and adhere to the high-Modernist aesthetics of image and montage. Both have economic ambitions and economists as presiding figures (Marx in one case, Gesell and Douglas in the other). Both authors have investments in antiquarian bodies of knowledge whose relevance to their own times they overestimate. Neither knows when to stop. And both were in the end consumed by the monster of fascism, Benjamin tragically, Pound shamefully.

It has been the fate of the *Cantos* to have a handful of anthology pieces excerpted, and the rest (Van Buren, the Malatestas, Confucius, etc.) quietly dropped. The fate of *The Arcades Project* may well be comparable. One can foresee a condensed, student edition drawn mainly from Convolutes B ('Fashion'), H ('The Collector'), I ('The Interior'), J ('Baudelaire'), K ('Dream City'), N ('On the Theory of Knowledge'), and Y ('Photography'), in which the quotations would be cut to a minimum and most of the surviving text will be by Benjamin himself. And that would be not wholly a bad thing.

Even on his chosen ground there is much for which Benjamin can be faulted. For someone who, if not exactly an economic historian, spent years of his life reading economic history, he was remarkably ignorant about those parts of the world where nineteenth-century capitalism most flourished, namely Britain and the United States. In his treatment of the department store he misses a crucial difference between the *grands magasins* of Paris and the department stores of New York and Chicago: whereas the former erected barriers to a mass clientèle, the latter saw it as their role to educate working-class shoppers into middle-class habits of consumption. He also makes nothing of the fact that arcades and department stores catered to the desires of women above all, while doing their best to form those desires and even create new ones.

The range of interests represented in the first two volumes of Benjamin's *Selected Writings* is broad. Besides the pieces focused on in this essay, there are a selection of his early, rather earnestly idealistic writings on education; numerous literary-critical essays, including two long pieces on Goethe, one of them an interpretation of *Elective Affinities*, the other a masterly overview of Goethe's career; excurses on various topics in philosophy (logic, metaphysics, aesthetics, philosophy of language, philosophy of history); essays on pedagogy, on children's books, on toys; an engagingly personal piece on book collecting; and a variety of travel pieces and forays into fiction. The essay on *Elective Affinities* stands out as a particularly strange performance: an extended aria, in supersubtle, mandarin prose, on love and beauty, myth and fate, brought to a high pitch of intensity by the secret resemblances Benjamin saw between the plot of the novel and a tragicomic erotic foursome he and his wife were involved in.

The third and fourth volumes of the *Selected Writings* include the 1935, 1938, and 1939 resumés of the Arcades Project; 'The Work of Art' in two versions; 'The Storyteller'; 'A Berlin Childhood'; the 'Theses on the Concept of History'; and a number of key letters to and from Adorno and Scholem, including the important 1938 letter on Kafka.

The translations, by various hands, are excellent throughout. If any one of the translators deserves to be singled out, it is Rodney Livingstone for his discreet efficiency in coping with the shifts of style and tone that mark Benjamin's development as a writer. The explanatory notes are of nearly the same high standard, but not quite. Information on figures referred to by Benjamin is sometimes out of date (Robert Walser) or incorrect: the dates for Karl

Korsch, on whom Benjamin relied heavily for his interpretation of Marx (Korsch was expelled from the German Communist Party for his maverick opinions), are given as 1892–1939 when they were in fact 1886–1961. (*V2*, p. 790 n5) There are errors in the Greek and Latin, and French sometimes fares badly: to call a gaggle of priests in their *soutanes* 'civilised crows' misses the point – better would be 'domesticated crows'. (*V2*, p. 354 note 35) Cryptic remarks – for instance, on 'the ominous spread of the cult of rambling' in Germany of the 1920s – are left unexplained. (*V1*, p. 454)

Some general practices of the editors and translators are also questionable. Benjamin had a habit of writing paragraphs pages long: surely the translator should feel free to break these up. Sometimes two drafts of the same piece are included, for reasons that are not made clear. Existing translations of German texts quoted by Benjamin are used when these translations are clearly not up to standard.[17]

What was Walter Benjamin: a philosopher? A critic? A historian? A mere 'writer'? The best answer is perhaps Hannah Arendt's: he was 'one of the unclassifiable ones . . . whose work neither fits the existing order nor introduces a new genre'.[18]

His trademark approach – coming at a subject not straight on but at an angle, moving stepwise from one perfectly formulated summation to the next – is as instantly recognisable as it is inimitable, depending on sharpness of intellect, learning lightly worn, and a prose style which, once he had given up thinking of himself as Professor Doctor Benjamin, became a marvel of accuracy and concision. Underlying his project of getting at the truth of our times is Goethe's ideal of setting out the facts in such a way that the facts will be their own theory. The Arcades book, whatever our verdict on it – ruin, failure, impossible project – suggests a new way of writing about a civilisation, using its rubbish as materials rather than its artworks: history from below rather than from above. And his call (in the 'Theses') for a history centred on the sufferings of the vanquished, rather than on the achievements of the victors, is prophetic of the way in which history-writing has begun to think of itself in our lifetime.

(2001)

5   Bruno Schulz

IN ONE OF his earliest childhood recollections, young Bruno Schulz sits on the floor ringed by admiring family members while he scrawls one 'drawing' after another over the pages of old newspapers. In his creative rapture, the child still inhabits an 'age of genius', still has unselfconscious access to the realm of myth. Or so it seemed to the man whom the child became; all of his mature strivings would be to regain touch with his early powers, to 'mature into childhood'.[1]

These strivings would issue in two bodies of work: etchings and drawings that would probably be of no great interest today had their deviser not become famous by other means; and two short books, collections of stories and sketches about the inner life of a boy in provincial Galicia, which propelled him to the forefront of Polish letters of the interwar years. Rich in fantasy, sensuous in their apprehension of the living world, elegant in style, witty, underpinned by a mystical but coherent idealistic aesthetic, *Cinnamon Shops* (1934) and *Sanatorium Under the Sign of the Hourglass* (1937) were unique and startling productions that seemed to come out of nowhere.

Bruno Schulz was born in 1892, the third child of Jewish parents from the merchant class, and named for the Christian saint on whose name-day his birthday fell. His home town, Drohobycz, was a minor industrial centre in a province of the Austro-Hungarian Empire that after World War I returned to being part of Poland.

Though there was a Jewish school in Drohobycz, Schulz was sent to the Polish *Gymnasium*. (Joseph Roth, in nearby Brody, had gone to a German *Gymnasium*.) His languages were Polish and German; he did not speak the Yiddish of the streets. At school he excelled at art, but was dissuaded by his family from following art as a profession. He registered to study architecture at the polytechnic in Lwow, but in 1914, when war was declared, had to break off his studies. Because of a heart defect he was not called up into the army. Returning to Drohobycz, he set about a programme of intensive self-education, reading and perfecting his draughtsmanship. He put together a portfolio of graphics on erotic themes entitled *The Book of Idolatry* and tried to sell copies, with some diffidence and not much success.

Unable to make a living as an artist, saddled, after his father's death, with a houseful of ailing relatives to support, he took a job as an art teacher at a local school, a position he held until 1941. Though respected by his students, he found school life stultifying and wrote letter after letter imploring the authorities for time off to pursue his creative work, pleas to which, to their credit, they did not always turn a deaf ear.

Despite his isolation in the provinces, Schulz was able to exhibit his artworks in urban centres and to enter into correspondence with kindred spirits. Into his thousands of letters, some 156 of which have survived, he poured much of his creative energy. Jerzy Ficowski, Schulz's biographer, calls him the last outstanding exponent of epistolary art in Poland.[2] All evidence indicates that the pieces that make up *Cinnamon Shops* began their life in letters to the poet Debora Vogel.

Cinnamon Shops was received with enthusiasm by the Polish

intelligentsia. On visits to Warsaw Schulz was welcomed into artistic salons and invited to write for literary reviews; at his school he was awarded the title 'Professor'. He became engaged to Józefina Szelińska, a Jewish convert to Catholicism, and, while not himself converting, withdrew formally from the Jewish religious community of Drohobycz. Of his fiancée he wrote: '[She] constitutes my participation in life. Through her I am a person, and not just a lemur and kobold . . . She is the closest person to me on earth.' (Ficowski, p. 112) Nevertheless, after two years the engagement fell through.

The first translation into Polish of Franz Kafka's *The Trial* appeared in 1936 under Schulz's name, but the actual work of translation had been done by Szelińska.

Sanatorium Under the Sign of the Hourglass, Schulz's second book, was for the most part cobbled together from early pieces, some of them still tentative and amateurish. Schulz tended to deprecate the book, though in fact a number of the stories are quite up to the standard of *Cinnamon Shops*.

Burdened with teaching and with familial responsibilities, anxious about political developments in Europe, Schulz was by the late 1930s descending into a state of depression in which he found it hard to write. Receipt of the Golden Laurel of the Polish Academy of Literature did not raise his spirits. Nor did a three-week visit to Paris, his only substantial venture outside his native land. He set off for what he would in retrospect call 'the most exclusive, self-sufficient, standoffish city in the world' in the dubious hope of arranging an exhibition of his artworks, but made few contacts and came away emptyhanded.[3]

In 1939, in terms of the Nazi-Soviet partition of Poland, Drohobycz was absorbed into Soviet Ukraine. Under the Soviets there were no opportunities for Schulz as a writer ('We don't need Prousts,' he was bluntly told). He was, however, commissioned to produce propaganda paintings. He continued to teach until, in the summer of 1941, the Ukraine was invaded by the Germans and all schools were closed. Executions of Jews began at once, and in 1942 mass deportations.

For a while Schulz managed to escape the worst. He had the luck to be adopted by a Gestapo officer with pretensions to art, thereby acquiring the status of 'necessary Jew' and the precious armband that protected him during roundups. For decorating the walls of his patron's residence and the officers' casino he was paid in food rations. Meanwhile he bundled his artworks and manuscripts in packages and deposited them among non-Jewish friends. Well-wishers in Warsaw smuggled money and false papers to him, but before he could summon up the resolve to flee Drohobycz he was dead, singled out and shot in the street during a day of anarchy launched by the Gestapo.

By 1943 there were no Jews left in Drohobycz.

In the late 1980s, as the Soviet Union was breaking up, news reached the Polish scholar Jerzy Ficowski that an unnamed person with access to the KGB archives had come into the possession of one of Schulz's packages, and was prepared to dispose of it for a price. Though the lead ran dry, it provided the basis for Ficowski's stubborn hope that lost writings of Schulz's might yet be recovered. Among the lost writings are an unfinished novel, *Messiah*, of which we know because Schulz had read extracts to friends, and notes that Schulz was taking up to the time of his death, memoranda of conversations with Jews who had seen at first hand the working of the execution squads and transports, intended to form the basis of a book about the persecutions. (A book of the very kind that Schulz was planning was published in 1997 by Henryk Grynberg.[4] Schulz himself figures as a minor character in the first of Grynberg's stories.)

In Poland Jerzy Ficowski (deceased 2006) was known as a poet and scholar of Gypsy life. His main reputation rests, however, on his work on Bruno Schulz. From the 1940s Ficowski indefatigably, against all obstacles, bureaucratic and material, scoured Poland, the Ukraine, and the wider world for what was left of Schulz. His translator, Theodosia Robertson, calls him an archaeologist, the leading archaeologist of Schulz's artistic remains. (Ficowski, p. 12) *Regions of the Great Heresy* is Robertson's translation of the third, revised edition (1992) of Ficowski's biography, to which he added two chapters – one on the lost novel *Messiah,* one on the fate of the murals that Schulz painted in Drohobycz in his last year – as well as a detailed chronology and a selection from Schulz's surviving letters.

Within her translation of *Regions of the Great Heresy,* Robertson has elected to retranslate all passages quoted from Schulz. She does so because, in the company of other US-based scholars of Polish literature, she has reservations about the existing English translations. These appeared from the hand of Celina Wieniewska in 1963: it is through them, under the collective title *The Street of Crocodiles*, that Schulz has hitherto been known in the English-speaking world.[5] Wieniewska's translations are open to criticism on a number of grounds. First, they are based on faulty texts: a dependable, scholarly edition of Schulz's writings appeared only in 1989. Second, there are occasions when Wieniewska silently emends Schulz. In the sketch 'A Second Autumn', for example, Schulz fancifully names Bolechow as the home of Robinson Crusoe. Bolechow is a town near Drohobycz; whatever Schulz's reasons for not pointing to his own town, it behoves his translator to respect them. Wieniewska changes 'Bolechow' to 'Drohobycz'. (*CW*, p. 190) Third and most seriously, there are numerous instances where Wieniewska cuts Schulz's prose to make it less florid, or universalises specifically Jewish allusions.

In Wieniewska's favour it must be said that her translations read very well. Her prose has a rare richness, grace, and unity of style. Whoever takes on the task of retranslating Schulz will find it hard to escape her shadow.

As a guide to *Cinnamon Shops*, we can do no better than go to the synopsis that Schulz himself wrote when he was trying to interest an Italian publisher in the book. (His plans came to nothing, as did plans for French and German translations.)

Cinnamon Shops, he says, is the story of a family told in the mode not of biography or psychology but of myth. The book can thus be called pagan in conception: as with the ancients, the historical time of the clan merges back into the mythological time of the forebears. But in his book the myths are not communal in nature. They emerge from the mists of early childhood, from the hopes and fears, fantasies and forebodings – what he elsewhere calls 'mutterings of mythological delirium' – that form the seedbed of mythic thinking. (*CW*, p. 370)

At the centre of the family in question is Jacob, by trade a merchant, but preoccupied with the redemption of the world, a mission he pursues through the means of experiments in mesmerism, galvanism, psychoanalysis, and other more occult arts belonging to what he calls the Regions of the Great Heresy. Jacob is surrounded by lumpish folk who have no grasp of his metaphysical strivings, led by his arch-enemy, the housemaid Adela.

In his attic Jacob rears, from eggs that he imports from all quarters of the world, squadrons of messenger birds – condors, eagles, peacocks, pheasants, pelicans – whose physical being he sometimes seems on the brink of sharing. But with her broom Adela scatters his birds to the four winds. Defeated, embittered, Jacob begins to shrink and dry up, metamorphosing at last into a cockroach. Now and again he resumes his original form in order to give his son lectures on such subjects as puppets, tailors' dummies, and the power of the heresiarch to bring trash to life.

This summary was not the limit of Schulz's efforts to explain what he was up to in *Cinnamon Shops*. For the eyes of a friend, the writer and painter Stanisław Witkiewicz, Schulz extended his account, producing a piece of introspective analysis of remarkable power and acuity amounting to a poetic credo.

He begins by recalling images from his own 'age of genius', his mythologised childhood, 'when everything blazed with godly colors'. (*CW*, p. 319) Two of these images still dominate his imagination: a horsedrawn cab with lanterns aglow emerging from a dark forest; and a father striding through the darkness, speaking soothing words to the child folded in his arms, though all the child hears is the sinister call of the night. The origin of the first image, he says, is obscure to him; the second comes from Goethe's ballad 'Der Erlkönig', which shook him to the bottom of his soul when his mother read it to him at age eight.

Images like these, he proceeds, are laid down for us at the threshold of life. They constitute 'an iron capital of the spirit'. For the artist they mark out the boundaries of his creative powers: all of the rest of his life consists in exploring and interpreting and trying to master them. After childhood we discover nothing new, we only go back again and again over the same ground in a struggle without resolution. 'The knot the soul got itself tied up in is not a false one that comes undone when you pull the ends. On the contrary, it draws tighter.' Out of the tussle with the knot emerges art. (*CW*, p. 368)

As for the deeper meaning of *Cinnamon Shops*, says Schulz, generally it is not good policy for a writer to subject his work to too much rational analysis. It is like demanding of actors that they drop their masks: it kills the play. 'In a work of art the umbilical cord linking it with the totality of our concerns has not yet been severed, the blood of the mystery still circulates; the ends of the blood vessels vanish into the surrounding night and return from it full of dark fluid.' (*CW*, pp. 368–9)

Nevertheless, if driven to give an exposition, he would say that the book presents a certain primitive, vitalistic view of the world in which matter is in a constant state of fermentation and germination. There is no such thing as dead matter, nor does matter remain in fixed form. 'Reality takes on certain shapes merely for the sake of appearance, as a joke or form of play. One person is human, another is a cockroach, but shape does not penetrate essence, is only a role adopted for the moment, an outer skin soon to be shed . . . [The] migration of forms is the essence of life.' Hence the 'all-pervading aura of irony' to be found in his world: 'the bare fact of separate individual existence holds an irony, a hoax.'

For this vision of the world Schulz does not feel he has to give an ethical justification. *Cinnamon Shops* in particular operates at a 'premoral' depth. 'The role of art is to be a probe sunk into the nameless. The artist is an apparatus for registering processes in that deep stratum where value is formed.' At a personal level, however, he will concede that the stories emerge from and represent 'my way of living, my personal fate', a fate marked by 'profound loneliness, isolation from the stuff of daily life'. (*CW*, pp. 369, 370)

The essay 'The Mythologizing of Reality', written a year later in 1936, presents in succinct form Schulz's thinking on the task of the poet, thinking which is itself mythic rather than systematic in its operations. The quest for knowledge, Schulz says, is at heart a quest to recover an original, unitary state of being, a state from which there had been some kind of fall into fragmentation. The way of science is to seek patiently, methodically, and inductively to put the fragments together again. Poetry seeks the same ends, but 'intuitively, deductively, with large, daring short cuts and approximations'. The poet – himself a mythic being involved in a mythic quest – works at the most basic level, the level of the word. The inner life of the word consists in 'tensing and stretching itself towards a thousand connections, like the cut-up snake in the legend whose pieces search for each other in the dark'. Systematic thought, by its nature, holds the parts of the snake apart to examine them; the poet, with his access to the 'old semantics', allows the word-parts to find their place again in the myths of which all knowledge is constituted. (*CW*, pp. 371–3)

On the basis of his two works of fiction, preoccupied as they are with a child's experience of the world, Schulz is often thought of as a naïve writer, a kind of urban folk artist. As his letters and essays demonstrate, however, he was an original thinker with remarkable powers of self-analysis, a sophisticated intellectual who, despite his provincial origins, could cross swords on terms of equality with confrères like Witkiewicz and Witold Gombrowicz.

In one exchange, Gombrowicz reports to Schulz a conversation with a stranger, a doctor's wife, who tells him that in her opinion the writer Bruno Schulz is 'either a sick pervert or a poseur, but most probably a poseur'. Gombrowicz challenges Schulz to defend himself in print, adding that he should regard the challenge as both substantive and aesthetic: for his reply he should find a tone that is neither haughty nor flippant nor laboured and solemn. (*CW*, p. 374)

In his reply Schulz ignores the task Gombrowicz has set him, coming at the question instead from a slant. What is it, he asks, that causes Gombrowicz, and artists in general, to pay attention to, and even take secret delight in, the stupidest, most philistine expressions of public opinion? (Why, for example, did Gustave Flaubert spend months and years collecting *bêtises*, stupidities, and arranging them in his *Dictionary of Received Opinions*?) 'Aren't you astonished,' he asks Gombrowicz, 'at [your] involuntary sympathy and solidarity with what at bottom is alien and hostile to you?' (*CW*, p. 377)

Unacknowledged sympathy with mindless popular opinion, Schulz suggests, comes from atavistic modes of thinking embedded in all of us. When some ignorant stranger dismisses him, Schulz, as a poseur, 'a dark, inarticulate mob rises up in you [Gombrowicz], like a bear trained to the sound of a gypsy's flute'. And this is because of the way the psyche itself is organised: as a multitude of overlapping subsystems, some more rational, some less so. Hence 'the confusing, multitrack nature' of our thinking in general. (*CW*, pp. 377, 378)

Schulz is also commonly thought of as a disciple, an epigone, or even an imitator of his older contemporary Franz Kafka. The similarities between his personal history and Kafka's are certainly remarkable. Both were born under Emperor Franz Joseph I into merchant-class Jewish families; both were sickly and found sexual relations difficult; both worked conscientiously at routine jobs; both were haunted by father figures; both died before their time, bequeathing complicated and troublesome literary estates. Furthermore, Schulz is (mistakenly) believed to have translated Kafka. Finally, Kafka wrote a story in which a man turned into an insect, while Schulz wrote stories in which a man is turned not only into one insect after another but into a crab too. (The crab-avatar of Jacob the father is thrown into boiling water by a maid, but then no one can bear to eat the jellified mess he becomes.)

Schulz's comments on his writing should make it clear how superficial these parallels are. His own orientation is toward the recreation, or perhaps fabulation, of a childhood conciousness, full of terror, obsession, and crazy glory; his metaphysics is a metaphysics of matter. Nothing of the kind is to be found in Kafka.

For Józefina Szelińska's translation of *The Trial* Schulz wrote an afterword that is notable for its perceptiveness and aphoristic power, but even more striking for its attempt to draw Kafka into the Schulzian orbit, to make of Kafka a Schulz *avant la lettre*.

'Kafka's procedure, the creation of a *doppelgänger* or substitute reality, stands virtually without precedent,' writes Schulz. 'Kafka sees the realistic surface of existence with unusual precision, he knows by heart, as it were, its code of gestures, all the external mechanics of events and situations, how they dovetail and inter-lace, but these to him are but a loose epidermis without roots, which he lifts off like a delicate membrane and fits onto his tran-scendental world, grafts onto his reality.'

Though the procedure Schulz describes here does not get to the heart of Kafka, as far as it goes it is admirably put. But he continues: '[Kafka's] attitude to reality is radically ironic, treacherous, profoundly ill-intentioned – the relationship of a prestidigitator to his raw material. He only simulates the attention to detail, the seriousness, and the elaborate precision of this reality in order to compromise it all the more thoroughly.' All of a sudden Schulz has left the real Kafka behind and begun to describe another kind of artist, the artist he himself is or would like to be seen as. It is a measure of his confidence in his own powers that he could try to refashion Kafka in his own image. (*CW*, p. 349)

The world that Schulz creates in his two books is remarkably unsullied by history. The Great War and the convulsions that followed upon it cast no backward shadow; there is no intima-tion, for example, that the sons of the barefoot peasant who, in the story 'Dead Season', is made fun of by the Jewish shop assist-ants, will decades later return to the same shop, ransack it, and beat the sons and daughters of the assistants.

There are hints that Schulz was aware that he could not for

ever live on the iron capital he had stored up in his childhood. Describing his state of mind in a 1937 letter, he says that he feels as if he is being dragged out of a deep sleep. 'The peculiarity and unusual nature of my inner processes sealed me off hermetically, made me insensitive, unreceptive to the world's incursions. Now I am opening myself up to the world . . . All would be well if it weren't for [the] terror and inner shrinking, as if before a perilous venture that might lead God knows where.' (*CW*, p. 408)

The story in which he most clearly turns his face to the wider world and to historical time is 'Spring'. The young narrator encounters his first stamp album, and in this burning book, in the parade of images from lands whose existence he had never guessed at – Hyderabad, Tasmania, Nicaragua, Abaracadabra – the fiery beauty of a world beyond Drohobycz suddenly reveals itself. Amidst the magical plenitude he comes upon the stamps of Austria, dominated by the image of Franz Joseph, emperor of prose (here the narrating voice can no longer pretend to be a child's), a dried-up, dull man used to breathing the air of chanceries and police stations. What ignominy to come from a land with such a ruler! How much better to be a subject of the dashing Archduke Maximilian!

'Spring' is Schulz's longest story, the one in which he makes the most concerted effort to develop a narrative line – in other words, to become a storyteller of a more conventional sort. Its basis is a quest story: the young hero undertakes to track down his beloved Bianca (Bianca of the slim bare legs) in a world modelled on the stamp album. As narrative it is formulaic; after a while it declines into a pastiche of costume drama and then peters out.

But halfway through, just as he is beginning to lose interest in the story he is concocting, Schulz turns his eyes inward and launches into a dense four-page meditation upon his own writing processes that one can only imagine as having been written in a trance, a piece of rhapsodic philosophising that develops one last time the imagery of the subterranean earthbed from which myth draws its sacred powers. Come to the underground with me, he says, to the place of roots where words break down and return to their etymologies, the place of anamnesis. Then travel deeper down, to the very bottom, to 'the dark foundations, among the Mothers', the realm of unborn tales. (*CW*, p. 140)

In these nether depths, which is the first tale to unfold its wings from the cocoon of sleep? It turns out to be one of the two foundation myths of his own spiritual being: the Erlkönig story, the story of the child whose parent has not the power to hold her (or him) back from the sweet persuasions of the dark – in other words, the story that, heard from his mother's lips, announced to the young Bruno that his destiny would entail leaving the parental breast and entering the realms of night.

Schulz was incomparably gifted as an explorer of his own inner life, which is at the same time the recollected inner life of his childhood and his own creative workings. From the first comes the charm and freshness of his stories, from the second their intellectual power. But he was right in sensing that he would not for ever be able to draw from this well. From somewhere he would have to renew the sources of his inspiration: the depression and sterility of the late 1930s may have stemmed precisely from a realisation that his capital was exhausted. In the four stories we have that postdate *Sanatorium*, one of them written not in Polish but in German, there is no indication that such a renewal had yet occurred. Whether for his *Messiah* he succeeded in finding new sources we will probably – despite Ficowski's best hopes – never know.

Schulz was a gifted visual artist within a certain narrow technical and emotional range. The early *Book of Idolatry* series in particular is a record of a masochistic obsession: hunched, dwarflike men, among whom Schulz himself is recognisable, grovel at the feet of imperious girls with slim, bare legs.

Behind the narcissistic challenge of Schulz's girls one can detect Goya's *Naked Maja*. The influence of the expressionists is also strong, Edvard Munch in particular. There are hints of the Belgian Félicien Rops. Curiously, in view of the importance of dreams to Schulz's fiction, the surrealists have left no mark on his drawings. Rather, as he matures, an element of sardonic comedy grows stronger.

The girls in Schulz's drawings are of a piece with Adela, the maid who rules the household in *Cinnamon Street* and reduces the narrator's father to childishness by stretching out a leg and proffering a foot to be worshipped. Fiction and artwork belong to the same universe; some of the drawings were meant to illustrate the stories. But Schulz never pretended that his visual art, with its restricted ambitions, was on a par with his writing.

Ficowski's book includes a selection of Schulz's drawings and graphics. A fuller selection is available in his edition of the *Collected Works*. All of Schulz's surviving drawings are available in reproduction in a handsome bilingual volume published by the Adam Mickiewicz Literary Museum.[6]

(2003)

6 Joseph Roth, the stories

AT THE APOGEE of a reign that commenced in 1848 and ran until 1916, Franz Joseph, Emperor of Austria and King of Hungary, ruled over some fifty million subjects. Of these, fewer than a quarter had German as their mother tongue. Even within Austria itself every second person was a Slav of one kind or another – Czech, Slovak, Pole, Ukrainian, Serb, Croat, or Slovene. Each of these ethnic nationalities had aspirations to become a nation-state in its own right, with all the appurtenances that go therewith, including a national language and a national literature.

The mistake of the imperial government, we can see with hindsight, was to take these aspirations too lightly, to believe that the benefits of belonging to an enlightened, prosperous, peaceful, multi-ethnic state would outweigh the pull of separatism and the push of anti-German (or, in the case of the Slovaks, anti-Magyar) prejudice. When war – precipitated by a spectacular act of terrorism by ethnic nationalists – broke out in 1914, the Empire found itself too weak to withstand the armies of Russia, Serbia, and Italy on its borders, and fell to pieces.

'Austro-Hungary is no more,' wrote Sigmund Freud to himself on Armistice Day, 1918. 'I do not want to live anywhere else . . . I shall live on with the torso and imagine that it is the whole.'[1] Freud spoke for many Jews of Austro-German culture. The dismemberment of the old Empire, and the redrawing of the map of eastern Europe to create new homelands based on ethnicity, worked to the detriment of Jews most of all, since there was no territory they could point to as ancestrally their own. The old supranational imperial state had suited them; the postwar settlement was a calamity. The first years of the new, stripped-down, barely viable Austrian state, with food shortages followed by levels of inflation that wiped out the savings of the middle class, and violence on the streets between paramilitary forces of Left and Right, only intensified their unease. Some began to look to Palestine as a national home; others turned to the supranational creed of communism.

Nostalgia for a lost past, and anxiety about a homeless future, are at the heart of the mature work of the Austrian novelist Joseph Roth. Roth looked back fondly on the Austro-Hungarian monarchy as the only fatherland he had ever had. 'I loved this fatherland,' he wrote in a foreword to *The Radetzky March*. 'It permitted me to be a patriot and a citizen of the world at the same time, among all the Austrian peoples also a German. I loved the virtues and merits of this fatherland, and today, when it is dead and gone, I even love its flaws and weaknesses.'[2] *The Radetzky March* is Roth's masterpiece, a great poem of elegy to Habsburg Austria composed by a subject from an outlying imperial territory; a great contribution to literature in the German language from a writer with barely a toehold in the German community of letters.

Moses Joseph Roth was born in 1894 in Brody, a middle-sized city a few miles from the Russian border in the imperial crown-land of Galicia. Galicia had become part of the Austrian Empire in 1772, when Poland was dismembered; it was a poor region densely populated with Ukrainians (known in Austria as

Ruthenians), Poles, and Jews. Brody itself had been a centre of the Haskala, the Jewish Enlightenment. In the 1890s, two thirds of its population was Jewish.

In German-speaking parts of the Empire, Galician Jews were held in low esteem. As a young man making his way in Vienna, Roth played down his origins, claiming to have been born in Schwabendorf, a predominantly German town (this fiction appears in his official papers). His father, he claimed, had been (variously) a factory owner, an army officer, a high state official, a painter, a Polish aristocrat. In fact Nachum Roth worked in Brody as an agent for a firm of German grain merchants. Moses Joseph never knew him: in 1893, shortly after his marriage, Nachum suffered a brainstorm of some kind on a train journey to Hamburg. He was taken to a sanatorium and from there passed into the hands of a wonder-working rabbi. He never recovered, never returned to Brody.

Moses Joseph was brought up by his mother in the home of her parents, prosperous assimilated Jews. He went to a Jewish community school where the language of instruction was German, then to the German-language *Gymnasium* in Brody. Half his fellow students were Jewish: to young Jews from the East, a German education opened the doors to commerce and to the dominant culture.

In 1914 Roth enrolled at the University of Vienna. Vienna at this time had the largest Jewish community in central Europe, some 200,000 souls living in what amounted to a ghetto of a voluntary kind. 'It is hard enough being an *Ostjude*,' a Jew from the East, remarked Roth; but 'there is no harder fate than being an *Ostjude* outsider in Vienna.' *Ostjuden* had to contend not only with anti-Semitism but with the aloofness of Western Jews.[3]

Roth was an outstanding student, particularly of German literature, though he looked down on most of his teachers, finding them servile and pedantic. This disdain is reflected in his early writings, which reflect the state-run education system as the preserve of careerists or else timid, uninspired plodders.

As a part-time job he tutored the young sons of a countess, and in the process picked up such dandyish mannerisms as kissing the hands of ladies, carrying a cane, wearing a monocle. He began to publish poems.

His education, which seemed to be leading him toward an academic career, was unfortunately terminated by the war. Overcoming pacifist inclinations, he enlisted in 1916, at the same time abandoning the name Moses. Ethnic tensions ran high enough in the imperial army for him to be transferred out of his German-speaking unit; he spent 1917–18 in a Polish-speaking unit in Galicia. His period of service became the subject of further fanciful additions to his biography, including stories he had been an officer and a prisoner of war in Russia. Years later he was still peppering his speech with officer-caste slang.

After the war Roth began to write for the press, and quickly gained a following among the Viennese. Before the war Vienna had been the capital of a great empire; now it was an impoverished city of two million in a country of barely seven million. Seeking better opportunities, Roth and his new wife Friederike moved to Berlin. There he wrote for liberal newspapers but also for the left-wing *Vorwärts*, signing his pieces 'Der rote Joseph', Joseph the Red. The first of his *Zeitungromane*, newspaper novels, came out, so called not only because they shared the themes of his journalism but also because the text was chopped up into short, snappy units. *The Spider's Web* (1923) deals presciently with the moral and spiritual menace of the fascist Right. It appeared three days before Hitler's first putsch.

In 1925 Roth was appointed Paris correspondent of the *Frankfurter Zeitung*, the leading liberal paper of the day, at a salary that made him one of the best-paid journalists in Germany. He had come to Berlin to make a career as a German writer, but in France he found that at heart he was French – 'a Frenchman from the East'.[4] He was enraptured by what he called the silkiness of French women, particularly the women he saw in Provence.

Even in his youth Roth had commanded a lucid, supple German. Now, using Stendhal and Flaubert – particularly the Flaubert of *Un Coeur simple* – as models, he perfected his characteristically exact mature style. (Referring to *The Radetzky March*, he remarked, 'Der Leutnant Trotta, der bin ich,' consciously echoing Flaubert's 'Madame Bovary, c'est moi.')[5] He even toyed with the idea of settling in France and writing in French.

After a year, however, the *Frankfurter Zeitung* replaced him in its Paris office. Disappointed, he put in for a trip to Russia. His habit of (in his words) 'handling in ironic fashion certain institutions, morals and customs of the bourgeois world' should not, he contended, be assumed to disqualify him from reporting on Russia and the 'dubious consequences' of the Russian revolution. His series of dispatches was a great success; reports from Albania, Poland, and Italy followed. He was proud of his journalistic work. 'I don't write so-called witty commentaries. *I sketch the features of the age* . . . I am a journalist, not a reporter, I am a writer, not a fashioner of lead articles.'[6]

Through all of this he continued to write fiction. In 1930 he published his ninth novel, *Job: The Story of a Simple Man*. Despite – or perhaps because of – its sentimental, fairytale ending – the ageing Mendel Singer, buffeted by the blows of fate and sinking into penury in the slums of New York, is whisked to safety by the idiot son he had abandoned in the Old World, a son who has unbeknown to him become a world-famous musician – *Job* became an international success (Roth confessed that he could not have penned the ending without recourse to drink). Purging the book of its Jewish elements, Hollywood turned *Job* into a movie under the title *Sins of Man*. *Job* was followed two years later by Roth's most ambitious book, *The Radetzky March*. Six more novels appeared in his lifetime, all of them smaller in scale, and a number of short fictions.

The Radetzky March, incomparably Roth's greatest novel and the only one on which he worked without undue haste, follows the fortunes of three generations of the Trotta family, servants of the Crown: the first Trotta a simple soldier elevated to the minor nobility for an act of heroism; the second a high provincial administrator; the third an army officer whose life dissolves into futility as the Habsburg mystique loses its hold on him, and who perishes without issue in the Great War.

The trajectory of the Trottas mirrors the trajectory of the Empire. The ideal of selfless service embodied in the middle Trotta falters in his son not because the Empire has gone wrong in any objective way but because there has been a change in the air that makes the old idealism unsustainable (it is the selfsame change in the air that is the starting point for the dissection of old Austria in Robert Musil's *The Man without Qualities*). The young Trotta, born in the 1890s, may represent the generation of Roth and Musil ('Der Leutnant Trotta, der bin ich'), but it is his father, who late in life has not only to swallow the shame of his son's failures but to discover – as he does with endearing humility – that the beliefs to which he has dedicated his life have fallen out of fashion, who is the most tragic figure in the book, and who shows how much more complex Roth is as a critical artist than as the apologist for the Habsburgs he later became.

In Roth's books, it is among its most marginal subjects that the Empire finds its most faithful followers. The Trottas, his exemplary Austro-Hungarians, are not German but Slovenian in origin.

Having killed off one line of this clan, Roth creates a distant Trotta cousin through whom to continue, in *Die Kapuzinergruft* (1938; translated as *The Emperor's Tomb*), a rather pale sequel to *The Radetzky March*, his fictional history of the decline of the imperial ideal into the cynicism and decadence of postwar Vienna.

Meanwhile Friederike Roth had become mentally ill and been hospitalised. She spent the 1930s in asylums in Germany and Austria; when the Nazis took control she would be one of those selected to be euthanised.

In 1933 Roth quit Germany for good, and, after roaming around Europe for a while, settled back in Paris. Translations of his work were coming out in a dozen languages; by most measures he was a successful author. His financial affairs were, however, in chaos. Furthermore, he had long been a heavy drinker, and by the mid 1930s had descended into alcoholism. In Paris he made his base in a tiny hotel room and spent his days in the café downstairs, writing, drinking, entertaining friends.

Hostile to both fascism and communism, he proclaimed himself a Catholic and involved himself in royalist politics, specifically in efforts to have Otto von Habsburg, grandnephew of the last emperor, restored to the throne. In 1938, with the threat of German annexation looming, he travelled to Austria as representative of the royalists to persuade the government to hand over the chancellorship to Otto. He had to depart ignominiously without being granted an audience. Back in Paris he urged the creation of an Austrian Legion to liberate Austria by force.

Opportunities to escape to the United States came up, but he let them pass. 'Why are you drinking so much?' asked a worried friend. 'Do you think you are going to escape? You too are going to be wiped out,' Roth replied.[7] He died in a Paris hospital in 1939, after days of delirium tremens. He was forty-four.

*

Though Roth tried his hand intermittently at short stories, his reputation in the English-speaking world has hitherto rested on his novels, above all on *The Radetzky March*. Then in 2001 his shorter fiction appeared in a translation by Michael Hofmann, with an introduction in which Hofmann puts in a claim for Roth as, at his best, the equal of Anton Chekhov.[8]

The title *The Collected Stories of Joseph Roth* would seem to make a promise, and an unambiguous one at that: that we are being offered all of Roth's stories. But what exactly are stories? Instead of trying to establish formal criteria – a hopeless task – Hofmann sensibly takes as his province all of Roth's fictional prose with the exception of his novels. In the relevant volumes of the canonical six-volume German *Werke* edited by Fritz Hackert there are eighteen pieces of fiction not labelled *Roman*, novel. The *Collected Stories* consists of seventeen of these eighteen pieces; it pays no attention to the fact that some of the eighteen are not proper stories with beginnings, middles, and ends, but fragments of abandoned larger projects; or the fact too that four of them appeared, either during Roth's lifetime or posthumously, as stand-alone books: *April: The History of a Love* (1925); *The Blind Mirror: A Short Novel* (1925); *The Legend of the Holy Drinker* (1939); and *The Leviathan* (printed in 1940, distributed only in 1945).

The missing eighteenth item is *The Legend of the Holy Drinker*, correctly classed by Hackert as a *Novelle*, a novella or long short story, rather than a *Roman*. The reason for its absence from the *Collected Stories*, tersely mentioned in the introduction, is that a translation (by Hofmann himself) is already on the market. The *Collected Stories* is therefore not, strictly speaking, the collected stories: it needs to be supplemented with either *The Legend of the Holy Drinker* (London: Chatto & Windus, 1989) or the composite volume *Right and Left* and *The Legend of the Holy Drinker* (New York: Overlook Press, 1992).

The first clear masterwork in the collection is 'Stationmaster Fallmerayer' of 1933. Fallmerayer is a cool, self-sufficient man of a type we find often in Roth, going dutifully but without feeling through the motions of love, marriage, and parenthood. Then fate intervenes. There is a train crash near the town in provincial Austria where he is stationmaster. One of the passengers, Countess Walewska, a Russian (an irritating feature of these translations is that German conventions are used to transliterate Russian names), is brought to his house to recuperate from shock. After her departure Fallmerayer recognises he has fallen in love with her.

Within months – the year is 1914 – Austria and Russia are at war. Fallmerayer fights on the eastern front, kept alive by his resolve to see the Countess again. In his spare time he teaches himself Russian. Sure enough, one day he finds himself in the vicinity of the Walewski estate. He announces himself; he and the Countess become lovers.

Their idyll is interrupted by the Bolshevik revolution. Fallmerayer saves the Countess from the Reds and escorts her across the seas to the safety of the Walewski villa in Monte Carlo. But just when their happiness seems assured, Count Walewski, whom they had thought dead, reappears. Old and crippled, he demands to be taken care of. His wife cannot refuse. Fallmerayer sums up the situation and without a word walks out. 'Nothing has ever been heard of him since.' (*Collected Stories*, p. 201)

Roth's feel for what can and what cannot be achieved in the short story form is sure. To the eye of a novelist – Tolstoy, for instance, whose impress is detectable not only on this story but on the just completed *Radetzky March* – the sequence of events from the first meeting of the stationmaster and the Countess to the arrival of the Count might seem merely to set the stage for the real question: what will a middle-aged Austrian who has abandoned family and country to follow a woman, and now finds himself adrift in postwar Europe, do with his life? Roth does not even broach the question. Without denying the power of love, even of *amour fou*, to make us into fuller human beings, he takes Fallmerayer to the brink of the *what next?* and leaves him there.

'The Bust of the Emperor' (1935) belongs squarely to Roth's ultra-conservative phase. Set in Galicia immediately after the Great War, it concerns the quixotic Count Franz Xaver Morstin who, despite the fact that his properties now fall within Poland, keeps a bust of Emperor Franz Joseph in front of his residence and goes around in the uniform of an Austrian cavalry officer. The story is told by an unnamed narrator who takes it as his task to commemorate this obscure, low-key protest against the course of history.

The narrator wastes no time in giving us his opinion of modern times. In the course of the nineteenth century, he observes caustically, it was discovered that 'every individual had to be a member of a particular race or nation'. 'All those people who had never been anything other than Austrians . . . began, in compliance with the "order of the day", to call themselves part of the Polish, the Czech, the Ukrainian, the German, the Romanian, the Slovenian, the Croatian "nation".' Among the few who continued to regard themselves as 'beyond nationality' was Count Morstin. (pp. 232, 233, 228)

Before the war the Count used to have some kind of social role as mediator between the people and the state bureaucracy. Now he is without power or influence. Yet the villagers – Jews, Poles, Ruthenians – continue to respect him. These folk are to be commended, advises the narrator, for resisting 'the incomprehensible caprices of world history'. 'The wide world is not so very different from the little village of Lopatyny as the leaders and the demagogues would have us believe,' he adds darkly. (p. 241)

Commanded by the new Polish authorities to remove the bust of the Emperor, Morstin supervises its solemn burial. Then he retires to the south of France to live out his days and write his memoirs. 'My former home, the monarchy . . . was a large house with many doors and many rooms for many different kinds of people,' he writes. 'This house has been divided, broken up, ruined. I have no business with what is there now. I am used to living in a house, not in cabins.' (p. 247)

Works like 'The Bust of the Emperor' and *The Emperor's Tomb* are conservative, not only in political outlook but in literary technique. Roth is not a modernist. Part of the reason is ideological, part temperamental, part, frankly, the fact that he did not keep up with developments in the literary world. Roth did not read much; he liked to quote Karl Kraus: 'A writer who spends his time reading is like a waiter who spends his time eating.'[9]

'The Leviathan' is an entirely different kind of story. Gone is Roth's reticence about his *Ostjude* origins. Set not in Galicia but in neighbouring Volhynia, in the Russian Empire, it is expansive, lyrical in tone, folkloric in manner. At its centre is the Jew Nissen Piczenik, who despite making a living selling coral beads to Ukrainian peasant women has never seen the sea. In the ocean of his imagination all living things, including the corals, are watched over by a fabulous beast, the Leviathan of Holy Scripture.

Piczenik makes friends with a young sailor, begins to visit taverns with him and miss prayers. He forsakes his family to go to Odessa with his new friend and stays there for weeks, fascinated with port life.

Back home, he finds he is losing trade to a rival who sells newfangled celluloid beads. Yielding to temptation, he begins to mix celluloid beads with the coral. But even this does not restore his fortunes. He decides to emigrate. En route to Canada his ship sinks. 'May he rest in peace beside the Leviathan until the coming of the Messiah,' run the last words of this most flamboyantly Jewish of Roth's stories. (p. 276)

'Stationmaster Fallmerayer', 'The Bust of the Emperor', and 'The Leviathan' are works of Roth's maturity. The earlier pieces in the *Collected Stories* are a miscellaneous lot, including humdrum pieces of naturalism, failed experiments, and abandoned fragments. Among the completed stories of this earlier phase, two stand out. 'The Honors Student' of 1916 is a remarkably confident debut. Set in small-town German Austria, it follows with a satirical eye the rise of Anton Wanzl, the honors student of the title, zealous, disciplined, obsequious, cunning – a being perfectly adapted to get ahead in the educational bureaucracy. Like many of these earlier pieces, however, it starts off full of ideas and energy, then loses its way and tails off.

The Wanzl character is rescued and reworked some fifteen years later in a first-person narrative entitled 'Youth'. The speaker comes across as cold-hearted, cynical, sensual yet mean with his emotions, excelling in literary study yet a stranger to the passions that animate great literature. 'Youth' scarcely pretends to be fiction: we seem to be reading a mordant, barely veiled piece of self-analysis on Roth's part.

'The Blind Mirror' (1925) is the story of a rather ordinary, dreamy, submissive, sexually naïve working-class girl, Fini, a *süße Mädel* in Viennese parlance. Here Roth goes in for a pastiche of novelette style, mitigating the syrupy sentiment with ironic touches and flashes of dark poetry. Fini works in a city office and lives in cramped quarters with a persecutory mother and a father invalided out of the army. Seduced by an older man, she soon finds how little fun there is in quasi-marital life with a lover who doesn't wash, wears slippers around the house, forgets to button his fly. 'Once a week, or maybe twice, they had congress on the studio sofa, a miserable surrender, silent and accompanied by silent weeping, like the desperate birthday celebrations of a terminal patient.' (p. 128)

Belatedly Fini finds true love in the arms of a dashing revolutionary. When this lover disappears, she drowns herself. Her story – an uneasy mix of parody, sentiment, and urban realism – comes to a close with her corpse on a dissecting table in a medical school.

In his letters of the 1920s Roth keeps mentioning a large-scale novel he is working on. The novel never got written; all that is left are two fragments, reprinted here – strings of anecdotes, fantastic in character and dotted with striking imagery, based on his early years in Galicia. Later Roth would transpose this material into a darker key and use it in a powerful short novel, *Das falsche Gewicht* (False Weight, translated into English as *Weights and Measures*), another work in which a man finds love too late in life to be able to enjoy it.

Michael Hofmann has translated Roth before, and has won prizes for his translations. Hofmann's English is as expressive, poised, and precise as Roth's German at its best. However, Roth did not always write as well as he could, and what Hofmann does when Roth is at less than top form is cause for concern.

In 'The Leviathan', for instance, Roth writes of the coral merchant Piczenik's wife's night attire, a 'long nightshirt, sprinkled with a number of irregular black spots, evidences of fleas'. Hofmann condenses this to a 'long flea-spotted nightgown'. In the same story Piczenik is greeted by his customers, in Roth's text, 'with embraces and kisses, laughing and crying, as if in him they were recovering a friend decades-long not seen, and long missed'. In Hofmann's version he is greeted 'with embraces and kisses, like a long-lost friend'. In both cases Hofmann seems to have decided that he can better render Roth's meaning by recasting or condensing the text than by translating every word. But is it part of a translator's job to give his author lessons in economy? (pp. 263, 260)

On occasion Hofmann improves on Roth to the point of rewriting him. In Hofmann we read of a pair of copper samovars 'burnished by the setting sun'. To burnish metal is to polish it, to make it shine. Inside the word 'burnish', by a neat linguistic accident, lies the word 'burn' – the copper shines because of the burning heat of the sun, so to speak. Any objection that English *burnish* derives from French *brunir*, to polish, which has nothing to do with burning, can be brushed aside, for it turns out that *burn-* and *brun-* words are tangled at the root in their Indo-European past. The only trouble is that none of this verbal ingenuity is to be found in Roth, in whose German the sun is merely reflected (*spiegelte sich*) in the samovars. (p. 261)

Sometimes Hofmann seems to nudge Roth in a direction in which Roth is not actually going: the pressure of a man's fingers on a girl's arm is 'insistent' when in the original it is merely soft. Sometimes, on the other hand, he misses a telling emphasis. To the narrator of 'The Bust of the Emperor', the generation that inherited power in Europe after 1918 was bad enough, but not as bad as (in Hofmann's version) 'the still more progressive and murderous inheritors' who succeeded it – a clear allusion to Mussolini, Hitler, and their cohort. But how can fascists be called progressive? In the German the word is *moderneren*, more modern: to Roth in his late phase, the *modern* line of thought that gave birth to the European nation-state also sanctioned the ethnic hatreds that would drive Europe to catastrophe. (pp. 105, 237)

Hofmann is British, and now and again uses British locutions whose meaning may escape the American reader. A young man plans to 'see off' (chase off) a rival for the affections of a girl. One girl asks another whether she has 'been poorly' yet (had her menstrual period). Someone 'havers' (hesitates) at the door of a hospital. Just as there is a case to be made for translating into the dialect of English that the translator commands most vividly, there is a contrary case to be made for using as linguistically neutral, as mid-Atlantic, a dialect as possible. (pp. 25, 102, 118)

(2002)

7 Sándor Márai

WE ARE WITH the old General, Henrik, in his castle in Hungary. The year is 1940. In twenty years, since the fall of the Habsburg monarchy, the General has not appeared in public. Now he is to have a visitor, his one-time bosom friend Konrad.

The General gazes at the portraits of his parents: his father the Guards officer, his mother the French noblewoman who did her best to fill this granite mausoleum in the woods with colour and music but in the end succumbed under its cold weight. In a long flashback he remembers how, as a boy, he was taken to Vienna to be enrolled in a military academy; how there he met Konrad, how the two became inseparable. During vacations back home he and Konrad rode together, fenced together, vowing to remain chaste. 'There is nothing to equal the delicacy of such a relationship. Everything that life has to offer later, sentimental yearnings or raw desire, intense feelings and eventually the bonds of passion, will all be coarser, more barbaric.'[1]

In due course the two young men graduated from the academy and joined the Guards. While Henrik led a conventional military-officer life, Konrad began to spend evenings alone, reading. Yet even after Henrik married the beautiful Krisztina, the bond between the two young men seemed unbroken.

The flashback ends. The old General opens a secret drawer and takes out a loaded revolver.

Out of the darkness Konrad arrives (how he has managed to cross German-occupied Europe he does not explain). Over dinner he describes his life since he and Henrik went their separate ways forty years ago. For years he worked in Malaya, for a British trading company. Now he is a British citizen and lives in England. In turn Henrik tells how, once the monarchy was abolished, he resigned his officer's commission.

The two agree that the post-1919 dispensation can inspire no feelings of loyalty in them. Konrad: 'My homeland was a feeling, and that feeling was mortally wounded . . . What we swore to uphold no longer exists . . . There was a world for which it was worth living and dying. That world is dead.' Henrik demurs: 'That world is still alive, even if in reality it no longer exists. It lives, because I swore an oath to uphold it.' (pp. 92–3)

Lightning strikes the electricity grid. In the castle the two old men continue their dinner by candlelight. A hundred pages have passed. We are halfway through *Embers* (Hungarian title: *The Candles Burn Down*). It is time for Hendrik to proceed to business.

All these past forty years, he tells Konrad, he has been plagued by a question to which he must now finally have an answer. In fact, if Konrad had not come tonight, he would have set out to find him, even in the bowels of hell. He reminds Konrad of what occurred on a certain fateful day in 1899 when he called at Konrad's bachelor apartment and to his surprise – he had never been there before, he was expecting a spartan set-up – found it full of beautiful objects, 'curtains and carpets, silver, ancient bronzes, crystal and furniture, rare woven materials'. (p. 118) As he stood marvelling, Krisztina stepped through the door, and the scales fell from his eyes.

Konrad and Krisztina had deceived and betrayed him – that was why Konrad fled the country. But had their treachery run even deeper? He cannot forget a moment when, out hunting with Konrad, a sixth sense told him that Konrad's gun was trained not on the deer but on the back of his head. (He had not turned: he did not want to experience 'the shame felt by the victim who is forced to look his killer in the eyes'.) Had they planned to murder him too, and if so why had their plan failed? Because Konrad had not the nerve to pull the trigger? (p. 148)

Henrik recalls his father's private verdict on Konrad: that at heart Konrad was not a soldier. Like Krisztina, dead these many years, Konrad had been a lover of music. Henrik has not shared that passion. Echoing the pathologically jealous hero of Tolstoy's *Kreutzer Sonata*, he denounces music as a call to libertinage and anarchy, a secret language used by 'select' people to express 'uninhibited, irregular things that are also probably indecent and immoral'. 'You killed something inside me,' he tells Konrad. 'Tonight, I am going to kill something inside you.' (pp. 178, 141)

Yet even as he has Konrad at his mercy, his desire for revenge seems to be waning. What, after all, will Konrad's death accomplish? With age, it seems, we begin to accept that our desires have found and will find no real echo in the world. 'The people we love do not love us, or not in the way we hope.' (p. 135) So of Konrad he demands no more than the truth. What was truly afoot between him and Krisztina?

To Henrik's questions, accusations, threats, and pleas Konrad makes no response. At dawn he departs. The last page is turned, the revolver remains unused.

Embers is a novel – really a novella – in which little happens. Of the trio of actors, Krisztina is a shadow, Konrad a stubborn silence. The castle, the storm, Konrad's night-time visit add up to no more than a setting and an occasion for Henrik to reflect aloud on the mutations undergone by his pain and jealousy over the course of time, and to utter his thoughts about life. The book reads like a sometimes clumsy narrative transcription of a stage play.

The topics on which Henrik utters his rather conventional thoughts include the newly erupted war (a world gone mad); primitive peoples (at least they have retained a sense of the sacral nature of killing); the masculine virtues of silence, solitude, the inviolability of one's word; friendship (a feeling known only to men, nobler than sexual desire because it demands nothing in return); and hunting (the sole arena left in which men can experience a forbidden joy, namely the urge, neither good nor evil in itself, to vanquish one's antagonist).

Henrik's opinions are those we might expect of any crusty retired general. But he is more than that. He is also a follower of the vulgarised interpretation of Nietzsche, with its romanticisation of violence and its homoerotic mystique, that held sway among the unreconstructed European military elite of the turn of the century. One way of reading *Embers* is as a work of irony, fashioned to allow the Henriks of the world to expose the crudity of their thought in their own words, without authorial intervention. But for such a reading to obtain, the reader must accept the book as a seamless piece of imposture in which Márai's own sentiments are deliberately silenced. The clichéd language would then mirror Henrik's own coarse sensibility, as would the crude *mis-en-scène*: the Gothic castle haunted by 'intangible presences'; the table adorned with 'exquisitely charming' porcelain; ties 'too deep for words' between the master and the ancient retainer who looks after his needs; 'ancient texts' that he consults in search of the meaning of life, etc., etc. (pp. 25, 83, 15, 111)

An alternative reading of this enigmatic book – enigmatic because so determinedly out of touch with its times (it appeared during the Second World War) – would give fuller weight to Márai's pessimism about our capacity to know other people, and his stoical resignation to not being known himself. 'In literature, as in life,' he writes in his memoir *Land, Land!* . . ., 'only silence is "sincere"'.[2] Once you give up your inmost secret, you have given up your self and in that sense cease to be yourself. (Hence Márai's disdain for psychoanalysis, with its therapeutic ambitions.) Even if in his heart the old General may feel he is not the caricature he seems to be, he may not protest or struggle, but must act out his role to the end. In a key passage Márai writes:

> We not only act, talk, think, dream, we also preserve our silence about something. All our lives we are silent about who we are, which only we know and about which we can speak to no one. Yet we know that who we are and what we cannot speak of constitutes the 'truth'. We are that about which we preserve our silence. (*Land, Land!* . . . , p. 83)

And elsewhere he observes that, in the arena of love, a woman yields up the secret of her self at the risk of losing the game.[3]

In the second reading of *Embers*, it is perhaps Konrad, with his studied refusal to excuse himself, and Krisztina, who from the fateful day of Konrad's flight until her death never speaks a word to her husband ('a strong personality,' he comments admiringly), who are truest to themselves. (*Embers*, p. 191)

Embers, published in Budapest in 1942, can profitably be read side by side with the novella *Eszter's Legacy*, first published three years earlier.[4] Like *Embers*, *Eszter's Legacy* seems to have been conceived as theatre. It has the same focus on a single character onstage throughout, a similar cryptic psychology issuing in an unexpected act: a middle-aged woman in straitened circumstances signing over her property to a man she knows perfectly well is bamboozling her with sentimental lies. As she notes with detached amusement, something within her seems to be compelling her to be fooled. She could resist, but to do so would be to act out of character. To resist would be to reject the caricatural version of womanliness, of woman as the one who loves to be lied to, who loves to yield. To resist the caricature would be to cry out against the theatre of life, to struggle to emerge from the sleepwalk of destiny. The deeper heroism, we infer, lies in stoical acceptance.

Eszter's Legacy is more straightforward than *Embers* in its narrative strategy, more transparent about its paternity – Chekhov, Strindberg – and therefore perhaps a less puzzling introduction to Márai's austere and radical fatalism.

Sándor Márai was born in 1900 in the provincial city of Kaschau (Hungarian Kassa), which after the end of the Dual Monarchy in 1919 ceased to be in Hungary and under the name Košice was allotted to the new state of Czechoslovakia. On the side of his father, a lawyer, the family was of Saxon origin: the name had been Grosschmidt, but in the wake of the uprisings of 1848, in which they had fought on the Hungarian nationalist side, they had changed it. At home they spoke German rather than Hungarian.

Márai's education was interrupted by the First World War. Called up at the age of seventeen, he seems to have spent most of his period of service hospitalised. After the war he flirted briefly with the student left, then went abroad. In Leipzig he enrolled at the newly created Institute for Journalism, but found the courses too academic, and moved to Frankfurt, where in a livelier intellectual atmosphere he felt more at home. He had a gift for making contacts, and was soon publishing in the prestigious *Frankfurter Zeitung*. He read Kafka and translated some of Kafka's stories into Hungarian.

From Frankfurt he progressed to Berlin, where he enrolled at the University of Berlin. His plan was to take a German degree, acculturate himself fully as German, then pursue a career as a German writer – in effect, to resume his Grosschmidt heritage. Instead he married a girl from Kaschau, abandoned his studies, and moved to Paris, there to follow the life of a free-floating intellectual of a loose Central European identity. For five years he used Paris as a base to travel extensively. He wrote for Hungarian newspapers; he also wrote a first novel, later to be repudiated.

In 1928 he returned to Hungary to settle and to re-learn Hungarian properly. He wrote voluminously, plays and novels. Between 1930 and 1939 sixteen books appeared, through which he began to win a substantial readership in both Hungary and the German-speaking world. He belonged to no political party, lived a private life. His tribute to the novelist Gyula Krúdy speaks to his own values: 'He was not prepared to write for a social class nor for the *Volk*, only for the class and *Volk* of independent people. He never cared to be the darling of the nation.'[5]

War broke out, but the stream of his publications continued unabated. These included a memoir of his return to Kaschau, now once again part of Hungary. In 1943, along with other Hungarian authors, he signed an open letter calling for the defence against outside influences of what he saw as a threatened Hungarian culture. He began a diary, written with publication in mind, the first volume, covering 1943–44, appearing in 1945.

Between the end of the war in 1945 and 1948 Márai published eight more books. But as the takeover of the country's institutions, directed from Moscow, moved into gear, the official attitude toward him grew frostier. Reading the writing on the wall, he withdrew into exile, first in Switzerland, then in Italy, then in New York. The Hungarian uprising of 1956 gave him new hope. He returned to Europe, only to be met by a stream of defeated refugees. In 1979 he and his wife followed their adopted son, a war orphan, to California. He died in 1989, by his own hand.

During his exile Márai was published in Hungarian by the Toronto publishing house of Vörösvary-Weller and in translation in France and Germany. In all, between 1931 and 1978, twenty-two of his books came out in German translation. The fact that appreciation for his writing was unaffected by changes in the political climate suggests that his notion of what it meant to be above the politics of the day found an echo among the German middle class. Meanwhile Márai continued to work on his *Diaries*: five further volumes appeared between 1958 and 1997. In 1990 he was posthumously awarded the Kossuth Prize, Hungary's highest honour.

The only book to emerge directly from Márai's American experience is *The Wind Comes from the West*, a collection of travel pieces based on a trip he took in the 1950s through the Southwest and South, with a dip into Mexico. One test of the quality of travel writing is whether it offers the natives a new perspective on themselves. This is a test that Márai fails. His information about the United States seems to come more from American newspapers than from personal observation; his commentary on what he sees is rarely fresh or striking. It is hard to imagine Americans finding this book of much interest, except perhaps tangentially as a record of how a European of Márai's generation and upbringing viewed their country (San Diego, for instance, is commended for its compact city centre, its South Italian elegance).[6]

Márai himself understood his commentary on America in a different light. In the old days, he wrote, a European visitor to America could pretend to be an explorer in an undiscovered land. But in today's America there is nothing left to discover because there is no such thing as the unknown. All that is left for the writer is to use the experience of travel to appreciate the fact that he is foreign to the continent, that he is a European.[7]

*

Márai's greatest popular success was with a book titled in German *Bekenntnisse eines Bürgers*, to be glossed as 'Confessions of a member of the old European middle class'. When it first came out in 1934, this was taken to be a work of autobiography. Alarmed, Márai added an authorial note to the third edition stressing that what he had written was a 'fictional biography' whose characters 'do not live and have never lived in the real world'. Nevertheless, the career of the hero of *Confessions* follows pretty closely the contours of Márai's early life as far as we know it, while his opinions are entirely consistent with Márai's own. It will be left to a future biographer to tease out what exactly was invented.

The first volume of the *Confessions* takes us through the unnamed hero's childhood and youth, first in his parents' comfortable home in Kaschau, then in boarding school in Budapest. This loving, leisurely evocation of a way of life long gone is the most attractive feature of the book. It is a way of life — that of the central European *Mittelstand*, hardworking, patriotic, socially responsible, respectful of learning — to the memory of which Márai clung even after it was gone.

The second volume follows the hero's *Wanderjahre* as he drifts through postwar Europe, first as a less than wholehearted student, later as a freelance writer, from Leipzig to Frankfurt to Berlin to Paris to Florence until, in 1928, he returns to Budapest to settle down seriously to the life of a writer.

In Berlin, with the mark plummeting and Hungarian forints in his pocket, he finds himself comfortably off. Together with some friends he hires an office and publishes a literary magazine. He has erotic adventures; he writes his first play. Never has life been so gay and carefree.

In Paris, he and his new wife try out *la vie bohème*. They are miserable. The food is poor, hygienic arrangements are unspeakable, they cannot understand Parisian speech. 'We lived like exiles in a primitive, tight-fisted city.' After a year they abandon the experiment: they move to the Right Bank, rent a comfortable apartment, import a maidservant from Kaschau, buy a car, live in greater style. He himself is still drawn to Montparnasse ('a university seminar, steambath, and open-air stage in one'), but preferably as an onlooker, not a participant.[8]

Gradually he learns to be more charitable to the French. They may be hardheaded and miserly, the war may have undermined their confidence, but they have not lost their quintessential sense of proportion, of what is good for them. Their modesty and lack of taste – 'self-conscious, almost humble' – becomes endearing. And it does not take much for them to open up and be warm. (p. 372)

As for the Germans, with their unexpiated, mythic sense of guilt, their mass tendencies, their complicated, nervous bellicosity, their disturbing uniforms, their pitiless craving for order and inner lack of order, they may well constitute a danger to Europe. Yet behind this 'pedantic, crazed' Germany glimmers an alternative, softer Germany, the Germany of Goethe and Thomas Mann. Who knows which is the real one? (p. 316)

The second volume ends with the hero ensconced in his study in Budapest, full of misgivings about the way the world is heading and about his own prospects. In the ten years he has been away he has lost his feel for his mother tongue. All over Europe the level of culture is sinking, civilised standards are waning, the herd instinct reigns. Yet even if it does make him sound like a premature sexagenarian, he will raise his voice on behalf of the bourgeois Enlightenment, 'an age, generations long, that proclaimed the triumph of reason over instinct and believed in the power of the spirit to resist and curb the drive to death'. (p. 420)

Read as a narrative fiction, *Confessions* is episodic and lacking in drama. As a memoir of artistic life in Berlin and Paris of the

1920s, it is short on observation and superficial in its judgements. It is best accepted as what its title proclaims it to be: a statement of faith by a young man who, having experimented with living as an expatriate bohemian, and having seen at first hand the disquieting political developments in Italy and Germany, confirms for himself what he seems to have known all along: that in every respect that matters he belongs to a dying breed, the progressive bourgeoisie of the Austro-Hungarian Empire.

Among Hungarians the consensus seems to be that Márai will ultimately be remembered for his six volumes of diaries. These are not yet available in English; the recent German edition has been pilloried for the sloppiness of its editing.

With the diaries can be included the unfortunately titled memoir *Land, Land! . . .* (in Hungarian as *Föld, Föld! . . .*), first published in Toronto in 1972. (The title recalls the cry of the sailor on watch aboard Columbus's flagship as he sighted the New World.) In 1996 *Land, Land! . . .* appeared in English under the limp title *Memoir of Hungary 1944–48.*[9] The 1996 translation is execrable, and is not used in this essay. Nonetheless, until we have translations of the diaries and more of the body of Márai's fiction, this will be the most substantial of his works to which English speakers have access, and our estimation of him will have to depend heavily on it.

Land, Land! . . . is a memoir of Márai's life from the arrival of the Red Army on the outskirts of Budapest in 1944 to his departure into exile in 1948. It is not strong on incident – Márai was not witness to any actual fighting, and for the Márai family the immediate postwar period was largely a matter of scraping by in a devastated city. It consists rather of a chronicle of political, social, and also spiritual change in the capital as the Communist Party tightened its grip on all aspects of life.

For some weeks in the summer of 1944 Márai had to share his villa north of Budapest with Russian soldiers, and the forced propinquity of the tall, elegant Middle European who spent his free time absorbed in Spengler's *Decline of the West* with Russian, Kirghiz, and Buryat peasant boys, their rudimentary exchanges mediated through a young woman who spoke Czech, was an eye-opener to both sides. 'You are not a bourgeois,' one of the more perceptive Russians tells Márai, '[because] you don't live on [inherited] wealth or on the labour of others, but from your own labours. Still . . . in your soul you are a bourgeois. You are holding fast to something that doesn't exist anymore.' (*Land, Land!* . . . , p. 53)

As for Márai, in his Spenglerian frame of mind he privately lumps Soviets with Chinese as 'Easterners'. Between Eastern and Western varieties of consciousness he posits an unbridgeable gulf: Eastern consciousness contains inner spaces created by vast geographies and histories of subjection where Westerners cannot follow. The Russians may have chased the Germans out of Hungary 'but freedom they could not bring, [they themselves] did not have it'. Young Russians are barely to be distinguished from the *Hitlerjugend:* 'In their souls the reflexes of inherited culture [have] died out.' (pp. 64–66, 19, 35)

Though well aware that the Nazis, whom he despised, used a vulgarised reading of Spengler as a pillar for their theory of history, Márai falls back on Spengler for his own historical interpretation of the westward expansion of Russia. Why? Partly because the interfusing of culture and race in Spengler is compatible with Márai's own notion of culture bred in the bone, partly because Spengler's pessimism about the fate of the West (that is, of western European Christendom) is congenial, but partly also because Spengler belongs to Márai's fund of reading and one of the more pigheaded articles of Márai's conservative credo is to yield up nothing without a fight.

Once the Germans have been chased out, Márai and his wife return to the city of Budapest, where they find their apartment in ruins, the library largely destroyed. They move to makeshift quarters, waiting along with their fellow citizens for the expected next step in their liberation, namely the return of Hungary to the fold of Christian, Catholic Europe. When the realisation dawns that they are waiting in vain (Beckett's *Waiting for Godot*, says Márai, captures the mood of the interregnum exactly), that Hungary has been abandoned to the Russians, a wave of randomly directed hatred spreads over the country. In fact, Márai contends, one of the features of the postwar period in general was the spread of waves of psychotic hatred – hence the rise of so many vengeful revolutionary movements all over the world.

More interesting than Márai's views on world history are the stories he has to tell of the lives of ordinary people in Budapest, first under Russian occupation, then under Hungarian communist rule. Inflation ravages not only the social but the moral life of the country. The secret police return, familiar despicable human types, recruited as before from among the 'proles' but dressed in new uniforms. There is a striking eight-page anecdote about a Jew, hunted during the war, now a powerful police officer, who sits down in the fashionable Café Emke and has the gypsy band play patriotic tunes for him from the fascist 1930s, smiling with pleasure while Kirghiz soldiers watch mistrustfully from the next table. 'Straight out of Dostoevsky,' comments Márai. (pp. 157, 145)

Was it a mistake to have returned to Hungary, Márai asks himself? He thinks back to the day in 1938 when the news came that Chancellor Schuschnigg of Austria had capitulated to Hitler's threats and resigned. Like everyone else, Márai knew the world was shifting beneath his feet. Yet the next day he played his usual game of tennis, followed by a shower and a massage. He is not proud of the way he behaved. 'One is always ashamed when one finds one is not a hero but a dupe – a dupe of history.' But what should he do now? Pour ashes over his head? Beat his breast? He refuses. 'All I regret is that, while I had the chance, I did not lead a more comfortable life with more variety.' (pp. 125, 127)

It takes a fair amount of self-confidence, even arrogance, to write like this. *Land, Land!* . . . , is a more deeply revealing *confessio* than the *Confessions* of 1934. About himself Márai is candid: like the rest of the Hungarian elite, he has failed to respond imaginatively to the crises of the twentieth century. He has behaved like a caricature of the bourgeois intellectual, scorning the rabble of the right and the rabble of the left, retreating into his private enjoyments.

Yet this failure, he argues, should not mean that the *Mittelstand* of Europe should be condemned to the scrapheap of history. Identity is not a purely personal matter. We are not just our private selves, we also participate in the caricatural version of ourselves that exists in social space. Since we cannot escape the caricature, we may as well embrace it. Besides, 'it was not only I who was a caricature in . . . the time between the two world wars: in the whole of life in Hungary – in its institutions, in the way people looked at things – there was something caricatural. It is good to know one is not alone.' (p. 132)

A year after the war's end Márai permits himself an excursion to Switzerland, Italy, and France. Switzerland gives rise to melancholy ruminations on the death of humanism, Europe's great gift to the world, in Auschwitz and Katyn. What does a Europe that has lost its sense of humanistic mission hold for a 'fringe-European' like himself? The Swiss look with scorn on their poor, shabby visitor. At least the Russians don't do that. (p. 196)

In France he is on the lookout for the 'courageous and exact self-criticism, the moral accounting' he expects of the French, but finds nothing of the kind. The French, it would seem, want only to take up where they left off in 1940, refusing to see that the four-hundred-year ascendancy of 'the white man' is at an end. (p. 206)

Back in Hungary the final crackdown has commenced. The secret police are everywhere. Márai ceases to write for newspapers, but does continue to publish books, including two volumes of a trilogy about the Hitler period, which Georg Lukács savages in a review, choosing to read what Márai has to say about the fascists as a veiled comment on the communists. Thereafter Márai falls silent, living modestly on his royalties. He spends his days immersed in the minor novelists of nineteenth-century Hungary, with their stories of the world of his childhood.

More and more pressure is brought to bear on bourgeois intellectuals to endorse the regime. It becomes clear that even the freedom to be silent, as a form of internal exile, will be taken away from people like him. He consults his beloved Goethe, and Goethe tells him that if he has a destiny it is his duty to live out that destiny. He makes preparations to leave. Strangely, no official obstacles are placed in his way.

Years pass in exile, years of impotence, cut off from 'the wonderful, lonely Hungarian language', yet his faith in the class into which he was born, and the historical mission of that class, remains unshaken:

I was a *Bürger* (even if only in caricature) and am still one today, though old and in a foreign country. To be a *Bürger* was for me never a matter of class status – I always regarded it as a vocation. The *Bürger* remained for me the best thing that modern Western culture produced, for the *Bürger* produced modern Western culture. (pp. 89, 86)

The recent flare-up of interest in Márai is not easy to explain. During the 1990s five books of his appeared in France without attracting more than respectful reviews. Then in 1998, promoted by Roberto Calasso of the publishing house of Adelphi, *Embers* in Italian shot up the best-seller lists. Taken up by the impresario of German literary reviewing, Marcel Reich-Ranicki, *Embers* in its German guise sold 700,000 copies in hardback. 'A new master,' enthused a reviewer in *Die Zeit*, 'whom in the future we will rank with Joseph Roth, with Stefan Zweig, with Robert Musil, with who knows what other of our faded demigods, perhaps even Thomas Mann and Franz Kafka.'[10]

Embers appeared in English in 2001, in a translation by Carol Brown Janeway not from the Hungarian but at second hand from the German translation – questionable professional practice. American reviewers seemed to accept without question claims by the publishers that *Embers* was 'unknown to modern readers' before 1999 (in fact a German translation had appeared in 1950 and a French translation in 1958, reissued in 1995), and treated Márai as a lost master, now recovered. The success of the book in Europe was repeated in the English-speaking world.

It is hard not to believe that this success is in large part a response to the popular-romance elements of the book – the castle in the forest, the story of passion and adultery and revenge, Konrad's sultry oriental paramour, the overblown language, and so forth – that is to say, to exactly that caricatural layer of kitsch which Márai, in his complexly ironical way, both distances himself from and accepts as unavoidable; though in the case of European readers one should not ignore a deeper historical tide, namely exhaustion or even mere impatience with a vision of the twentieth century in which everything either leads up to or leads away from the black hole of the Holocaust, and a corresponding nostalgia for times when moral questions still had manageable dimensions.

In 2004 a second novel by Márai, *Vendégjáték Bolzanóban* (1940) ('Guest-play in Bolzano'), appeared in English translation under two different titles: *Conversations in Bolzano* in the UK, *Casanova in Bolzano* in the USA.[11]

The action of *Conversations in Bolzano* is exiguous, and it is part of the conception of the book that it should be so. It begins with the arrival of Giacomo Casanova in Bolzano. He has just escaped from prison in Venice, and he has unfinished business in mind. Five years ago he fought a duel with the Duke of Parma over the Duke's fifteen-year-old fiancée, Francesca. The Duke had warned him then never to come back. Now here he is.

Apprised of his presence, the Duke pays him a visit in his room in the inn. He offers a deal: in return for the freedom to woo Francesca and perhaps spend a single night with her, Casanova must undertake never to see her again. For his pains he will receive ten thousand ducats and a letter of safe conduct.

What is in it for you? asks Casanova. It will be my gift to my wife, the Duke replies: the experience of a night with a great artist in love, and a lesson in how little capable of true love he is. As the fruit of that lesson the Duke expects to win his wife's gratitude and affection.

Casanova accepts what the Duke regards as a deal but he himself sees as a challenge.

Soon after the Duke's departure, Francesca appears. Her husband underestimates her, she says. She is prepared to throw up everything to live with Casanova and show him what true love can be. But she can see that his passion is no match for hers. His only fidelity is to his art. Taking her leave, she foretells a wretched old age for him, filled with regrets.

The substance of *Conversations in Bolzano* is made up of these two extended conversations, which are pretty much monologues (the Duke's running to a full fifty pages), and Casanova's ruminations upon them. As the original title suggests, the novel plays with the idea of the celebrity performance, seeming to look forward to the performance to take place at the Duke's masked ball and perhaps afterwards in the Duchess's bedroom; whereas the prologue, set in Casanova's room and addressed to the subject of whether there is to be any performance at all, turns out to be the only performance there will be. In its static quality – instead of action in the present we have memory of action in the past and reflection upon the possibility of action in the future – and its thin narrative line, *Conversations in Bolzano*, like *Embers*, reveals an author more at home in the theatre of the nineteenth century than in the novel.

As in *Embers* too, there is little of what one would call development. All three of the characters, even the young Duchess, have set positions from which they speak, and their speeches do no more than enunciate these positions. Individually and collectively (as participants in the performance) they are exemplary Máraisians. 'You, like me,' says the Duke to Casanova, 'are merely a cat's-paw, an actor, the tool of the fate that is playing with us both, a fate whose purpose sometimes appears unfathomable.' (p. 202) Francesca may urge Casanova to rebel against the role prepared for him – that of the heartless seducer – but her urgings carry no hint that she hopes to change him. The lovers seem aware that they are playing out a tragedy of sorts in which the promise of love will be smothered in the name of domesticity on the one hand and sensuality on the other; nevertheless they do not, themselves, aspire to rebel against their roles in it. A melancholy stoicism takes the place of tragic courage.

Márai nowhere suggests that the memoirs the historical Casanova left behind prove him a great artist. Nevertheless, in his attractiveness to women and in the instinctive unease he awakes in the authorities – he was jailed in Venice not for anything he had done but for 'his entire manner of being, his soul' – Casanova embodies the Romantic artist-rebel as conceived in the popular imagination. (p. 107) The intellectual heart of *Conversations in Bolzano* consists in the confrontation between the naïve conception – kept alive by Francesca – of the artist as the figure of truth and the Casanovan counterexample of the artist who submits, ethically as well as aesthetically, to the practice of illusion, even illusion of the most clichéd kind. The artist in seduction gets his way, Casanova suggests, neither because he opens the girl's eyes to who she really is nor because he blinds her with lies but because both he and she sense that lies repeated by seducers generation after generation come to have a truth of their own.

When Francesca and Casanova take the stage for their big scene, they do so (as the consequence of some unconvincing plotting) in disguise: Francesca masked and costumed as a man, Casanova as a woman. Francesca sets out the naïve position on the subject of love: love entails the stripping away of illusion and the embrace of the naked truth of the beloved. 'We are still only masked figures, my love,' she says, 'and there are many more masks between us, each of which must, one by one, be discarded, before we can finally know each other's true, naked faces.' (p. 261)

In his farewell letter to the Duke, Casanova in effect gives the artist's response. Love relies on illusion, he says. 'There was yet something else I knew that the duchess of Parma could not yet know: that the truth can only survive as long as the hidden veils of desire and longing draw a curtain before her and cover her.' (p. 291) The melancholy truth into which Casanovan art initiates us is that not only are we always masked but we cannot survive in an unmasked state.

Conversations in Bolzano begins as historical fiction of a routine kind, but the busy filling-in of background and recreation of milieu is happily soon over and the book can settle down to being what Márai wants it to be: a vehicle for expressing his ideas on the ethics of art. Further translations from Márai's fictional *oeuvre* are promised; but nothing made available thus far to readers without Hungarian contradicts the impression that, however thoughtful a chronicler of the dark decade of the 1940s he may have been, however bravely (or perhaps just unabashedly) he may have spoken up for the class into which he was born, however provocative his paradoxical philosophy of the mask may be, his conception of the novel form was nevertheless old-fashioned, his grasp of its potentialities limited, and his achievements in the medium consequently slight.

(2002)

8 Paul Celan and his translators

PAUL ANTSCHEL WAS born in 1920 in Czernowitz in the territory of Bukovina, which after the break-up of the Austro-Hungarian Empire in 1918 had become part of Romania. Czernowitz was in those days an intellectually lively city with a sizeable minority of German-speaking Jews. Antschel was brought up speaking High German; his education, partly in German, partly in Romanian, included a spell in a Hebrew school. As a youth he wrote verse and revered Rilke.

After a year (1938–39) at medical school in France, where he encountered the Surrealists, he came home on vacation and was trapped there by the outbreak of war. Under the Hitler-Stalin pact Bukovina was absorbed into the Ukraine: for a brief while he was a Soviet subject.

In June of 1941 Hitler invaded the USSR. The Jews of Czernowitz were driven into a ghetto; soon the deportations commenced. Apparently forewarned, Antschel sought hiding the night his parents were taken. The parents were shipped to labour camps in occupied Ukraine, where both died, his mother by a bullet to the head when she became unfit for work. Antschel himself spent the war years doing forced labour in Axis Romania.

Liberated by the Russians in 1944, he worked for a while as an aide in a psychiatric hospital, then in Bucharest as an editor and translator, adopting the pen-name Celan, an anagram of Antschel in its Romanian spelling. In 1947, before Stalin's iron curtain came down, he slipped away to Vienna and from there moved to Paris. In Paris he passed his examinations for the Licence ès Lettres and was appointed lecturer in German literature at the prestigious École Normale Supérieure, a position he held until his death. He married a Frenchwoman, a Catholic from an aristocratic background.

The success of this move from East to West was soon dampened. Among the writers Celan had been translating was the French poet Yvan Goll (1891–1950). Goll's widow Claire took issue with Celan over his versions, and went on to accuse him publicly of plagiarising certain of Goll's German poems. Though the accusations were malicious and perhaps even crazy, Celan brooded over them to the point of convincing himself that Claire Goll was part of a conspiracy against him. 'What must we Jews yet endure?' he wrote to his confidante Nelly Sachs, like him a Jew writing in German. 'You have no idea how many should be counted among the base, no Nelly Sachs, you have no idea! . . . Should I name names? You would stiffen with horror.'[1]

His reaction cannot just be put down to paranoia. As postwar Germany began to feel more confident, anti-Semitic currents were again beginning to flow, not only on the right but, more disturbingly, on the left. Celan suspected, not without reason, that he had become a convenient focus for the campaign for the Aryanisation of German culture that had not given up in 1945, merely gone underground.

Claire Goll never relented in her campaign against Celan, pursuing him even beyond the grave; her persecutions poisoned his days and contributed heavily to his eventual breakdown.

Between 1938 and his death in 1970 Celan wrote some eight hundred poems in German; in addition there is a body of early work in Romanian. Recognition of his gifts came soon, with the publication of *Mohn und Gedächtis* (Poppy and Memory) in 1952. He consolidated his reputation as one of the more important young German-language poets with *Sprachgitter* (Speech Grille; 1959) and *Die Niemandsrose* (The No-One's Rose; 1963). Two more volumes appeared during his lifetime, and three posthumously. This later poetry, out of phase with the leftward swing of the German intelligentsia after 1968, was not quite so enthusiastically received.

By the standards of international modernism, Celan up to 1963 is quite accessible. The later poetry, however, becomes strikingly difficult, even obscure. Baffled by what they took to be arcane symbolism and private references, reviewers called the later Celan hermetic. It was a label he vehemently rejected. 'Not in the least hermetic,' he said. 'Read! Just keep reading, understanding comes of itself.'[2]

Typical of the 'hermetic' Celan is the following posthumously published poem, untitled, which I quote in John Felstiner's translation.[3]

> You lie amid a great listening,
> enbushed, enflaked.
>
> Go the Spree, to the Havel,
> go to the meathooks,
> the red apple stakes
> from Sweden –
>
> Here comes the gift table,
> it turns around an Eden –
>
> The man became a sieve, the Frau
> had to swim, the sow,
> for herself, for no one, for everyone –

The Landwehr Canal won't make a murmur.
Nothing
    stops.

What, at the most elementary level, is this poem about? Hard to say, until one becomes privy to certain information, information supplied by Celan to the critic Peter Szondi. The man who became a sieve is Karl Liebknecht, 'the Frau . . . the sow' swimming in the canal is Rosa Luxemburg. 'Eden' is the name of an apartment block built on the site where the two activists were shot in 1919, while the meathooks are the hooks at Plötzensee on the Havel River on which the would-be assassins of Hitler in 1944 were hanged. In the light of this information, the poem emerges as a pessimistic comment on the continuity of right-wing murderousness in Germany, and the silence of Germans about it.

The Rosa Luxemburg poem became a minor *locus classicus* when the philosopher Hans-Georg Gadamer, defending Celan against charges of obscurity, gave a reading of it through which he argued that any receptive, open-minded reader with a German cultural background can understand what it is important to understand in Celan without assistance, that background information should take second place to 'what the poem [itself] knows'.[4]

Gadamer's argument is a brave but losing one. What he forgets is that we cannot be sure that the information that unlocks the poem – in this case, the identities of the dead man and woman – is of secondary importance until we know what it is. Yet the questions Gadamer raises are important ones. Does poetry offer a kind of knowledge different from that offered by history, and demand a different kind of receptivity? Is it possible to respond to poetry like Celan's, even to translate it, without fully understanding it?

Michael Hamburger, one of the most eminent of Celan's translators, seems to think so. Though scholars have certainly illumined Celan's poetry for him, Hamburger says, he is not sure he 'understands', in the normal sense of the word, even those poems he has translated, or all of them.[5]

'[It] asks too much of the reader,' is the verdict of Felstiner on the Rosa Luxemburg poem. On the other hand, he continues, 'what is too much, given this history?' This, in a nutshell, is Felstiner's own response to accusations of hermeticism against Celan. Given the enormity of anti-Semitic persecutions in the twentieth century, given the all-too-human need of Germans, and of the Christian West in general, to escape from a monstrous historical incubus, what memory, what knowledge is it *too much* to demand? Even if Celan's poems were totally incomprehensible (this is not something that Felstiner says, but it is a valid extrapolation), they would nevertheless stand in our way like a tomb, a tomb built by a 'Poet, Survivor, Jew' (the subtitle of Felstiner's study), insisting by its looming presence that we remember, even though the words inscribed on it may seem to belong to an undecipherable tongue. (Felstiner, p. 254)

At stake is more than a simple confrontation between a Germany impatient to forget its past and a Jewish poet insisting on reminding Germany of that past. Celan was made famous by, and is still most widely known for, the poem 'Todesfuge' ('Death Fugue'):

Black milk of daybreak we drink you at night
we drink you at noon death is a master from Germany
we drink you at sundown and in the morning we drink
    and we drink you
death is a master from Germany his eyes are blue
he strikes you with leaden bullets his aim is true

(I quote from Hamburger's translation, in *Poems of Paul Celan*, p. 63, because Felstiner's version of the passage, quite as riveting in its own way, is controversial out of context.) 'Death Fugue' was Celan's first published poem: it was composed in 1944 or 1945 and first appeared, in Romanian translation, in 1947. It absorbs from the Surrealists everything that is worth absorbing. It is not entirely Celan's brainchild: here and there he takes over phrases, among them 'Death is a master from Germany', from fellow poets of his Czernowitz days. Nevertheless, its impact has been immediate and universal. 'Death Fugue' is one of the landmark poems of the twentieth century.

'Death Fugue' has been widely read in the German-speaking world, anthologised, studied in schools, as part of a programme of what is called *Vergangenheitsbewältigung*, coming to terms with, or overcoming, the past. At the public readings Celan gave in Germany 'Death Fugue' was always in demand. It is the most direct of Celan's poems in naming and blaming: naming what went on in the death camps, blaming Germany. Some of Celan's defenders argue that he is labelled 'difficult' only because readers find the encounter with him too emotionally bruising. It is an argument that needs to account for the reception of 'Death Fugue', a reception with apparently open arms.

In fact, Celan himself never trusted the spirit in which he was welcomed and even fêted in West Germany. In the line that German critics took with 'Death Fugue' – to quote one eminent critic, that it showed he had '[escaped] history's bloody chamber of horrors to rise into the ether of pure poetry' – he sensed that he was being misinterpreted, and in the deepest historical sense, wilfully misinterpreted.[6] Nor was he pleased to hear that in the classroom German students were being directed to ignore the content of the poem and concentrate on its form, particularly its imitation of musical (fugal) structure.

When Celan writes of the 'ashen hair' of Shulamith, he is invoking the hair of Jews that fell as ash on the Silesian country-side; when he writes of 'the sow' bobbing in the waters of the Landswehr Canal, he is referring, in the voice of one of her murderers, to the body of a dead Jewish woman. Against pressure to recuperate him as a poet who had turned the Holocaust into something higher, namely poetry, against the critical orthodoxy of the 1950s and early 1960s, with its view of the ideal poem as a self-enclosed aesthetic object, Celan insists that he practises an art of the real, an art that 'does not transfigure or render "poetical"; it names, it posits, it tries to measure the area of the given and the possible.'[7]

With its repetitive, hammering music, 'Death Fugue' is as direct as verse can be in its approach to its subject. It also makes two huge implicit claims about what poetry in our time is, or should be, capable of. One is that language can measure up to any subject whatsoever: however unspeakable the Holocaust may be, there is a poetry that can speak it. The other is that the German language in particular, corrupted to the bone during the Nazi era by euphem-ism and a kind of leering doublespeak, is capable of telling the truth about Germany's immediate past.

The first claim was dramatically rejected in Theodor Adorno's pronouncement, issued in 1951 and reiterated in 1965, that 'to write poetry after Auschwitz is barbaric.'[8] Adorno might have added: doubly barbaric to write a poem in German. (Adorno took back his words, grudgingly, in 1966, perhaps as a concession to 'Death Fugue'.)

Celan avoids the word 'Holocaust' in his writing, as he avoided all usages that might seem to imply that everyday language is in a position to name, and thereby limit and master, that towards which it gestures. Celan gave two major public addresses during his lifetime, both acceptance speeches for prizes, in which, with great scrupulousness of word choice, he responded to doubts about the future of poetry. In the first address, in 1958, he spoke of his halting faith that language, even the German language, had survived 'that which happened' under the Nazis.

> There remained in the midst of the losses this one thing: language.
>
> It, the language, remained, not lost, yes in spite of everything. But it had to pass through its own answerlessness, pass through frightful muting, pass through the thousand darknesses of deathbringing speech. It passed through and gave back no words for that which happened; yet it passed through this happening. Passed through and could come to light again, 'enriched' by all this. (*SPP*, p. 395)

Coming from a Jew, such an expression of faith in German might seem odd. Yet Celan was by no means alone: even after 1945, numbers of Jews continued to claim the German language and intellectual tradition as their own. Among them was Martin Buber. Celan paid a visit to the aged Buber to ask Buber's counsel about continuing to write in German. Buber's response – that it was only natural to write in one's mother tongue, that one should take a forgiving stance toward the Germans – disappointed him. As Felstiner puts it, 'Celan's vital need, to hear some echo of his plight, Buber could not or would not grasp.'[9] His plight was that if German was 'his' language, it was his only in a complex, contested, and painful way.

During his time in Bucharest after the war, Celan had improved his Russian and had translated Lermontov and Chekhov into Romanian. In Paris he continued to translate Russian poetry, finding in the Russian language a welcome, counter-Germanic home. In particular he read Osip Mandelstam (1891–1938) intensively. In Mandelstam he met not only a man whose life-story corresponded in what he felt were uncanny ways to his own, but a ghostly interlocutor who responded to his deepest needs, who offered, in Celan's words, 'what is brotherly – in the most reverential sense I can give that word'. Setting aside his own creative work, Celan spent most of 1958 and 1959 translating Mandelstam into German. His versions constitute an extraordinary act of inhab-iting another poet, though Nadezhda Mandelstam, Mandelstam's widow, is right to call them 'a very far cry from the original text'. (Felstiner, pp. 131, 133)

Mandelstam's notion of poem as dialogue did much to reshape Celan's own poetic theory. Celan's poems begin to address a Thou who may be more or less distant, more or less known. In the space between the speaking I and the Thou they find a new field of tension.

> (I know you, you're the one bent over low,
> and I, the one pierced through, am in your need.
> Where flames a word to witness for us both?
> You – wholly real. I – wholly mad.)

(This is Felstiner's translation. In the freer version by Heather McHugh and Nikolai Popov, the last line reads: 'You're my reality. I'm your mirage.'[10])

If there is one theme that dominates John Felstiner's biography of Celan, it is that Celan developed from being a German poet whose fate it was to be a Jew to being a Jewish poet whose fate it was to write in German; that he outgrew kinship with Rilke and Heidegger to find in Kafka and Mandelstam his true spiritual fore-bears. Though Celan continued during the 1960s to visit Germany to give readings, any hope that he might develop an emotional involvement with a re-arisen Germany faded, to the point that he would call it 'a most tragic and indeed most childish error'. (Felstiner, p. 226) He began to read Gershom Scholem on the Jewish mystical tradition, Buber on Hasidism. Hebrew words – *Ziv*, the unearthly light of God's presence; *Yizkor*, memory – appeared in his poetry. The theme of testifying, witnessing, came to the fore, along with the bitter personal subtheme: 'No one / bears witness for the / witness.' (*SPP*, p. 261) The 'Thou' of his now insistently dialogical poetry became, intermittently but unmistakably, God; echoes emerged of the Kabbalistic teaching that the whole of creation is a text in the divine language.

The capture of Jerusalem by Israeli forces in the 1967 war filled Celan with joy. He wrote a celebratory poem that was widely read in Israel:

> Just think: your
> own hand
> has held
> this piece of
> habitable earth,
> again suffered
> up into life. (*SPP*, p. 307)

In 1969 Celan visited Israel for the first time ('So many Jews, only Jews, and not in a ghetto,' he marvelled ironically). (Felstiner, p. 268) He gave talks and readings, met Israeli writers, resumed a romantic relationship with a woman from his Czernowitz days.

As a child Celan had for three years attended a Hebrew school. Though he studied the language unwillingly (he associated it with his Zionist father rather than his beloved Germanophile mother), his command ran surprisingly deep. Aharon Appelfeld, by then an Israeli but by origin a Czernowitzer like Celan, found Celan's

Hebrew 'rather good'. (Felstiner, p. 327) When Yehuda Amichai read out his translations of Celan's poems, Celan was able to suggest improvements.

Back in Paris, Celan wondered whether, in staying behind in Europe, he had not made the wrong choice. He toyed with the idea of accepting a teaching position in Israel. Memories of Jerusalem gave rise to a brief burst of composition, poems that are at the same time spiritual, joyful, and erotic.

Celan had long been troubled by fits of depression. In 1965 he had entered a psychiatric clinic, and later underwent electroshock therapy. At home he was, as Felstiner puts it, 'sometimes violent'. He and his wife agreed to live apart. A friend visiting from Bucharest found him 'profoundly altered, prematurely aged, taciturn, frowning'. 'They're doing experiments on me,' he said. To his Israeli lover he wrote, in 1970: 'They've healed me to pieces.' Two months later he drowned himself. (Felstiner, pp. 243, 330)

To the historian Erich Kahler, with whom Celan had corresponded, Celan's suicide proved that to be 'both a great German poet and a young Central European Jew growing up in the shadow of the concentration camps' was a burden too great for one man to bear.[11] In a profound sense this verdict on Celan's suicide is true. But we cannot discount more mundane causes like Claire Goll's prolonged, mad vendetta, or the nature of the psychiatric care he underwent. Felstiner does not comment directly on the treatment to which Celan's doctors subjected him, but from Celan's own bitter asides it is clear they have much to answer for.

Even during Celan's lifetime there had developed a busy scholarly trade, principally in Germany, based upon him. That trade has today grown to an industry. As Kafka is to German prose, so Celan has become to German poetry.

Despite the pioneering translations of Jerome Rothenberg,

Michael Hamburger, and others, Celan did not really penetrate the English-speaking world until he had been taken up in France; and in France Celan was read as a Heideggerian poet, that is to say, as if his poetic career, culminating in suicide, exemplified the end of art in our times, an end in parallel to the end of philosophy as diagnosed by Heidegger.

Though Celan is not what one would call a philosophical poet, a poet of ideas, the link with Heidegger is not fanciful. Celan read Heidegger attentively, as Heidegger read Celan; Hölderlin was a formative influence on both. Celan approved of Heidegger's view of poetry's special claims to truth. His own explanation of why he wrote – 'so as to speak, to orient myself, to find out where I was and where I was meant to go, to sketch out reality for myself' – is fully in tune with Heidegger. (*SPP*, p. 396)

Despite Heidegger's National Socialist past and his silence on the subject of the death camps, Heidegger was important enough to Celan for Celan, in 1967, to call on him at his retreat in the Black Forest. Afterwards he wrote a poem ('Todtnauberg') about that meeting and the 'word / in the heart' he hoped to hear from Heidegger, but failed to get.

What might have been the word Celan was expecting? 'Pardon', suggests Philippe Lacoue-Labarthe in his book on Celan and Heidegger. But he soon revises his guess. 'I was wrong to think . . . that it was enough to ask forgiveness. [The extermination] is absolutely *unforgivable*. That is what [Heidegger] should have said.'[12]

To Lacoue-Labarthe, Celan's poetry is 'in its entirety, a dialogue with Heidegger's thought'. (p. 33) It is this approach to Celan, dominant in Europe, that has done most to take him out of the orbit of the ordinary educated reader. But there is an opposing school, to which Felstiner clearly adheres, which reads Celan as a fundamentally Jewish poet whose achievement it has been to force back into German high culture (with its ambition to locate its ideal origins in classical Greece), and into the German language, the memory of a Judaic past that a line of German thinkers culminating in Heidegger had tried to obliterate. In this view Celan certainly *answers* Heidegger but, having answered him, leaves him behind.

Celan began his professional life as a translator and continued to do translations to the end, principally from French into German but also from English, Russian, Romanian, Italian, Portuguese, and (in collaboration) Hebrew. Two volumes of his six-volume *Collected Works* are given over to his translations. In English Celan devoted himself particularly to Emily Dickinson and Shakespeare. Though his German Dickinson is less rhythmically jagged than the original, he seemed to find in her a kind of compression, syntactic and metaphorical, that he could learn from. As for Shakespeare, he returned again and again to the sonnets. His versions are breathless, urgent, questioning; they do not try to imitate Shakespeare's grace. As Felstiner puts it, Celan sometimes '[edges] beyond dialogue with the English into argument', rewriting Shakespeare in accord with his sense of his own times. (p. 205)

For his own translations of Celan, Felstiner takes hints – as no translator before him has done – from Celan's manuscript revisions and recorded readings, as well as from French versions approved by Celan. An example will show what use he makes of these researches. Celan's longest poem, 'Engführung' ('Stretto'), begins with the words 'Verbracht ins / Gelände / mit der untrüglichen Spur', removed into the terrain (or territory) with the unerring (or unmistakable) track (or trace). What is the best translation of *verbracht*? A French translation of the poem overseen by Celan uses the word *déporté*. However, if we check Celan's German version of the voice-over to Alain Resnais' documentary film about the death camps, *Night and Fog*, we find French *déporter* translated by German *deportieren*. *Deportieren* is the word regularly used in official documents for the deportation of prisoners or populations, where it has an abstract and euphemistic colour. To avoid such euphemism, Felstiner eschews the cognate English word *deported*. Instead, recalling the idiomatic use of *verbracht* by internees, he translates it as 'taken off': 'Taken off into / the terrain . . .' (*SPP*, pp. 118–19)

Many of the translations in *Felstiner's Selected Poems and Prose of Paul Celan* already appear embedded in the text of *Paul Celan: Poet, Survivor, Jew*, but for republication they have been revised and in most cases refined. Part of Felstiner's enterprise in the earlier book was to explain, in terms that a reader without German will understand, the nature of problems that Celan sets for a translator, from unexplained allusions on the one hand to compressed or compounded or invented words on the other, and how he, Felstiner, has responded case by case. Inevitably this entails justifying his own strategies and word-choices, and thus to one of the more unfortunate features of the book: an element of self-promotion.

Among recent translators of Celan, Felstiner, Popov and McHugh (hereafter Popov-McHugh), and Pierre Joris stand out. If Joris is less immediately engaging than the other two, that may be because he has set himself a more difficult task: whereas Felstiner and Popov-McHugh claim the freedom to select the poems they find most congenial (and, by implication, to avoid those that frustrate their best efforts), Joris gives us the two late collections *Atemwende* (*Breathturn*; 1967) and *Fadensonnen* (*Threadsuns*; 1968) in their entirety, some two hundred poems in all. Since it is by now accepted that Celan composed in sequences and cycles, with poems within a given volume referring backward and forward to other poems, his project is to be applauded. It does, however, bring problems in its train. There are plenty of incompletely achieved poems in Celan, and, more to the point, plenty of moments of near total obscurity. The temperature of Joris's pages is, understandably, not always white hot.[13]

Felstiner selects and translates about a hundred and sixty poems, distributed over the whole of Celan's career, among them some moving early lyrics. Popov-McHugh's selections come mainly from the late work. The overlap between their two volumes is slight: fewer than twenty poems. Only a handful of poems are common to all three translators.

Between Felstiner and Popov-McHugh it is hard to choose. The solutions that Popov-McHugh find to the problems set by Celan are sometimes dazzlingly creative, but Felstiner has his brilliant moments too, most notably in his 'Deathfugue', where the English is in the end drowned out by German ('Death is ein Meister aus Deutschland'). (*SPP*, pp. 31–33) Now and again there are substantive differences on how to parse, and therefore to understand, Celan's knotted, compacted syntax; in such cases Felstiner is usually the more dependable.

Felstiner is a redoubtable Celan scholar, but Popov-McHugh are no slouches in the scholarly department themselves. Felstiner's limitations emerge when Celan calls for a light touch, for instance in the poem 'Selbdritt, selbviert', which relies on folk-song patterns and nonsense formulas. Popov-McHugh's version is witty and lyrical, Felstiner's too sobersided.

Celan's is not an expansive music: he seems to compose word by word, phrase by phrase, rather than in long breath units. While giving each word and phrase its full weight, the translator has to create rhythmic momentum too.

> ich ritt durch den Schnee, hörst du,
> ich ritt Gott in die Ferne – die Nahe, er sang,
> es war
> unser letzter Ritt . . .

writes Celan.

> I rode through the snow, do you hear,
> I rode God into the distance – the nearness, he sang.
> it was
> our last ride . . .

writes Felstiner. (*SPP*, pp. 138-9)

> I rode through the snow, do you read me,
> I rode God far – I rode God
> near, he sang.
> it was
> our last ride . . .

write Popov-McHugh. (p. 5)

Felstiner's lines are rhythmically lifeless. Popov-McHugh's 'I rode God far – I rode God / near' is not there in the original, but it would be hard to argue that its forward drive is inappropriate.

There are many places, on the other hand, when the roles are reversed and Felstiner emerges as the more daring and inventive. 'Wenn die Totenmuschel heranschwimmt / will es hier läuten,' writes Celan: when the shell of the dead comes swimming up / there will be peals of bells here. 'When death's shell washes up on shore,' write Popov-McHugh, merely going through the motions. (p. 1) 'When the deadman's conch swims up,' writes Felstiner, leaping from shell to conch and to the conch's trumpet-like, annunciatory function. (*SPP*, p. 89)

There are also seemingly obvious points that Popov-McHugh miss. In one poem a *Wurfholz*, a throwing-stick, is flung out into space and returns. Felstiner translates the word by 'boomerang', Popov-McHugh inexplicably by 'flung wood'. (*SPP*, p. 179; Popov-McHugh p. 11)

In another poem Celan writes of a word that falls into the pit behind his forehead and continues to grow there: he compares the word to the 'Siebenstern' (seven-star), the flower whose learned name is *Trientalis europea*. In an otherwise excellent version, Popov-McHugh translate *Siebenstern* simply as 'starflower', failing to pick up the specifically Jewish resonances with the six-pointed Star of David and the seven-branched menorah. Felstiner expands the word to 'sevenbranch starflower'. (*SPP*, p. 195; Popov-McHugh p. 12)

On the other hand, the flower known in German as *die Zeitlose*, the timeless (*Colchicum autumnale*), is unimaginatively translated by Felstiner as 'the meadow saffron', while Popov-McHugh, with justifiable liberty, rename it 'the immortelle'. (*SPP*, p. 201; Popov-McHugh p. 13)

Sometimes, then, it is Felstiner who hits on exactly the right formulation, sometimes Popov-McHugh, to the point where one feels one could stitch together from their respective versions – with the occasional hint from Joris – a composite text that would improve on all three. Such a procedure would not be far-fetched or impracticable, given the stylistic commonality of their versions, a commonality stemming of course from Celan.

All three – Felstiner in his biography of Celan, Popov-McHugh in their notes, Joris in his two introductions – have illuminating things to say about Celan's language. Joris is particularly telling on Celan's agonistic relation to German:

> Celan's German is an eerie, nearly ghostly language; it is both mother-tongue, and thus firmly anchored in the realm of the dead, and a language the poet has to make up, to re-create, to re-invent, to bring back to life . . . Radically dispossessed of any other reality he set about to create his own language – a language as absolutely exiled as he himself. To try to translate it as if it were current, commonly spoken or

available German – i.e. to find a similarly current English or American 'Umgangssprache' – would be to miss an essential aspect of the poetry. (*Breathturn*, pp. 42–3)

Celan is the towering European poet of the middle decades of the twentieth century, one who, rather than transcending his times – he had no wish to transcend them – acted as a lightning rod for their most terrible discharges. His unremitting, intimate wrestlings with the German language, which form the substrate of all his later poetry, come across in translation as, at best, overheard rather than heard directly. In this sense translation of the later poetry must always fail. Nevertheless, two generations of translators have striven, with striking resourcefulness and devotion, to bring home in English what can be brought. Others will without doubt follow.

(2001)

9 Günter Grass and the *Wilhelm Gustloff*

GÜNTER GRASS BURST upon the literary scene in 1959 with *The Tin Drum*, a novel which, with its mix of the fabulous – a child hero who as a protest against the world around him refuses to grow – and the realistic – a densely textured realisation of prewar Danzig – announced the arrival in Europe of magic realism.

Made financially independent by the success of *The Tin Drum*, Grass threw himself into campaigning for Willy Brandt's Social Democrats. After the Social Democrats came to power in 1969, however, and particularly after Brandt resigned in 1974, Grass grew estranged from mainstream politics, occupying himself more and more with feminist and ecological issues. Throughout this evolution he nevertheless remained a believer in reasoned debate and in deliberate if cautious social progress. His chosen totem was the snail.

Having been among the first to attack the consensus of silence about the complicity of ordinary Germans in Nazi rule – a silence whose causes and consequences have been explored by Alexander and Margarete Mitscherlich in their groundbreaking work of psychohistory *The Inability to Mourn* – Grass is freer than most to enter the current debate in Germany about silence and silencing, taking up, in a characteristically cautious and nuanced way, a position that until the turn of the century only the radical right had dared to champion in public: that ordinary Germans – not just those who perished in the camps or died opposing Hitler – have a claim to be numbered among the victims of World War II.

Questions about victimhood, about silence, and about the rewriting of history are at the heart of Grass's 2003 novel, *Crabwalk*, whose main character and narrator arrives in the world during the dying throes of the Third Reich. Paul Pokriefke's birthday is January 30, a date with some symbolic resonance in German history. On January 30, 1933, the Nazis took power. And on the same day in 1945 Germany suffered its worst maritime disaster ever, a real-life disaster in the midst of which the fictional Paul was born. Paul is thus a kind of midnight's child in Salman Rushdie's sense, a child fingered by fate to give voice to his times.

Paul, however, would prefer to shirk his destiny. Sliding through life unnoticed suits his taste. A journalist by trade, he trims his sails to the political wind blowing strongest. In the 1960s he writes for the conservative Springer press. When the Social Democrats come to power he becomes a rather half-hearted left liberal; later he takes up ecological issues.

There are, however, two powerful people behind him, both nagging him to write the story of the night on which he was born: his mother and a shadowy figure so like the writer Günter Grass that I will call him 'Grass'.

Pokriefke is Paul's mother's name; his father's identity is unknown even to his mother. But from his mother Paul learns that he is connected in an accidental way with an important Nazi, *Landesgruppenleiter* (regional commander) Wilhelm Gustloff. Gustloff – a real-life personage – was in the 1930s stationed in Switzerland with orders to gather intelligence and recruit expatriate Germans and Austrians to the fascist cause. In 1936 a Jewish student of Balkan background named David Frankfurter called at Gustloff's home in Davos and shot him dead, after which he gave himself up to the police. 'I fired the shots because I am a Jew. I . . . have no regrets,' Frankfurter reportedly said.[1] Tried by a Swiss court and sentenced to eighteen years, Frankfurter was expelled from the country after serving half his time. He went to Palestine and subsequently worked in the Israeli defence ministry.

Back in Germany the death of Gustloff was seized upon as an opportunity to create a Nazi martyr and stir up anti-Jewish feeling. The body was ceremonially brought back from Switzerland and the ashes buried in a memorial grove on the shore of Lake Schwerin with a four-metre high memorial stone. Streets and schools were named after Gustloff, even a ship.

The cruise ship *Wilhelm Gustloff* was launched in 1937 as part of the National Socialist programme of recreation for the working class, a programme known as *Kraft durch Freude*, strength through joy. It carried 1,500 passengers at a time in classless accommodation on trips to the Norwegian fjords, Madeira, and the Mediterranean. Soon, however, more pressing uses were found for it. In 1939 it was sent to bring back the Condor Legion from Spain. When war broke out it was outfitted as a hospital ship. Later it became a training ship for the German navy, and finally a refugee transport.

In January of 1945 the *Gustloff* sailed from the German port of Gotenhafen (now Polish Gdynia), heading westward and crammed with some ten thousand passengers, for the most part German civilians fleeing the advancing Red Army, but also wounded soldiers, trainee U-boat sailors, and members of the Women's Auxiliary. Its mission was therefore not without a military side. In the icy waters of the Baltic it was torpedoed by a Soviet submarine under the command of Captain Aleksandr Marinesko. Some twelve hundred survivors were picked up; everyone else died. The death toll makes it the worst maritime disaster in history.

Among the survivors is a girl (fictional) named Ursula ('Tulla') Pokriefke in an advanced state of pregnancy. In the boat that rescues her Tulla gives birth to a son, Paul. Put ashore with her baby, she tries to make her way west through the Russian lines but ends up in Schwerin in the Russian zone, site of the Gustloff memorial.

By birth, then, Paul is tenuously linked to Wilhelm Gustloff. A more disturbing link emerges decades later, in 1996, when, idly browsing the Internet, Paul comes across a website called www.blutzeuge.de, where the 'Comrades of Schwerin' keep Gustloff's memory alive. (A *Blutzeuge* is a blood oath. Blutzeuge day, November 9, was a sacred date on the Nazi calendar, the day on which the SS reaffirmed their oath.) From familiar turns of phrase he begins to suspect that the so-called Comrades are no more and no less than his son Konrad, a high school student, whom he rarely sees now that the boy has elected to live with his grandmother Tulla in Schwerin.

Konrad, it emerges, has become obsessed with the Gustloff affair. For his history class he has written a paper on the *Kraft durch Freude* programme, which his teachers have banned him from reading on the grounds that the topic is 'inappropriate' and the paper itself 'severely infected with Nationalist Socialist thinking'. He has tried to present the same paper at a meeting of the local neo-Nazis, but it is too scholarly for his shaven-headed, beer-swilling audience. Since then he has restricted himself to his website, where under the code-name 'Wilhelm' he proposes Gustloff to the world as an authentic German hero and martyr, and repeats his grandmother's claim that the classless *Kraft durch Freude* cruise ships were an embodiment of true socialism. (pp. 196, 202)

'Wilhelm' soon meets with a hostile response. Writing back to the website under the name 'David', a respondent asserts that Frankfurter was the true hero of the story, a hero of Jewish resistance. On his computer screen Paul watches as his son and the putative Jew argue back and forth.

But a mere contest of words proves not to be enough for Konrad. He invites 'David' – who turns out to be of his own age – to Schwerin, and on the site of the demolished Gustloff monument shoots him as Frankfurter had shot Gustloff. Soon it emerges that his victim's real name was Wolfgang, and that he was not a Jew at all but had been so possessed by feelings of guilt over the Holocaust that he had tried to live as a Jew in his German household, wearing a yarmulke and demanding that his mother keep a kosher kitchen.

Konrad is unmoved by the revelation. 'I shot because I am a German,' he says at his trial, echoing Frankfurter's words, 'and because the eternal Jew spoke through David.' Cross-examined, he admits he has never met a real Jew, but denies that is relevant. While he has nothing against Jews in the abstract, he says, Jews belong in Israel, not in Germany. Let Jews honour Frankfurter if they wish, and Russians Marinesko; it is time for Germans to honour Gustloff. (p. 204)

The court bends over backward to see Konrad as a puppet of forces beyond his ken. Tulla makes a dramatic appearance on the witness stand to defend her grandson and denounce his parents for neglecting him. She does not tell the court that it was she who gave the youth the murder weapon.

Surveying the proceedings, Paul is convinced that Konrad is the only participant not afraid to speak his mind. Among the lawyers and judges he detects a smothering blanket of repression. Worst are the dead boy's parents, impeccable liberal intellectuals who blame no one but themselves and deny any desire for revenge. Their son craved to be a Jew, Paul finds, precisely because of his father's habit of seeing two sides to every question, including the question of the Holocaust.

Sentenced to seven years in juvenile detention, Konrad proves a model prisoner, using his time to study for his university entrance examinations. The only friction arises when his request to have a picture of *Landesgruppenleiter* Gustloff in his cell is refused.

Tulla Pokriefke, born in 1927, the same year as Günter Grass, first makes her appearance in *Cat and Mouse* (1961), though Lucy Rennwand of *The Tin Drum* can be regarded as a forerunner. In *Cat and Mouse* she is 'a spindly little [ten year old] with legs like toothpicks' who goes swimming with the boys in Kaisershafen harbour and is permitted to watch their masturbation contests.[2] In *Dog Years* (1963), now a high school student, she maliciously denounces one of her teachers to the police: he is sent to the Stutthof labour camp and dies there. On the other hand, when a malodorous pall descends over Kaisershafen, it is Tulla alone who utters what everyone privately knows: that the smell comes from truckloads of human bones from Stutthof.

By the last year of the war Tulla is working as a streetcar conductor and doing her best to get pregnant. Thereafter she disappears from view: in *The Rat* (1986) the ex-drummer boy Oskar Matzerath, now going on for sixty, remembers her as 'a very special kind of bitch' who, to the best of his knowledge, went down with the *Gustloff*.[3]

Tulla's politics are hard to reduce to any coherent system. A trained carpenter and impeccable proletarian, she has thrown herself into Party affairs in the new East German state and been recognised and rewarded for her activism. An unquestioning follower of the Moscow line, she weeps when Stalin dies in 1953 and lights candles for him. Yet while in one breath she can hail the crew of the submarine that nearly killed her as 'heroes of the Soviet Union allied to us workers in friendship', in the next she can describe Wilhelm Gustloff as 'the tragically murdered son of our beautiful city of Schwerin' and put forward *Kraft durch Freude* as a model for communists to follow. (pp. 149, 93)

Despite her incorrectness, she retains her position in the collective, held in affection by her comrades but also feared. When, after the collapse of the regime in 1989, what Grass calls 'die Berliner Treuhand' and his translator ingeniously calls 'the Berlin Handover Trust' moves into the old East to buy up state enterprises, she makes sure that she gets her cut. By the end of the book she has managed to work Catholicism into her eclectic belief system: in the living room of her home on Gagarin Street not far from the Lenin monument she has a shrine in which Uncle Joe smokes his pipe side by side with the Virgin Mary.

Paul sees his mother as the last true Stalinist. What exactly he means by that he does not spell out; but Tulla emerges from his account as unprincipled, canny, scheming, tenacious, impatient of theory, unforgiving, hard to kill, a nationalist first and last, and an anti-Semite, which constitutes a not inaccurate profile of a Stalinist. She also gave birth to a child at sea on a night when she witnessed thousands of dead children floating head down in their ineffectual lifejackets, and heard the collective last cry of the doomed passengers of the *Wilhelm Gustloff* as they slid overboard. 'A cry like that – you won't ever get it out of your ear,' she says. As if to prove it, her hair turned white that night. Besides being a Stalinist, Tulla is thus also a stricken soul: stricken by what she saw and heard, and unable to get over her grief until the taboo on representing what happened on January 30, 1945, is broken and the dead can be mourned as they deserve. (p. 155)

Tulla Pokriefke is the most interesting character in *Crabwalk* – perhaps, after Oskar, the boy with the tin drum, the most interesting in Grass's whole *oeuvre*, not only at a human level but also for what she stands for in greater German society: an ethnic populism that survived better in the East than in the West but evades capture by the right as by the left; that has its own story of what happened in Germany and the world in the twentieth century, a story that may be slanted, self-interested, and chaotic, but is deeply felt nonetheless; that resents being banned from polite discourse and generally repressed by the *bien-pensants*; and that will not go away.

Ugly though we may consider the Tulla Pokriefke phenomenon to be, *Crabwalk* presents for scrutiny a considered argument for allowing the Tullas and Konrads of Germany to have their heroes and martyrs and memorials and ceremonies of remembrance. The case against repression, the case for an all-inclusive national history, is one that Paul, faced with the fate of his son, comes to appreciate more and more, namely that if deep-seated passions are repressed they emerge elsewhere in new, unpredictable forms. Refuse to allow Konrad to read his paper to the class and he becomes a killer; lock him away and a new website pops up on the Internet: www. kameradschaft-konrad-pokriefke.de with its blood oath, 'We believe in you, we will wait for you, we will follow you.' (p. 234)

The most personal parts of *Crabwalk* are those in which Grass or 'Grass' looms over Paul Pokriefke's shoulder and we learn how Paul's narrative, namely *Crabwalk*, comes to be written. As a student in West Berlin thirty years ago, Paul attended a course in creative writing taught by 'Grass'. Now 'Grass' contacts him again, urging him to write the *Gustloff* book, arguing that as the offspring of that tragic night he is peculiarly fitted for the task. Years ago 'Grass' collected materials for a *Gustloff* book of his own, but then decided 'he'd had it with the past' and did not write it, and now it is too late. (p. 80)

People of his generation kept a discreet silence about the war years, 'Grass' confides, because their personal sense of guilt was overwhelming and because 'the need to accept responsibility and show remorse took precedence'. But now he realises that was a mistake: the historical memory of Germany's sufferings was thereby surrendered to the radical right. (p. 103)

'Grass' has working sessions with Paul in which he presses him to find words to describe the horrors of the last months of the war, as fleeing Germans perished by the hundreds of thousands, perhaps millions. For Paul's guidance 'Grass' even produces a specimen passage (deceptive guidance, however, for the passage describes not what really happened but what he saw in a film about the end of the *Gustloff*).

Paul is not inclined to accept the pleas of 'Grass' at face value. The reason why 'Grass' has not written the book is, he suspects, that his energies have dried up. Furthermore, he suspects, the real pressure comes from the obsessed Tulla behind 'Grass', twisting his arm. 'Grass' claims to be a mere casual acquaintance of Tulla's from the old days in Danzig. The truth, he suspects, is that 'Grass' was her lover and may be his father. His suspicions are strengthened by a comment that 'Grass' makes on his drafts: that Tulla should be given more mystery, more of a 'diffuse glow'. 'Grass' seems still to be under the spell of the witch-woman with the white hair. (p. 104)

'Who sows the wind will reap the storm,' runs the German proverb. It is not so much in the storm – the atrocities committed upon ethnic Germans in their flight from the east, the *Schrecklichkeit* of the fire-bombing of German cities, the coldhearted indifference of the Allies to the sufferings of the German population after the war – that the German radical right has found wellsprings of enduring resentment to exploit, as in the silence demanded of those who see themselves as victims or heirs of victims – a silence first imposed by outsiders, then adopted as a considered political measure by Germans themselves.

This taboo is today being re-examined in an extended national debate. *Crabwalk* was a best-seller when it came out in Germany in early 2002. This was not because the Gustloff/*Gustloff* story had never been tackled before. On the contrary, barely a year after Wilhelm Gustloff's death the popular author Emil Ludwig published, in German though not in Germany, a novel about the affair in which Frankfurter emerges as a hero, a man who by striking down a prominent Nazi hopes to inspire Jews to resistance. In 1975 the Swiss director Rolf Lyssy made a film, *Konfrontation*, on the same theme.

The last voyage of the *Gustloff* was the basis for the film *Night Fell over Gotenhafen* (1959) by the German American director Frank Wisbar. A survivor of that voyage, Heinz Schön, has year after year been publishing his researches into the fateful event and the identities of those who died. In English there has been *The Cruelest Night: Germany's Dunkirk and the Sinking of the Wilhelm Gustloff* (1979) by Christopher Dobson, John Miller, and Thomas Payne. Grass himself has referred to the *Gustloff* in several of his books, starting with *The Tin Drum*, as well as to the sinking by British planes of another erstwhile cruise ship, the *Cap Arcona*, carrying concentration camp survivors.

Thus neither Gustloff nor the *Gustloff* is forgotten in the sense of having been cut or allowed to fall out of the record. But there is a difference between being part of the record and being part of collective memory. The anger and resentment of people like Tulla Pokriefke grows out of a sense that their suffering has not been given its due, that an event catastrophic enough to be a cause of public mourning has been forced to remain a source of private grief. Her plight, and the plight of thousands like her, is captured most poignantly when, wanting to commemorate the dead, she can find nowhere to put her flowers but on the site of the old Nazi memorial. The question she asks, in its most emotive form, is: Is the reason why we are not allowed to lament, together and in public, the deaths of those thousands of drowned children simply that they were German children?

Ever since 1945 the question of collective guilt has been a divisive one in Germany, and Grass is at pains to confront it not directly but sideways, crabwise. *Crabwalk* is billed as *eine Novelle*, a novella or short fiction; its subject is not the sinking of the *Gustloff* but the need to write, and the coming to be written of, the story of the sinking of the *Gustloff*.

It is here that Günter Grass and the shadowy 'Grass' figure come closest to merging: through 'Grass', Grass presents his apology for not having written and, sadly, for no longer having it in his power to write the great German novel in which the multitude of Germans who perished in the death throes of the Third Reich are brought back to life so that they can be buried and mourned fittingly, and, the work of mourning having been completed, a new page in history can at last be turned, in an act of remembrance that will still the inarticulate, smouldering resentment of the Tulla Pokriefkes of Germany and liberate their grandchildren from the burden of the past.

But what does it in fact mean for the story of the *Gustloff* to be written by a Paul Pokriefke? It is one thing to relive the terrible last hours in the imagination and then render them in words that will bring their terrors home to readers, which is the task that 'Grass' seems to set before Paul. But the writing project before which Paul wavers is larger and more taxing: to become the writer who at the present moment in history – the early years of the twenty-first century – chooses to make the loss of the *Gustloff* his subject, that is to say, who chooses to break the taboo on asserting that a war crime or at least an atrocity was visited on Germans that night.

Paul's reluctance to write the greater story, and the crabwise dance he performs in telling the story of his reluctance – a dance during which, by sideways motion, the greater story somehow gets told – is justified. For an obscure journalist named Pokriefke who by lucky or unlucky accident happened to be born on the scene to retell the story means nothing. For the present, stories about the sufferings of Germans during the war remain inseparable from who tells them and for what motive. The best person to tell how nine thousand innocent or 'innocent' Germans died is not Pokriefke nor even 'Grass' but Günter Grass, doyen of German letters, winner of the Nobel Prize, steadiest practitioner and most enduring exemplar of democratic values in German public life. For Grass to tell the story at the opening of the new century means something. It may even signal that it is acceptable, appropriate, proper for all the stories of what happened in those terrible years to enter the public arena.

Günter Grass has never been a great prose stylist or a pioneer of fictional form. His strengths lie elsewhere: in the acuteness of his observation of German society at all levels, his ability to access the deeper currents of the national psyche, and his ethical steadiness. The narrative of *Crabwalk* is put together from bits and pieces that work efficiently in their present order though without any great feel of aesthetic inevitability. The authorial device of tracking the submarine and its prey step by step as they converge on the fatal crossroads as though directed by a higher destiny is a particularly creaky one. As a piece of writing *Crabwalk* suffers by comparison with some of Grass's other forays into the *Novelle* form, notably *Cat and Mouse* and, most recently, *The Call of the Toad* (1992), an elegantly constructed fiction hovering between the satiric and the elegiac, in which a decent, elderly couple found an association to allow Germans expelled from Danzig (now Polish Gdansk) to be interred in the city of their birth, only to have their enterprise swept away from under their feet and turned into a money-spinning racket.[4]

Ralph Manheim was Grass's first and best English translator, admirably attuned to Grass's language. After Manheim's death in 1992 the mantle was taken over first by Michael Henry Heim and then by Krishna Winston. Though there are one or two points one might quibble over – Tulla owns a master craftsman's certificate (*Meisterbrief*), not a 'master's diploma', which sounds too academic; Captain Marinesko is not 'degraded' (*degradiert*) on his return to port but reduced in rank – Winston's version of *Crabwalk* is a faithful one, down to the occasional clumsy, Grassian turn of phrase. (pp. 191, 180)

The main challenge to Winston's ingenuity is provided by Tulla Pokriefke. Tulla speaks a demotic East German German with echoes of the working-class suburbs of prewar Danzig. Finding an equivalent in American English is a thankless task. Locutions like 'Ain't it good enough that I'm out here breaking my back for them no-goods?' have a quaintly dated feel; but perhaps Germans from the West find Tulla's speech quaintly dated too. (p. 69)

(2003)

W. G. SEBALD was born in 1944 in the corner of southern Germany where Germany, Austria, and Switzerland converge. In his early twenties he travelled to England to further his studies in German literature, and spent most of his working life teaching in England at a provincial university. By the time of his death in 2001 he had a solid body of academic publication to his name, mainly on the literature of Austria.

But in his middle years Sebald also blossomed as a writer, first with a book of poetry, then with a sequence of four prose fictions. The second of these, *The Emigrants* (1992; English translation 1996), brought him wide attention, particularly in the English-speaking world, where its blend of storytelling, travel record, fictive biography, antiquarian essay, dream, and philosophical rumination, executed in elegant if rather lugubrious prose and supplemented with photographic documentation of endearingly amateurish quality, struck a decidedly new note (the German reading public was accustomed by this time to the crossing and indeed trampling of boundaries between fiction and nonfiction).[1]

The people in Sebald's books are for the most part what used to be called melancholics. The tone of their lives is defined by a hard-to-articulate sense that they do not belong in the world, that perhaps human beings in general do not belong here. They are humble enough not to claim they are preternaturally sensitive to the currents of history – in fact they tend to believe there is something wrong with them – but the tenor of Sebald's enterprise is to suggest that his people are prophetic, even though the fate of the prophet in the modern world is to be obscure and unheard.

What is the basis of their melancholy? Again and again Sebald suggests they are labouring under the burden of Europe's recent history, a history in which the Holocaust looms large. Internally they are racked by conflict between a self-protective urge to block off a painful past and a blind groping for something, they know not what, that has been lost.

Although in Sebald's stories the overcoming of amnesia is often figured as the culmination of a labour of research – burrowing in archives, tracking down witnesses – the recovery of the past only confirms what at the deepest level his people already know, as their steady melancholy in the face of the world already expresses, and as, in their intermittent breakdowns or catalepsies, their bodies have all along been saying in their own language, the language of symptom: that there is no cure, no salvation.

The form that the crisis of melancholy in Sebald takes is well defined. There is a lead-up full of compulsive activity, often consisting of nocturnal walking, dominated by feelings of apprehension. The world seems full of messages in some secret code. Dreams come thick and fast. Then there is the experience itself: one is on a cliff or in an aircraft, looking down in space but also back in time; man and his activities seem tiny to the point of insignificance; all sense of purpose dissolves. This vision precipitates a kind of swoon in which the mind collapses.

Vertigo (1990), Sebald's first long prose work, emphasises the apocalyptic dimension of this mental crisis. In the final section of the book the 'I' narrator takes a trip to his birthplace, the town of W. There, as he pores over a clutter of objects in a dusty attic, a flood of memories is released, followed by intimations that retribution is about to be visited on the town. Fearing madness, he flees. The homeward trip through southern Germany is eerie. The landscape has an alien air; people at the train station look like refugees from doomed cities; before his eyes someone reads a book that, as his later bibliographical researches prove, does not exist.[2]

In Sebald, 1914 often appears as the year when Europe took the wrong turn. But, looked at more closely, the pre-1914 idyll reveals itself to be without foundation. Did the true wrong turn take place earlier, then, with the triumph of Enlightenment reason and the enthronement of the idea of progress? While there is plenty of historical awareness in Sebald – the cities and landscapes through which his people move are ghost-ridden, layered with signs of the past – and while part of his general gloom is about the destruction of habitat in the name of progress, he is not conservative in the sense of harking back to a golden age when mankind was at home in the world in a good, natural way. On the contrary, he subjects the concepts of home and being at home to continual sceptical scrutiny. One of his literary-critical books is a study of the notion of *Heimat* (homeland) in Austrian literature. Playing on the ambiguity of the word *unheimlich* (unhomelike, unfamiliar, hence uncanny), he suggests that for today's Austrians, citizens of a notional country whose territory and population have altered with each turn in modern European history, there ought to be something ghostly in feeling at home.[3]

The Rings of Saturn (1995) comes the closest among Sebald's books to what we usually think of as nonfiction. It is written to tame the 'paralyzing horror' that overtakes its author – that is to say, its 'I' figure – in the face of the decline of the eastern region of England and the destruction of its landscape. (Of course the 'I' in Sebald's books is not to be identified with the historical W. G. Sebald. Nevertheless, Sebald as author plays mischievously with similarities between the two, to the point of reproducing snap-shots and passport photographs of 'Sebald' in his texts.)[4]

After a walking tour through the region, Sebald or 'I' is hospi-talised in a cataleptic state, with symptoms that include a sense of utter alienation linked to hallucinations of being in a high place looking down on the world. To this vertigo he gives a metaphys-ical rather than a merely psychological interpretation. 'If we view ourselves from a great height,' he says, 'it is frightening to realise how little we know about our species, our purpose and our end.' A spinning of the mind followed by mental collapse is what happens when we see ourselves from God's point of view. (p. 92)

Sebald did not call himself a novelist – prose writer was the term he preferred – but his enterprise nevertheless depends for its success on attaining lift-off from the biographical or the essay-istic – the prosaic in the everyday sense of the word – into the realm of the imaginative. The mysterious ease with which he is able to achieve such lift-off is the clearest proof of his genius. But *The Rings of Saturn* does not always succeed in this respect. Chapters on Joseph Conrad, Roger Casement, the poet Edward Fitzgerald, and the last empress of China, all of whom – surprisingly – have links with East Anglia, remain anchored in the prosaic.

In the earlier books the subject of time is not treated in any depth, perhaps because Sebald is not sure his medium will bear the weight of too much philosophising. When the subject is broached, it tends to be via references to the idealist paradoxes of Jorge Luis Borges, or, in *The Rings of Saturn*, to one of Borges's mentors, the neo-Platonist Sir Thomas Browne. But in *Austerlitz* (2001), Sebald's most ambitious book, time is confronted full on.[5]

Time has no real existence, asserts Jacques Austerlitz, a professor of European art and architecture who lost his past when his Jewish parents packed him off to England as a small child to escape the coming catastrophe. Instead of the continuous medium of time, says Austerlitz, there exist interconnected pockets of space-time whose topology we may never understand, but between which the so-called living and the so-called dead can travel and thus meet one another. A snapshot, he goes on, is a kind of eye or node of linkage between past and present, enabling the living to see the dead and the dead to see the living, the survivors. (This denial of the reality of time provides a retrospective rationale for the photographs that pepper Sebald's prose texts.)

One consequence of the denial of time is that the past is reduced to a set of interlocking memories in the minds of the living. Austerlitz is haunted by the knowledge that each day a quantum of the past, including his own past, vanishes as people die and memories are extinguished. Here he echoes the anxiety expressed by Rainer Maria Rilke in his letters about the duty of the artist as bearer of cultural memory. Indeed, behind Sebald's scholar hero, so out of place in the late twentieth century, loom several dead masters from the last years of Habsburg Austria: Rilke, the Hugo von Hofmannsthal of the 'Letter to Lord Chandos', Kafka, Wittgenstein.

Shortly before his death Sebald published a book of poems with images by the artist Tess Jaray.[6] It is a work of no great ambition, suggesting that verse-writing was a mere hobby to him. Yet his first book of poetry, *Nach der Natur* (1988), translated as *After Nature*, is a work of considerable scope. Though its imagery is more challenging than anything in Sebald's prose works, the verse retains the Sebaldian virtues of rhetorical elegance and clarity, and sits well in English translation, as indeed does everything he wrote.[7]

After Nature is made up of three long poems. The first is about Mathias Grünewald, the sixteenth-century painter, whose life-story Sebald cobbles together from scanty historical sources and observations on his paintings. Chief among the paintings is the altarpiece Grünewald executed for the Antonine monastery of Isenheim in Alsace, in his time the home of a hospital for plagues of various kinds. In the darkest of the Isenheim paintings – the temptation of Saint Anthony, the crucifixion and deposition of Jesus – Sebald's Grünewald sees creation as a field of experiment for blind, amoral natural forces, one of nature's crazier productions being the human mind itself, capable not only of mimicking its creator and inventing ingenious methods of destruction, but of tormenting itself – as in the case of Grünewald – with visions of the insanity of life.

Equally bleak is Grünewald's *Crucifixion* in Basel, where the strange, murky lighting creates an effect of time rushing backward. Behind the painting, Sebald suggests, lie premonitions of apocalypse stemming from an eclipse of the sun in central Europe in 1502, a 'secret sickening away of the world, / in which a phantasmal encroachment of dusk / in the midst of daytime like a fainting fit / poured through the vault of the sky.' (p. 30)

The darkness of Grünewald's vision is not just a matter of an idiosyncratically melancholy temperament. Via connections with the messianic prophet Thomas Münzer, Grünewald knew and responded to the horrors of the Thirty Years War, which included a widespread atrocity any artist would shudder at, the gouging out of eyes; furthermore, through his wife, a convert born in the Frankfurt ghetto, he had intimate experience of the persecution of Europe's Jews.

The coda of this first poem consists of a single image: the world overtaken by a new ice age, white and lifeless, which is all that the brain sees when the optic nerve is torn.

The second of the *After Nature* poems is again about vastness and blankness and iciness. Its hero, Georg Wilhelm Steller (1709–1746), is a child of the Enlightenment, a young German intellectual who has abandoned theology to study natural science. In pursuit of his ambition of cataloguing the fauna and flora of the frozen north, Steller travels to St Petersburg, a city that looms like a phantom out of 'the future's resounding emptiness', where he joins the expedition led by Vitus Bering to map the sea passage from Russia's Arctic ports to the Pacific. (p. 48)

The expedition is successful. Steller even sets foot for a few brief hours on the North American land mass. On the way back to Russia, however, the voyagers suffer shipwreck. The melancholy Bering dies; the survivors make their way home in a makeshift craft, all but Steller, who goes off into the Siberian interior to collect specimens and familiarise himself with the native peoples. There he too dies, leaving behind a list of plants and a manuscript destined to become a guidebook for hunters and trappers.

The aims of the Grünewald and Steller poems are not biographical or historical in any ordinary sense. Though the scholarship behind them is thorough – Sebald had publications on art-historical subjects to his name; he clearly did his homework on the Bering expedition – scholarship takes second place to what he intuits about his subjects and perhaps projects upon them (this may give a clue as to how Sebald constructed characters in his later prose fictions). Instance one: his claim that Grünewald, though married, was secretly homosexual, involved for many years in 'a male friendship wavering / between horror and loyalty' with a fellow painter named Matthis Nithart, is, among specialists, highly contentious: 'Matthis Nithart' may simply be Grünewald's own baptismal name. Instance two: the historical Steller appears to have been a vain and supercilious young man, interested mainly in making a name for himself, who met his death when he fell into a drunken stupor in sub-zero temperatures. None of this is in Sebald.

It is thus best to think of Grünewald and Steller as personae, masks that enable Sebald to project back into the past a character type, ill at ease in the world, indeed in exile from it, that may be his own but that he feels possesses a certain genealogy which his reading and researches can uncover. The Grünewald persona, with his Manichean view of the creation, is more fully worked out than the Steller persona, which is little more than a set of gestures, perhaps because Sebald could find – or create – no believable depths in the latter's character.

'Dark Night Sallies Forth', the third of the poems in *After Nature*, is more overtly autobiographical. Here Sebald, as 'I', takes stock of himself as individual but also as inheritor of Germany's recent history. In images and in fragments of narrative, the poem tells his story from his birth in 1944 under the sign of Saturn, the cold planet, to the 1980s. Some of the images – we are familiar with the practice by now from Sebald's prose fictions – come from Europe's cultural treasure chest, in this case two paintings by Albrecht Altdorfer (1480–1538): of the destruction of Sodom; and of the battle of Arbela, fought between Alexander of Macedon and Darius, king of Persia.

Seeing the Sodom painting for the first time precipitates a *déjà vu* experience, which Sebald connects with the bombing of Germany's cities in World War II and the refusal of his parents to speak about the subject. The general willed amnesia of his parents' generation, the chief source of his grievance against and alienation from them, forces him to do their remembering for them. (Putting an end to this spell of historical amnesia became a matter of gathering national concern in Germany at the turn of the century. It is the theme of Sebald's own *Luftkrieg und Literatur*, 1999, translated as *On the Natural History of Destruction*.[8])

In the poem the spectacle of the destruction of Sodom leads to a personal crisis ('I nearly went out of my mind'), which Sebald links to his recurrent episodes of vertigo. With hindsight we can see that it will also lead to the labour of reparation constituted by his four prose works, and particularly by his biographies of Jews, both imaginary (the people in *The Emigrants*; Austerlitz) and real (his friend and now his translator Michael Hamburger in *The Rings of Saturn*). (p. 91)

The most clearly narrative section of *After Nature*, written with a nod in the direction of 'The Prelude', William Wordsworth's poem about his formative years, tells the story of Sebald's first sojourn in the Manchester of the 1960s, a city in which early industrial Europe survives into the late twentieth century as a kind of necropolis or kingdom of the dead ('These images / often plunged me into a quasi / sublunary state of deep / melancholia'). (p. 103)

The East Anglian landscape where Sebald later finds himself is equally bleak: farms have been replaced with asylums or prisons or homes for the aged or testing ranges for weapons. Nor is modern England unique in its ugliness. Flying over Germany, he has another of his darkly visionary experiences.

> Cities phosphorescent
> on the riverbank, industry's
> glowing piles waiting
> beneath the smoke trails
> like ocean giants for the siren's
> blare, the twitching lights
> of rail- and motorways, the murmur
> of the millionfold proliferating molluscs,
> wood lice and leeches, the cold putrefaction,
> the groans and the rocky ribs,
> the mercury shine, the clouds that
> chased through the towers of Frankfurt,
> time stretched out and time speeded up,
> all this raced through my mind

> and was already so near the end
> that every breath of air made my
> face shudder. (p. 118)

Visions like this led him to think of himself as Icarus, the boy who, sailing high above the earth with the homemade wings, sees what no ordinary mortal is allowed to see. When he falls, as he is doomed to do, will anyone pay attention, or, as in Brueghel's famous painting, will the world simply go on with its business?

Vertigo points him backward to childhood problems with keeping his balance, and forward to the second Altdorfer painting, *The Battle of Arbela*, a panorama of slaughter on a huge scale rendered in detail of hallucinatory, vertigo-inducing minuteness. The painting ought to precipitate another of his melancholic collapses. Instead it leads to the rather unconvincing transcendence with which the poem ends: an opening out of vision beyond horizons of unending warfare, East versus West, to a new future:

> . . . still further in the distance,
> towering up in the dwindling light,
> the mountain ranges,
> snow-covered and ice-bound,
> of the strange, unexplored,
> African continent.

After Nature has its dead patches and moments of empty portentousness, but in all it is a work of great power and seriousness fully worthy to stand beside the prose works of Sebald's last decade.

(2002)

11   Hugo Claus, poet

IN ONE OF Hugo Claus's later poems, a celebrated poet agrees to be interviewed by a younger man, also a poet. A few drinks soon unleash the malice and envy that lie behind the visit. Just between the two of us, asks the younger man, why do you keep the modern world at arm's length? Why do you pay so much attention to the dead masters? And why are you so obsessed with technique? Don't be offended, but sometimes I find you much too hermetic. And your rhyme patterns: they are so obvious, so childish. What is your philosophy, your basic idea, in a nutshell?

The older man's mind roams back to his childhood, to the dead masters Byron, Ezra Pound, Stevie Smith. 'Stepping stones,' he says.

'Pardon?' says the puzzled interviewer.

'Stepping stones for the poem to tread on.' He leads the young man to the door, helps him on with his coat. From the doorstep he points up at the moon. Uncomprehending, the young man stares at the pointing finger.[1]

In this wry look at himself through the eyes of a dismissive younger generation, Claus manages to summarise the more obvious features of his poetry. He does indeed keep his distance from the modern world (though in a more nuanced way than his rival cares to recognise); he is indeed highly conscious of how his own work relates to literary tradition, national and European; he is indeed a master of verse form, to a point where he can make difficult feats seem childishly easy; he is indeed sometimes hermetic – in fact, sometimes writes within a hermetic tradition; and readers looking for a neat message, some Clausian 'philosophy' that will sum up his life's work, are likely to come away empty-handed.

Now in his seventies, Claus has a hugely productive artistic career behind him during which he has been showered with honours and awards, not only in his native Belgium and in the Netherlands, but more widely in western Europe. His dramatic *oeuvre* – original plays, translations, and adaptations – has made him a major theatrical presence. He has conducted notable forays into cinema and into art and art criticism. But the creations by which he will ultimately be remembered are, first, *The Sorrow of Belgium* (1983), one of the great novels of postwar Europe, and second, a corpus of poetry that in his collected *Poems 1948–2004* runs to some 1,400 pages.

Hugo Claus was born in 1929 in Brugge (Bruges) in Flanders, the son of a printer with a passion for the theatre. Several of his schoolteachers during the Occupation were right-wing nationalists; he himself was drawn into the fascist Flemish youth movement. After the liberation his father was briefly interned for his wartime political activities. This background is drawn on in *The Sorrow of Belgium*.

Claus received a sound *Gymnasium*-type education with an emphasis on classical and modern languages but did not proceed to university. He began his career in the arts as a book illustrator, then at the age of eighteen published a first book of verse and a year later a first novel. Among his early literary idols were Antonin Artaud and the French surrealists; he soon became active in the

COBRA (Copenhagen-Brussels-Amsterdam) art movement.

During the decade of the 1950s Claus lived in France and Italy as well as his native Belgium. In 1959 he was invited on a tour of the United States by the Ford Foundation, along with a group of up-and-coming European writers including Fernando Arrabal, Günter Grass, and Italo Calvino. 'A verse from Luke won't help you here,' he recorded, faced with the impersonal hugeness of Chicago.[2]

Talented in a range of artistic spheres and hugely energetic, Claus continued to write poetry and fiction and to paint while at the same time developing his skills as a playwright, screenplay writer, theatre and cinema director, and art critic. With the publication of his *Poems 1948–1963* he signalled the close of the first phase of his poetic career, a phase of which *The Sign of the Hamster* (1963), a rambling retrospective look at his life on the lines of François Villon's 'Great Testament', emerges as the high point. Along with Remco Campert, Gerrit Kouwenaar, Simon Vinkenoog, and Lucebert, he had by now established himself in the front rank of the new generation of Dutch-language poets, a generation that made its mark in the early 1950s by espousing an anti-traditional, anti-rational, anti-aesthetic, experimental art receptive to New World influences but by the 1960s had split apart, its members going their various individual ways.

The revolutionary tumult of 1968 did not leave Claus untouched. He paid a visit – obligatory, at the time, for left-inclined European intellectuals – to the socialist utopia of Cuba, and praised its achievements, though more guardedly than some of his fellows. Back in Belgium a law court found one of his theatrical productions injurious to public morals and sentenced him to four months in prison (after a public outcry the sentence was suspended). An ill-starred love affair engendered a book of poems, *Morning, you* (1971), notable as much for its sexual explicitness as for its searing emotional intensity. For years thereafter Claus's private life would be subject to the prying of the tabloid press.

While Claus has not been a political poet in any narrow sense, the poems of his first phase certainly reflect the apocalyptic mood and alienation from mainstream politics of the European intelligentsia during the darkest years of the Cold War, a war whose reality – given that Brussels was the headquarters of NATO – was hard for any Belgian to ignore. In this respect Claus is close to his German contemporary, the poet Hans Magnus Enzensberger. But Claus's vision remains uniquely Netherlandic. The spirit that broods over his trampled motherland is that of Hieronymus Bosch: he harks back to the same late-medieval folk-imagination, with its bestiaries and gnomic sayings, upon which Bosch drew for his vision of a world gone mad.

In the poetry of Claus's later phase it is the exploration of relations between the sexes, at both a personal and a symbolic level, that comes to the fore. The spirit of this work is anything but autumnal: like W. B. Yeats, Claus rages against the decay of the physical self while desire remains untamed. In these explorations Claus calls upon the resources of myth, Indian as well as Greek. His theatrical work of the same period concentrates on adaptations of Greek and Roman tragedy. It would not be going too far to say that the late Clausian universe is dominated by a struggle between male and female principles (this in spite of the poet's own warning that he has no 'philosophy' to peddle).

Hugo Claus is not a great lyricist, and though his style is crisp and pointed he cannot be called a great satirist or epigrammatist either. From the beginning, however, his poetry has been marked by an uncommon mix of intelligence and passion, given expression in a medium over which he has such light-fingered control that art becomes invisible. Many of the shorter pieces in his *oeuvre* are merely fugitive or occasional. Nevertheless, scattered throughout in some abundance are poems whose verbal concentration, intensity of feeling, and intellectual range bring their author into the first rank of European poets of the late twentieth century.

(2005)

12   Graham Greene, *Brighton Rock*

TO THE WIDER world, Brighton of the 1930s presented the face of an attractive seaside resort. But behind that face lay another Brighton: tracts of shoddily built houses, dreary shopping areas, and desolate industrial suburbs. This 'other' Brighton bred disaffection and criminality, much of the latter concentrated on the race-track and its lucrative pickings.

Graham Greene made a number of trips to Brighton with the purpose of soaking in its atmosphere and gathering material for his fiction. This research was first drawn on in *A Gun for Sale* (1936), a novel in which Battling Kite, leader of a gang that extorts money from bookmakers in return for protection, has his throat slit by the rival Colleoni gang.

Out of the murder of Kite grows the action of *Brighton Rock* (1938), which was initially planned as just another crime novel of a kind that might easily be adapted for the screen. The book starts with the hunting down of Fred Hale, a reporter used by Colleoni as an informer, by the Kite gang. In an act that is not described, Kite's lieutenant, a youth named Pinkie Brown, kills Hale, perhaps by pushing a stick of the hard red-and-white candy known as Brighton Rock down his throat. The body is unmarked: the doctor who conducts the post mortem concludes that Hale died of a heart attack.

But for Ida Arnold, an easygoing *demi-mondaine* whom Hale meets on the last day of his life, and but for Rose, the young waitress who unwittingly reveals the flaw in Pinkie's alibi, the case would be closed. The action of the novel thus moves in two converging lines: Pinkie's attempts to ensure Rose's silence, first by marrying her, then by talking her into a suicide pact; and Ida's quest, first to get to the bottom of the mystery of Hale's sudden death, then to save Rose from Pinkie's machinations.

Pinkie is a product of the 'other' Brighton. His parents are dead; the schoolyard, with its hierarchies of power and its casual sadism, rather than the schoolroom, has afforded him his education. The gangster Kite has been his adopted father or big brother, Kite's gang his surrogate family. Of the world beyond Brighton he is utterly ignorant.

Amoral, charmless, prim, seething with resentment against 'them' and against the 'bogies' (police) used by 'them' to keep him down, Pinkie is a chilling figure. He distrusts women, who in his view have nothing on their minds but marriage and babies. The very thought of sex revolts him: he is haunted by memories of his own parents' Saturday night tussle under the bedclothes, to which he had to listen from his own bed. While the men he commands now that Kite is dead have transitory relationships with women, he is locked into a virginity of which he is ashamed but from which has no idea of how to escape.

Into his life comes Rose, a plain, timid girl ready to worship any boy who takes notice of her. The story of Pinkie and Rose is the story, on Pinkie's side, of a struggle to bar the entry of love into his heart, on Rose's of dogged persistence in loving her man in defiance of all prudence. To preclude her from testifying against him if he is ever brought to trial, Pinkie marries Rose in a civil ceremony that both know to be an offence against the Holy Ghost. Not only does Pinkie marry Rose, he grimly goes through with the ordeal of consummating the marriage; and, before the veil of misogynistic hatred and contempt once again descends, finds that lovemaking is not all that bad, that he can look back on it with a kind of pleasure, a kind of pride.

Only one more time does Pinkie have to repulse the batterings of redemption upon his walled-in heart. As he drives Rose to the lonely spot where, if his plan works, she will shoot herself, he feels 'an enormous emotion . . . like something trying to get in; the pressure of gigantic wings against the glass . . . If the glass broke, if the beast – whatever it was – got in, God knows what it would do.'[1]

What holds Pinkie and Rose together is the fact that they are both 'Romans', children of the True Church, of whose teachings they have the merest smattering but which gives them nevertheless an unshakable sense of inner superiority. The teaching on which they rely most heavily is the doctrine of grace, summed up in an anonymous poem that has impressed itself on the memories of both:

> My friend judge not me,
> Thou seest I judge not thee:
> Betwixt the stirrup and the ground,
> Mercy I asked, mercy I found.

God's grace, in Catholic teaching, is unknowable, unpredictable, mysterious; to rely on it for salvation – to postpone repentance until the moment between the stirrup and the ground – is a deep sin, a sin of pride and presumption. One of Greene's achievements in *Brighton Rock* is to raise his unlikely lovers, teenage hoodlum and anxious child bride, to moments of comical yet awful Luciferian pride.

Is Pinkie damned? Within the purview of the novel the

question makes no sense: of what happens in Pinkie's soul while he tumbles down the cliff at the end of the book we are given no hint. Who are we anyhow to say that, in some cases, reliance on God's mercy may not come out of a genuinely spiritual intuition of how the mystery of grace works? For what it is worth, however, Greene did later in life put it on record that he did not accept the doctrine of eternal damnation. The world contained enough suffering, he said, to qualify as a purgatory in itself.

Brighton Rock is a novel without a hero. But in the person of Ida Arnold, the woman whom the desperate Fred Hale picks up on the last day of his life, Greene creates not only an unconventional detective, shrewd, dogged, and unflappable, but also a stout ideological antagonist to the Catholic axis of Pinkie and Rose. Pinkie and Rose believe in Good and Evil; Ida believes in more down-to-earth Right and Wrong, in law and order, though of course with a bit of fun on the side. Pinkie and Rose believe in salvation and damnation, particularly the latter; in Ida the religious impulse is tamed, trivialised, and confined to the ouija board. In the scenes in which Ida, full of motherly concern, tries to wean Rose away from her demonic lover, we see the rudiments of two world views, the one eschatological, the other secular and materialist, uncomprehendingly confronting each other.

Though Ida's view seems in the end to triumph, it is one of Greene's subtler achievements to put that view in doubt as perhaps blinkered and tyrannical. In the end the story belongs not to Ida but to Rose and Pinkie, for they are prepared, in however juvenile a way, to confront ultimate questions, while she is not.

Rose's faith in her lover never wavers. To the end she identifies Ida, not Pinkie, as the subtle seducer, the evil one. '*She* ought to be damned . . . She doesn't know about love.' (p. 267) If the worst comes to the worst, she, Rose, would rather suffer in hell with

Pinkie than be saved with Ida. (As we will never know the fate of Pinkie's soul, so we will never know whether Rose's faith will be proof against the hateful words, preserved on a vinyl disk, that Pinkie speaks to her from beyond the grave: 'God damn you, you little bitch.') (p. 193)

Graham Greene belonged to a generation whose vision of modern urban life was deeply influenced by T. S. Eliot's *The Waste Land*. No mean poet himself, Greene brings Brighton to life in imagery of sombre expressionist power: 'The huge darkness pressed a wet mouth against the panes.' (p.252) In later books Greene tended to rein in the poetry when it became obtrusive.

Even more pervasive in his fiction is the influence of cinema. The late 1930s were a time of growth for the British film industry. By law, cinemas had to screen a quota of British films. A system of subsidies rewarded films of quality. A genuinely British school of film reflecting the realities of British life grew up, a development that Greene welcomed. In 1935 he became the film critic for the *Spectator*, and during the next five years some four hundred film reviews appeared over his name. Later he was to work on adaptations of his own novels, including *Brighton Rock* itself, filmed by Carol Reed in 1947 and distributed in the United States under the title *Young Scarface*.

From as early as *Stamboul Train* (1932) Greene's novels had borne the imprint of the cinema: a preference for observation from the outside without commentary, tight cutting from scene to scene, equal emphasis for the significant and the non-significant. 'When I describe a scene,' he said in an interview, 'I capture it with the moving eye of the cine-camera rather than with the photographer's eye – which leaves it frozen . . . I work with the camera, following my characters and their movements.'[2] In *Brighton Rock* the influence of the visual style of Howard Hawks can be felt in the handling of the violence at the race-track. The ingenious use of the itinerant photographer to advance the plot suggests Alfred Hitchcock. Chapters characteristically end with the focus being pulled back from human actors to the greater natural scene – the moon over city and beachfront, for instance.

At the time he wrote *Brighton Rock* Greene was also refining his narrative technique, using Henry James and Ford Madox Ford as his masters and *The Craft of Fiction* by Percy Lubbock as his textbook. While *Brighton Rock* may not be technically perfect – there are lapses during which Pinkie's inner narration is invaded by the narrator's comments and judgments – it is, in its concentration on intimate evil, clearly of the Jamesian school.

The novel has other failings too. While Greene's sympathies are clearly on the side of the demoralised, unemployed poor, the one big scene in which he might have explored the texture of their life – the visit to Rose's parents – is less disturbing in its impact than grotesque. And the pace of the action slackens toward the end – too many pages are devoted to the individual destinies of Pinkie's gang.

Given the taciturn ethos of his characters, Greene has little occasion in *Brighton Rock* to display his skill as a writer of dialogue. The exception is the lawyer Prewitt, who is articulate enough to take on a Dickensian verbal life of his own.

For the 1970 collected edition, Greene retouched the original text in places. In 1938 he had felt at liberty to use terms like 'Jewess' and 'nigger' ('niggers' with 'cushiony' lips). In the circles in which he moved at the time, such racial epithets were acceptable currency. After the war they no longer were. Accordingly he turned 'niggers' into 'negroes' and 'Jewesses' in some contexts into 'women', in others into 'bitches'. Colleoni's 'old Semitic face' becomes his 'old Italian face'. The cushiony lips remain.

The fact that Greene thought the insult could be removed with a few strokes of the pen indicates that in his mind it belonged to the mere verbal surface of the novel, not to its underlying attitudes and ideas.

Graham Greene was born in 1904 into a family of some intellectual distinction. On his mother's side he was related to Robert Louis Stevenson. His father was headmaster of a public school; one of his brothers became Director-General of the BBC.

At Oxford University he read history, wrote poetry, enrolled briefly in the Communist Party, and toyed with the idea of entering the spying trade. After graduating he took a night job on *The Times* as a sub-editor, writing fiction by day. His first novel was published in 1929; *Brighton Rock* was his ninth.

In 1941, after a spell as an air raid warden, Greene joined SIS, the Secret Intelligence Service, where his immediate superior was Kim Philby, later to be uncovered as in the pay of the Russians. After the war he worked in publishing until his income from book royalties, screenplay writing, and the sale of film rights made it unnecessary for him to hold down a job.

Greene continued to serve SIS informally for years after the war, reporting on what he picked up on his extensive travels. To a degree he was only a dilettante secret agent. Nevertheless, the information he supplied was valued.

Brighton Rock was his first serious novel, serious in the sense of working with serious ideas. For a while Greene maintained a distinction between his forays into the serious novel and his so-called entertainments. Of the twenty-odd further volumes of fiction he published before his death in 1991, *The Power and the Glory* (1940), *The Heart of the Matter* (1948), *The End of the Affair* (1951), *A Burnt-Out Case* (1961), *The Honorary Consul* (1973), and *The Human Factor* (1978) have attracted the most critical attention.

In this body of work Greene carved out a territory of his own,

'Greeneland', in which men as imperfect and divided as any have their integrity and the grounds of their belief tested to the limit, while God, if he exists, remains hidden. The stories of these dubious heroes are told grippingly enough and searchingly enough to engage readers by the million.

Greene was fond of quoting Robert Browning's Bishop Blougram:

> Our interest's in the dangerous edge of things,
> The honest thief, the tender murderer,
> The superstitious atheist . . .

If he had to choose an epigraph for his whole *oeuvre*, he said, it would be that. Although he revered Henry James ('as solitary in the history of the novel as Shakespeare in the history of poetry'), his immediate descent is from the Joseph Conrad of *The Secret Agent*. Of his progeny, John le Carré has been the most distinguished.[3]

Greene is often thought of as a Catholic novelist, one who interrogates the lives of his characters from a specifically Catholic viewpoint. He certainly felt that without a religious awareness, or at least without an awareness of the possibility of sin, the novelist could not do justice to the human condition: this is the essence of his criticism of Virginia Woolf and E. M. Forster, whose worlds he found 'paper-thin', cerebral.[4]

Greene's account of how from being a Catholic and a novelist he became a Catholic novelist was elaborated late in life and should not necessarily be taken at face value. In this account, though he converted to Catholicism as a young man,[5] religion remained for him a private affair between the believer and God until he witnessed at first hand the persecution of the Church in Mexico and saw how religious belief could take over and sacramentalise the whole of people's lives.

What is left out of this account is the attraction, romantic in nature and attested to in his early fiction, that Catholicism exerted on him – the sense that Catholics have unique access to an ancient body of wisdom and that English Catholics in especial, members of a once persecuted sect, are as a result inherent outsiders.

However ill educated Greene's Pinkie Brown may be (not so badly educated, however, that he cannot compose sentences in Latin), his sense of self is wrapped up with possessing a secret knowledge, unavailable to the hoi polloi, of having a higher fate reserved for him. This sense of election, shared by many other Greene characters, gives rise to criticism such as George Orwell's: Greene 'appears to share the idea, which has been floating around ever since Baudelaire, that there is something rather *distingué* in being damned'.[6] But such criticism is not wholly fair: if at moments Greene seems to tremble on the edge of endorsing Pinkie's romantic conception of Catholicism as the creed of the Byronic outsider, there are other moments when Pinkie's eschatological apparatus seems a mere rickety defence erected against the ridicule of the world – ridicule of his shabby clothes, his gaucherie, his working-class speech, his youth, his ignorance of sex. Pinkie may do his best to elevate his acts to the sphere of sin and damnation, but to the doughty Ida Arnold they are simply crimes that deserve the punishment of the law; and in this world, the only world we have, it is Ida's view that tends to prevail.

(2004)

13 Samuel Beckett, the short fiction

ALTHOUGH *WATT*, WRITTEN in English during the war years but published only in 1953, is a substantial presence in the Beckett canon, it can fairly be said that Beckett did not find himself as a writer until he switched to French and, in particular, until the years 1947–51, when in one of the great creative outpourings of modern times he wrote the prose fictions *Molloy*, *Malone Dies*, and *The Unnamable* ('the trilogy'), the play *Waiting for Godot*, and the thirteen *Texts for Nothing*.[1]

These major works were preceded by four stories, also written in French, about one of which – 'First Love' – Beckett had his doubts. (He might also have queried the ending of 'The End': usually a master of restraint, Beckett indulges here in an uncharacteristic dip into plangency.)

In these stories, in the novel *Mercier and Camier* (written in French in 1946), and in *Watt*, the outlines of the late-Beckettian world, and the procedures by which Beckettian fictions are generated, begin to become visible. It is a world of confined spaces or else bleak wastes, inhabited by asocial and indeed misanthropic monologuers helpless to terminate their monologue, tramps with failing bodies and never-sleeping minds condemned to a purgatorial treadmill on which they rehearse again and again the great themes of Western philosophy; a world that comes to us in the distinctive prose that Beckett, using French models in the main, though with Jonathan Swift whispering ghostly in his ear, was in the process of perfecting for himself, lyrical and mordant in equal measures.

In *Texts for Nothing* (the French title *Textes pour rien* alludes to the orchestral conductor's initial beat over silence) we see Beckett trying to work himself out of the corner into which he had painted himself in *The Unnamable*: if 'the Unnamable' is the verbal sign for whatever is left once every mark of identity has been stripped from the series of antecedent monologuers (Molloy, Malone, Mahood, Worm and the rest of them), who/what comes when the Unnamable is stripped too, and who after that successor, and so forth; and – more important – does the fiction itself not degenerate into a record of an increasingly mechanical stripping process?

The problem of how to concoct some verbal formula that will pin down and annihilate the unnamable residue of the self and thus at last achieve silence is formulated in the sixth of the *Texts*. By the eleventh text, that quest for finality – hopeless, as we know and Beckett knows – is in the process of being absorbed into a kind of verbal music, and the fierce comic anguish that accompanied it is in the process of being aestheticised too. Such is the solution that Beckett seems to arrive at, a makeshift solution if ever there was one, to the question of what to do next.

The next three decades will see Beckett, in his prose fictions, unable to move on – stalled, in fact, on the very question on what it means to move on, why one should move on, who it is that should do the moving on. A dribble of publications continues: brief quasi-musical compositions whose elements are phrases and sentences. *Ping* (1966) and *Lessness* (1969) – texts built up from repertoires of set phrases by combinatorial methods – represent the extreme of this tendency. Their music happens to be harsh;

but as the fourth of the *Fizzles* of 1975 proves, Beckett's compositions can also be of haunting verbal beauty.

The narrative premise of *The Unnamable*, and of *How It Is* (1961), is held onto in these short fictions: a creature constituted of a voice attached, for reasons unknown, to some kind of body enclosed in a space more or less reminiscent of Dante's Hell, is condemned for a certain length of time to speak, to try to make sense of things. It is a situation well described by Heidegger's term *Geworfenheit*: being thrown without explanation into an existence governed by obscure rules. *The Unnamable* was sustained by its dark comic energy. But by the late 1960s that comic energy, with its power to surprise, had reduced itself to a relentless, arid self-laceration. *The Lost Ones* (1970) is hell to read and was perhaps hell to write too.

Then, with *Company* (1980), *Ill Seen Ill Said* (1981), and *Worstward Ho* (1983), we emerge miraculously into clearer water. The prose is suddenly more expansive, even, by Beckettian standards, genial. Whereas in the preceding fictions the interrogation of the trapped, *geworfen* self had had a mechanical quality, as though it were accepted from the beginning that the questioning was futile, there is in these late pieces a sense that individual existence is a genuine mystery worth exploring. The quality of thought and of language remains as philosophically scrupulous as ever, but there is a new element of the personal, even the autobiographical: the memories that float into the mind of the speaker clearly come from the early childhood of Samuel Beckett himself, and these are treated with a certain wonder and tenderness even though – like images from early silent film – they flicker and vanish on the screen of the inner eye. The key Beckettian word 'on', which had earlier had a quality of grinding hopelessness to it ('I can't go on, I'll go on') begins to take on a new meaning: the meaning, if not of hope, then at least of courage.

The spirit of these last writings, optimistic yet humorously sceptical about what can be achieved, is well captured in a 1983 letter of Beckett's: 'The long crooked straight is laborious but not without excitement. While still "young" I began to seek consolation in the thought that then if ever, i.e. now, the true words at last, from the mind in ruins. To this illusion I continue to cling.'[2]

Though it is not a description he would have accepted, Beckett can justly be called a philosophical writer, one whose works can be read as a series of sustained sceptical raids on Descartes and the philosophy of the subject that Descartes founded. In his suspicion of Cartesian axiomatics Beckett aligns himself with Nietzsche and Heidegger, and with his younger contemporary Jacques Derrida. The satiric interrogation to which he subjects the Cartesian cogito (I am thinking, therefore I must exist) is so close in spirit to Derrida's programme for exposing the metaphysical assumptions behind Western thought that we must speak, if not of Beckett's direct influence on Derrida, then of a striking case of sympathetic vibration.

Starting out as an uneasy Joycean and an even more uneasy Proustian, Beckett eventually settled on philosophical comedy as the medium for his uniquely anguished, arrogant, self-doubting, scrupulous temperament. In the popular mind his name is associated with the mysterious Godot who may or may not come but for whom we wait anyhow, passing the time as best we can. In this he seemed to define the mood of an age. But his range is wider than that, and his achievement far greater. Beckett was an artist possessed by a vision of life without consolation or dignity or promise of grace, in the face of which our only duty − inexplicable and futile of attainment, but a duty nonetheless − is not to lie to ourselves. It was a vision to which he gave expression in language of a virile strength and intellectual subtlety that marks him as one of the great prose stylists of the twentieth century.

(2005)

14 Walt Whitman

IN AUGUST OF 1863 · Private Erastus Haskell of the 141st New York Volunteers died of typhoid fever in Armory Square Hospital, Washington, DC. Shortly thereafter his parents received a long letter from a stranger. 'I was very anxious [Erastus] should be saved,' the stranger wrote,

> and so were they all – he was well used by the attendants . . . Many nights I sat in the hospital by his bedside . . . – he always liked to have me sit there, but never cared to talk – I shall never forget those nights, it was a curious and solemn scene, the sick and wounded lying around in their cots . . . and this dear young man close at hand . . . I do not know his past life, but what I do know, and what I saw of him, he was a noble boy – I felt he was one I should get very much attached to . . .
>
> I write you this letter, because I would do something at least in his memory – his fate was a hard one, to die so – He is one of the thousands of our unknown young American men in the ranks about whom there is no record or fame, no fuss about their dying so unknown, but I find in them the real precious and royal ones . . . Poor dear son, though you were not my son, I felt to love you as a son, what short time I saw you sick and dying there.

The letter was signed 'Walt Whitman', with a Brooklyn address.[1]

Writing letters of condolence was just one of the duties that Whitman took upon himself as a Soldiers' Missionary. Doing the rounds of the hospitals in Washington, he brought the soldiers gifts of fresh underwear, fruit, ice cream, tobacco, postage stamps. He also chatted to them, consoled them, kissed and embraced them, and if they had to die tried to ease their dying. 'I never before had my feelings so thoroughly and (so far) permanently absorbed, to the very roots, as by these huge swarms of dear, wounded, sick, dying boys,' he wrote. 'I have formed attachments in hospital, that I shall keep to my dying day, & they will the same, without doubt.'[2]

Between 1862 and 1865, Whitman by his own count ministered to some one hundred thousand men. Though his interventions were not universally welcomed – 'That odious Walt Whitman, [come] to talk evil and unbelief to my boys,' wrote one nurse – he was nowhere denied entry. One might wonder whether in our day a middle-aged man, a reputed pornographer, would be allowed to haunt the wards, drifting from the bedside of one attractive young man to another, or whether he would not soon find himself hustled to the door by a couple of aides.[3]

Whitman kept notes on his Washington experiences, later working these up into newspaper articles and lectures, which in 1876 he published in a limited edition under the title *Memoranda During the War*. This in turn became part of *Specimen Days* (1882). Not everything in the *Memoranda* comes from first-hand experience. Though Whitman gives the impression that he witnessed the assassination of Abraham Lincoln in Ford's theatre and provides a dramatic description of the event, he was not in fact there. But he did believe he enjoyed a special relationship with Lincoln. Both men were tall. Whitman was often present when Lincoln passed through the streets and was convinced that, over the heads of the crowd, the elected leader of the people recognised and nodded back to the unacknowledged legislator of mankind (like Shelley, Whitman had elevated ideas about his calling).

As a young man Whitman had been much impressed by the new science of phrenology. He took the standard phrenological test and came out with high scores for Amativeness and Adhesiveness, middling scores for language skills. He was proud enough of his scores to publish them in advertisements for *Leaves of Grass*.

In phrenological jargon, amativeness is sexual ardour; adhesiveness is attachment, friendship, comradeship. The distinction became important to Whitman in his erotic life, where it gave a name and in effect a respectability to his feelings for other men. It also gave body to his conception of democracy: as a variety of love not confined to the sexual couple, adhesiveness could constitute the grounding of a democratic community. Whitmanian democracy is adhesiveness writ large, a nationwide network of fraternal affection much like the loving comradeship that he witnessed among young soldiers marching out to war, and that he detected in his own heart when he tended them afterwards. In the preface to the 1876 *Leaves of Grass* he would write: 'It is by a fervent, accepted development of comradeship, the beautiful and sane affection of man for man, latent in all young fellows . . . and by what goes directly and indirectly along with it, that the United States of the future . . . are to be most effectually welded together, intercalated, anneal'd into a living union.'[4]

To Whitman, adhesiveness was not simply amativeness in sublimated form but an autonomous erotic force. The most attractive feature of Whitman's dreamed-of United States is that it does not demand of its citizens the sublimation of eros in the interest of the state. In this it differs from other nineteenth-century utopias.

Whitman was not only highly adhesive but, if one goes by what he wrote, highly amative too: 'I turn the bridegroom out of bed and stay with the bride myself, / I tighten her all night to my thighs and lips.' The question of exactly what physical form his amativeness took has exercised Whitman scholars more and more openly of late. (*LoG*, p. 65)

In the postwar years Whitman formed significant attachments to younger men, among which two stand out: with Peter Doyle, a conductor on the Washington railway; and with Harry Stafford, a printer's apprentice. The relationship with Doyle – who was near illiterate and according to Whitman thought *Leaves of Grass* 'a great mass of crazy talk and hard words, all tangled up without sense or meaning' – seems to have caused Whitman considerable anguish. In a coded notebook entry Whitman admonishes himself:

Give up absolutely & for good, from this present hour, this feverish, fluctuating, useless undignified pursuit of [Doyle] – too long (much too long) persevered in – so humiliating . . . Avoid seeing her [*sic*], or meeting her, or any talk or explanations – or any meeting, whatever, from this hour forth, for life.

(In the course of censoring his papers, Whitman painstakingly erased culpable masculine pronouns and substituted the feminine.)[5]

The attachment to Harry Stafford appears to have been more tranquil – Whitman was nearly forty years Stafford's senior. Whitman was accepted by the Stafford family: he stayed as a paying guest on their farm, where he could at leisure practise his morning ritual of a mudbath followed by a dip in the spring, all accompanied by loud singing.

If one reads the so-called Live Oak poems of 1859 autobiographically, there would also appear to have been an important attachment in the late 1850s, one that brought Whitman to realise that his feelings towards other men could not forever be kept private: 'An athlete is enamoured of me, and I of him, / But toward him there is something fierce and terrible in me eligible to burst forth, / I dare not tell it in words, not even in these songs.' (*LoG*, p. 132)

In the form in which they survive in manuscript, the twelve Live Oak poems tell the story of this attachment. But when it came to publication Whitman lost his nerve and distributed them, out of order, among a larger set of poems entitled 'Calamus', which, broadly speaking, celebrate adhesiveness more than amativeness.

Perhaps for strategic reasons, Whitman liked it to be thought that he had affairs with women. He even circulated rumours of children he had fathered out of wedlock in New Orleans and elsewhere. Women certainly found him attractive; and it is hard to believe that the poet of 'I Sing the Body Electric' was ignorant of the pleasures of heterosexual sex: 'Bridegroom night of love working surely and softly into the prostrate dawn, / Undulating into the willing and yielding day, / Lost in the cleave of the clasping and sweetflesh'd day.' (*LoG*, p. 96)

The erotic passages in *Leaves of Grass*, particularly passages of narcissism and exhibitionism, where humorous sallies are easily mistaken for boasting, troubled many of Whitman's friends, not least Ralph Waldo Emerson, the older contemporary to whom Whitman owed most. Emerson saw Whitman's genius from the first, and stood by his protégé even when Whitman shamelessly used Emerson's name to promote his book. But Emerson's mild advice that Whitman tone down the sex for the 1860 edition was ignored.

What surprises us about contemporary responses to *Leaves of Grass* is that it was the apparently heterosexual sex, rather than the homoeroticism behind the Calamus poems, that gave offence, and that eventually provoked the Boston district attorney to threaten action unless the 1881 edition was purged.

By this time Whitman had a considerable following among gay intellectuals, particularly in England: on a tour of the United States, Oscar Wilde visited Whitman and came away with, he claimed, a kiss fresh upon his lips. The essayist John Addington Symonds pressed Whitman to admit that the veiled subject of the Calamus poems was a love affair with a man. But Whitman, more, one suspects, out of canniness than out of fear, refused. The poems, he replied frostily, would bear no such 'morbid inferences − [which] are disavow'd by me & seem damnable'.[6]

Were readers of Whitman's day then more tolerant of sexual love between men than we usually give them credit for, as long as it did not proclaim itself too blatantly? Was the poet of the body electric tacitly recognised as gay? 'I am the poet of the woman the same as the man . . . / I am he that walks with the tender and growing night, / I call to the earth and sea half-held by the night. / Press close bare-bosom'd night − press close magnetic nourishing night! / Night of south winds − night of the large few stars! / Still nodding night − mad naked summer night.' (*LoG*, p. 49)

In an afterword to a reprint of the 1855 *Leaves of Grass*, David Reynolds makes fun of Anthony Comstock, the campaigner against indecent literature, who denounced the heterosexual sex in the 1881 edition while ignoring the Calamus poems. How, Reynolds asks, could Comstock have missed what today seems an obvious homosexual substrate? 'The answer would seem to be that same-sex love was not interpreted in the same way then as it is now.' 'Whatever the nature of [Whitman's] relations with [young men], most of the passages of same-sex love, in his poems were not out of keeping with then-current theories and practices that underscored the healthiness of such love.'[7]

Reynolds reiterates this position in his book *Walt Whitman*:

Although Whitman evidently had one or two affairs with women, he was mainly a romantic comrade who had a series of intense relationships with young men, most of whom went on to get married and have children. Whatever the nature of his physical relationships with them, most of the passages of same-sex love in his poems were not out of keeping with then-current theories and practices that underscored the healthiness of such love.[8]

In similarly cautious vein, Jerome Loving, in his 1999 biography, writes that Peter Doyle 'may or may not have been Whitman's lover'. 'It is impossible to know the intimate details of their relationship.' Of Harry Stafford, Loving writes: 'Today our views of Whitman's relationship with [Stafford] may reflect . . . the current interest in Whitman's possible homosexual tendencies more than the actual facts.'[9]

Both Reynolds and Loving seem to me to treat the question too simply. What Loving calls 'the intimate details' and Reynolds somewhat more delicately 'the nature of [Whitman's] physical relationships' with young men can refer to only one thing: what Whitman and the young men in question did with their organs of amativeness when they were alone together. If Comstock can be treated as a figure of fun, it is because he stupidly missed the amative content underlying the lofty adhesive locutions of the Calamus poems.

Without siding with the censors (though to ridicule Comstock for being 'bewhiskered and paunchy', as Reynolds does, is hardly to the point – Whitman was bewhiskered and more than a little paunchy himself), might one not argue that, among readers who did not take offence at the Calamus poems, some might have missed the amative content not because they were blinded by preconceptions about what intimacy between men had to consist in but because they did not feel they needed to ask themselves what the amative content of that intimacy might be, that is, because their notion of intimacy did not boil down to what the men in question did with their sexual organs?[10]

It is a post-Victorian commonplace that from their early years Victorians were taught to repress certain thoughts, particularly thoughts about 'the facts of life', until the very air became clouded with sexual repression. But the anathema on repression is part of the Freudian agenda, one of the weapons Sigmund Freud forged in his intimate war with his parents' generation. *Pace* Freud, it is perfectly possible to refrain from having fantasies about the private lives of other people, even of our parents, without having to repress those fantasies and to bear the consequences of repression – the notorious return of the repressed – in our own psychic life. We pay no psychic price when, for example, we refrain from ruminating on 'the intimate details', 'the actual facts', of what other people do when they visit the bathroom.

In other words, believing that contemporary readers of Whitman's poems of love missed what those poems were really about may reveal more about simple-minded notions of what it means to be 'really about' something than it reveals about Whitman's readers.

Peter Coviello's response to the question of how Whitman got away with writing poems of same-sex love is more subtle than Loving's or Reynolds's but in the end also misses the mark. The attachments that underlie the Calamus poems and the *Memoranda*, Coviello writes, 'frustrate the available taxonomies of intimate relations'.

There has been I think a good deal of misbegotten hand-wringing over these attachments, born partially of a wish not to describe anachronistically kinds of relations – desiring same-sex relations – in terms that were not current in Whitman's time. But this well-meaning hesitancy oughtn't to lead us to mantle Whitman's relations among the soldiers with a counterfeit chastity. (To do this is to forget, in the first place, the relative latitude afforded to mid-century men . . . in an era before the more explicitly punishing language of sexual deviancy had gained broad currency.)[11]

Mid-nineteenth-century men did indeed have a freedom that mid-twentieth-century men did not: they could kiss in public, they could hold hands, they could write poems to each other born out of the deepest love (Tennyson's 'In Memoriam' is a case in point), they could even share a bed, all without being ostracised by society or punished by the law. But Coviello's implicit point seems to be that such behaviour would not have been punished because it would not have been misinterpreted: specifically, it would not have been interpreted as a sign of unchaste hanky-panky with the amative organs when the lights were out.

The question to ask instead is whether such behaviour would have been interpreted at all, that is, subjected to interrogation for chastity or unchastity. There is a certain sophistication, governed by unspoken social consensus, whose nature lies in taking things simply for what they seem to be. It is this sort of social wisdom, whose other name might be tact, that we are in danger of denying to our Victorian forebears.

Scholars seem agreed that some time after 1880 a new paradigm of heterosexual versus homosexual, part of what Coviello calls the 'punishing language of sexual deviancy', made its way into everyday discourse from the sexological ('scientific') literature, and took over as the primary distinction to be made between varieties of the erotic. What paradigm it supplanted is less clear. Jonathan Ned Katz suggests that in early Victorian times the reigning distinction was moral in character rather than sexological: between the passionate on the one hand and the sensual on the other, between high and low, love and lust. Passionate relationships between men or between women were not subjected to interrogation as long as they were of the higher, loving sort.[12]

Whitman, born in 1819, was raised in a family of radical Democrats. Throughout his life he believed in an America of yeoman farmers and independent artisans, even though this Jacksonian social ideal became increasingly fanciful as, by mid-century, the new industrial economy took hold and the native artisan class – to say nothing of streams of immigrants from the Old World – were turned into wage labourers in factories.

As a journalist and newspaper editor in the 1840s and early 1850s, Whitman involved himself from the radical side in the politics of the Democratic Party. By 1855, however, disenchanted with the evasiveness of the Democrats on the issue of slavery, he had dropped out of political life. In their essentials his political beliefs were by now fixed: the world might change around him but he would not change.

Despite his opposition to slavery, it would be too much to say that in his views on race Whitman was ahead of his times. He was never an abolitionist – indeed he thundered against the 'abominable fanaticism' of the abolitionists.[13] The point of conflict between North and South was the extension of slaveholding to the new western states. Because slavery was anti-democratic in its effects, because a slave economy was in his eyes the antithesis of an economy of independent yeoman farmers, Whitman supported war against the slaveholders. He did not support the war in order to win for black slaves a rightful place in a democratic order.

Nor was the condition of the South in the wake of the war a source of celebration to him. He lamented the 'measureless degradation and insult' of Reconstruction, he deplored 'black domination, but little above the beasts', such as could not be allowed to continue. If slavery had presented a terrible problem to his century, he wrote in an 1876 note to his *Memoranda*, 'how if the mass of the blacks in freedom in the U.S. all through the ensuing century, should present a yet more terrible and more deeply complicated problem?' While he did not reiterate his pre-war proposal that the best solution to the 'problem' of blacks in America would be to create a national home for them elsewhere, he did not withdraw it either.[14]

The long celebratory catalogues of Americans at work that we find in 'Song of Myself' and 'A Song for Occupations' are therefore tilted toward a diversity in everyday working life that even when *Leaves of Grass* first came out in 1855 no longer reflected reality: 'The carpenter dresses his plank . . . / The mate stands braced in the whale-boat . . . / The spinning-girl retreats and advances to the hum of the big wheel, / The farmer . . . looks at the oats and rye . . .' Yet it is this vision that Whitman is concerned to project as the future of the nation. To be the poet of America, the national poet, he had to make his vision of a world already receding into the past prevail over a reality increasingly dictated by the market in human labour and by an ideology of competitive individualism. (*LoG*, p. 41)

What is most striking in the face of this insuperable task is Whitman's optimism. To his dying day he seems to have believed that the force that had given birth to the republic, a force to which he gave the name democracy, would prevail. His faith came out of a conviction, growing stronger as his interest in politics waned, that democracy was not one of the superficial inventions of human reason but an aspect of the ever-developing human spirit, rooted in eros. 'I cannot too often repeat that [democracy] is a word the real gist of which still sleeps . . . It is a great word, whose history,

I suppose, remains unwritten, because that history has yet to be enacted.'[15]

Whitman's democracy is a civic religion energised by a broadly erotic feeling that men have for women, and women for men, and women for women, but above all that men have for other men. For this reason the social vision expressed in his poetry (the prose is another story) has a pervasive erotic colouring. The poetry does its work by a kind of erotic spellbinding, drawing its readers into a world in which a more or less benign, more or less promiscuous affection of all for all reigns. Even the call of death in poems like 'Out of the Cradle' has its erotic allure.

It is no wonder that by his middle years Whitman had become enveloped in the aura of prophet and sage (the flowing beard helped), or that he attracted not so much admirers of his poetic art as disciples, Whitmanians, held together by a disaffection from modern life, aspirations toward the cosmic, and a longing for more and better sex. In his biography, Loving suggests that Whitman even introduced to American shores the phenomenon of the groupie, quoting one Susan Garnet Smith from Hartford, Conn., who out of the blue wrote to the gay poet informing him that her womb was 'clean and pure' and ready for his child. 'Angels guard the vestibule,' she assured him, 'until thou comest to deposit our and the world's most precious treasure.'[16]

Meanwhile under the presidency of Ulysses S. Grant the United States was descending into the unrestrained money-grubbing and ostentation of the Gilded Age. Whitman saw all of this clearly enough. Nevertheless, in the role of the Sage of Camden and in a spirit of what Paul Zweig calls 'frozen optimism' he continued to enounce cosmic-sounding prophecies, to which a reading of Hegel seems to have contributed, of the triumph of adhesive democracy.[17]

★

Though Whitman had only a rude formal education, it would be a mistake to think of him as uncultivated or intellectually parochial. For most of his life he was pretty much master of his own time, and used that time to read omnivorously. Despite his pose as a working man, he hung around with artists and writers as much as with what he liked to call roughs. During his years as a newspaperman he reviewed hundreds of books, including serious works of philosophy and social criticism. He followed the main British reviews and was up to date with currents in European thought. In the 1840s he fell under the spell of Thomas Carlyle – as did many other restless young people – and took on board Carlyle's critique of capitalism and industrialism. The failures of the European revolutions of 1848 jolted him badly. Of the writers of his day, the two who influenced him most deeply and to whom he found it hardest to acknowledge his indebtedness were an American, Emerson, and an Englishman, Tennyson.

Though he proclaimed, and indeed trumpeted, the cultural autonomy of America, he was sorely attracted by the idea of a triumphal lecture tour of England. If such a tour never took place, it was not because he lacked adherents in England but because as a form of entertainment the celebrity lecture never caught on there as it did in the United States. For the sake of publication in England he submitted to having *Leaves of Grass* purged of its more risqué items, something he never allowed in the United States.

To collect one's poems, to bring out a Collected Poems, does not mean to republish all the poems one has written in a lifetime. By convention, the collector is entitled to revise old poems and quietly omit those he or she no longer cares to acknowledge. The Collected Poems is thus a handy way to shape one's own past.

Whitman seems to have had it in mind from the beginning

that *Leaves of Grass* would be an ongoing Collected Poems, growing and changing as his self-conception changed. It went through six editions in all, several of which occur in variant forms as Whitman had new poems stitched into already printed volumes. It is hard to know – and in a way it is a mistake to ask – which of the six is the best, the one we ought to read to the exclusion of others, since they represent six formulations and reformulations of who Walt Whitman was. A simple example: whereas in 1855 he was 'Walt Whitman, an American, one of the roughs, a kosmos', by 1881 he was 'Walt Whitman, a kosmos, of Manhattan the son'.[18] ('That [Whitman] was a kosmos, is a piece of news we were hardly prepared for. Precisely what a kosmos is, we trust [he] will take an early occasion to inform the impatient public,' wrote Charles Eliot Norton in a review of the 1855 edition.)[19]

The rule of thumb in the scholarly world is to take an author's last revision, his or her last word, as definitive. But there are exceptions, cases where the critical consensus is that the late revision is inferior to or even traduces the original. Thus we tend to read the 1805 version of Wordsworth's autobiographical poem *The Prelude* in preference to the 1850 revision. In much the same way, one might argue in favour of reading Whitman's early poems in their first published form, since his tendency after 1865 was to revise in the direction of the 'poetic' (i.e., the Tennysonian) in the hope of winning a wider readership.

Whitman intended the sixth edition of *Leaves of Grass* to be the definitive one. Published in Boston in 1881, the edition was withdrawn from sale when threatened with prosecution on the grounds of obscenity. Whitman found himself a new publisher in Philadelphia, where its sudden notoriety did wonders for the book's sales.

This sixth edition contains some three hundred poems, grouped together under themes and in numbered series. Its core consists

of the survivors of the twelve-poem first edition of 1855, princi-
pally the long poem later titled 'Song of Myself', plus 'Crossing
Brooklyn Ferry' (added in 1856); 'Out of the Cradle Endlessly
Rocking' and the amative poems (added in 1860); and 'When
Lilacs Last in the Dooryard Bloom'd' and the 'Drum-Taps' poems
(added to various issues of the 1867 edition).

This core is not large. Despite all the labour he put into re-
evaluating and revising and re-ordering and retitling and reissuing
his poems, and despite the claims he liked to repeat in his later
years that there was a hidden, cathedral-like structure to *Leaves of
Grass* toward which he had all his life been groping, it seems likely
that, except to specialists, Whitman will always be known for a
few individual poems rather than as the author of a single great
book, the new poetic bible of America.

(2005)

15 William Faulkner and his biographers

'NOW I REALISE for the first time,' wrote William Faulkner to a woman friend, looking back from the vantage point of his mid-fifties, 'what an amazing gift I had: uneducated in every formal sense, without even very literate, let alone literary, companions, yet to have made the things I made. I don't know where it came from. I don't know why God or gods or whoever it was, selected me to be the vessel.'[1]

The disbelief Faulkner here lays claim to is a little disingenuous. For the kind of writer he wanted to be, he had all the education, even all the book-learning, he needed. As for company, he stood to gain more from garrulous oldsters with gnarled hands and long memories than from effete *littérateurs*. Nevertheless, a measure of astonishment is in order. Who would have guessed that a boy of no great intellectual distinction from small-town Mississippi would grow up to be not only a famous writer, cele-brated at home and abroad, but the *kind* of writer he in fact became: one of the most radical innovators in the annals of American fiction, a writer to whom the avant-garde of Europe and Latin America would go to school?

Of formal education Faulkner certainly had a minimum. He dropped out of high school in his junior year (his parents seem not to have kicked up a fuss), and though he briefly attended the

University of Mississippi, that was only by grace of a dispensation for returned servicemen (of Faulkner's war service, more below). His college record was undistinguished: a semester of English (grade: D), two semesters of French and Spanish. For this explorer of the mind of the post-bellum South, no courses in history; for the novelist who would weave Bergsonian time into the syntax of memory, no studies in philosophy or psychology.

What the rather dreamy Billy Faulkner gave himself in place of schooling was a narrow but intense reading of *fin-de-siècle* English poetry, notably Swinburne and Housman, and of three novelists who had given birth to fictional worlds lively and coherent enough to rival the real one: Balzac, Dickens, and Conrad. Add to this a familiarity with the cadences of the Old Testament, Shakespeare, and *Moby-Dick*, and, a few years later, a quick study of what his older contemporaries T. S. Eliot and James Joyce were up to, and he was fully armed. As for materials, what he heard around him in Oxford, Mississippi turned out to be more than enough: the epic, told and retold endlessly, of the South, a story of cruelty and injustice and hope and disappointment and victimisation and resistance.

Billy Faulkner had barely quit school when the First World War broke out. Captivated by the idea of becoming a pilot and flying sorties against the Hun, he applied in 1918 to be taken into the Royal Air Force. Desperate for fresh manpower, the RAF recruiting office sent him to Canada on a training course. Before he could make his first solo flight, however, the war ended.

He returned to Oxford wearing an RAF officer's uniform and sporting a British accent and a limp, the consequence, he said, of a flying accident. To friends he also confided that he had a steel plate in his skull.

He sustained the aviator legend for years; he began to play it down only when he became a national figure and the risk of exposure loomed too large. His dreams of flying were not abandoned, however. As soon as he had the money to spare, in 1933, he took flying lessons, bought his own plane, and briefly operated a flying circus: 'WILLIAM FAULKNER'S (Famous Author) AIR CIRCUS,' ran the advertisement.[2]

Faulkner's biographers have made much of his war stories, treating them as more than just the concoctions of a puny and unprepossessing youth desperate to be admired. Frederick R. Karl believes that 'the war turned [Faulkner] into a storyteller, a fictionist, which may have been the decisive turnabout of his life.' (p. 111) The ease with which he duped the good people of Oxford, Karl says, proved to Faulkner that, artfully contrived and convincingly expounded, a lie can beat the truth, and thus that one can make not only a life but a living out of fantasy.

Back home, Faulkner drifted. He wrote poems about 'epicene' (by which he seems to have meant narrow-hipped) women and his unrequited longings for them, poems that, even with the best will in the world, one cannot call promising; he began to sign his name not 'Falkner', as he was born, but 'Faulkner'; and, following the pattern of the male Falkners, he drank heavily. For some years, until he was dismissed for poor performance, he held a sinecure as postmaster of a small station, where he spent office hours reading and writing.

For someone so determined to follow his own inclinations, it is odd that, rather than packing his bags and heading for the bright lights of the metropolis, he chose to remain in the town of his birth, where his pretensions were regarded with sardonic amusement. Jay Parini, his most recent biographer, suggests that he found it hard to be out of reach of his mother, a woman of some sensibility who seems to have had a deeper relation with her eldest son than with a dull and spineless husband.[3]

On forays to New Orleans Faulkner developed a circle of bohemian friends and met Sherwood Anderson, chronicler of Winesburg, Ohio, whose influence on him he was later at pains to minimise. He began to publish short pieces in the New Orleans press; he even dipped into literary theory. Willard Huntingdon Wright, a disciple of Walter Pater, made a particular impression on him. In Wright's *The Creative Will* (1915) he read that the true artist is solitary by nature, 'an omnipotent god who moulds and fashions the destiny of a new world, and leads it to an inevitable completion where it can stand alone, self-moving, independent', leaving its creator exalted of spirit.[4] The type of the artist-demiurge, suggests Wright, is Balzac, much to be preferred to Émile Zola, a mere copyist of a pre-existing reality.

In 1925 Faulkner made his first trip abroad. He spent two months in Paris and liked it: he bought a beret, grew a beard, began work on a novel – soon to be abandoned – about a painter with a war wound who goes to Paris to further his art. He hung out at James Joyce's favourite café, where he caught a glimpse of the great man but did not approach him.

All in all, nothing in the record suggests more than a would-be writer of unusual doggedness but no great gifts. Yet soon after his return to the United States he would sit down and write a 14,000-word sketch bursting with ideas and characters which would lay the groundwork for the series of great novels of the years 1929–42. The manuscript contained, in embryo, Yoknapatawpha County.

As a child Faulkner had been inseparable from a slightly older friend named Estelle Oldham. The two were in some sense betrothed. When the time came, however, the Oldham parents, disapproving of the shiftless youth, married Estelle off to a lawyer with better prospects. Thus when Estelle returned to the parental home it was as a divorced woman of thirty-two with two small children.

Though Faulkner seems to have had doubts about the wisdom of taking up with Estelle again, he did not act on them. Before long the two were married. Estelle must have had doubts of her own. During the honeymoon she may or may not have tried to drown herself. The marriage itself turned out to be unhappy, worse than unhappy. 'They were just terribly unsuited for each other,' their daughter, Jill, told Parini many years later. 'Nothing about the marriage was right.' (Parini, p. 130) Estelle was an intelligent woman, but she was used to spending money freely and to having servants carry out her every wish. Life in a dilapidated old house with a husband who spent his mornings scribbling and his afternoons replacing rotten timbers and putting in plumbing must have come as a shock to her. A child was born but died at two weeks. Jill was born in 1933. Thereafter sexual relations between the Faulkners seem to have ceased.

Together and separately, William and Estelle drank to excess. In late middle age Estelle pulled herself right and went on the wagon; William never did. He had affairs with younger women which he was not competent or careful enough to conceal. From scenes of raging jealousy the marriage by degrees dwindled into, in the words of Faulkner's first biographer, Joseph Blotner, 'desultory domestic guerrilla warfare'. (p. 537)

Nevertheless, for thirty-three years, until Faulkner's death in 1962, the marriage endured. Why? The most mundane explanation is that, until well into the 1950s, Faulkner could not afford a divorce – that is to say, could not, in addition to the troops of Faulkners or Falkners, to say nothing of Oldhams, dependent on his earnings, afford to support Estelle and three children in the style she would have demanded, and at the same time relaunch himself decently in society. Less easily demonstrable is Karl's claim that at some deep level Faulkner needed Estelle. 'Estelle could never be disentangled from the deepest reaches of [Faulkner's] imagination,' Karl writes. 'Without Estelle . . . he could not have continued [to write].' She was his 'belle dame sans merci' – 'that ideal object man worships from a distance who is also . . . destructive'. (p. 86)

By choosing to marry Estelle, by choosing to make his home in Oxford amid the Falkner clan, Faulkner took on a formidable challenge: how to be patron and breadwinner and paterfamilias to what he privately called '[a] whole tribe . . . hanging like so many buzzards over every penny [I] earn', while at the same time serving his inner daimon. Despite an Apollonian ability to immerse himself in his work – 'a monster of efficiency,' Parini calls him – the project wore him down. To feed the buzzards, the one blazing genius of American literature of the 1930s had to put aside his novel-writing, which was all that really mattered to him, first to churn out stories for popular magazines, later to write screenplays for Hollywood. (Parini, pp. 319, 139)

The trouble was not so much that Faulkner was unappreciated in the community of letters as that there was no room in the economy of the 1930s for the profession of avant-garde novelist (today Faulkner would be a natural for a major fellowship). Faulkner's publishers, editors, and agents – with one miserable exception – had his interests at heart and did their best on his behalf, but that was not enough. Only after the appearance of *The Portable Faulkner*, a selection skilfully put together by Malcolm Cowley in 1945, did American readers wake up to what they had in their midst.

The time spent writing short stories was not all wasted. Faulkner was an extraordinarily tenacious reviser of his own work (in Hollywood he impressed by his ability to fix up dud scripts by other writers). Revisited and reconceived and reworked, material that made its first appearance in *The Saturday Evening Post* or *The Woman's Home Companion* resurfaced transmogrified in *The Unvanquished* (1938), *The Hamlet* (1940), and *Go Down, Moses* (1942), books that straddle the line between story collection and novel proper.

The same buried potential cannot be claimed of his screenplays. When Faulkner arrived in Hollywood in 1932, riding on his passing notoriety as the author of *Sanctuary* (1931), he knew nothing of the industry (in his private life he disdained movies as much as he disliked loud music). He had no gift for putting together snappy dialogue. Furthermore, he soon acquired a reputation as an undependable lush. From a high of $1,000 a week his salary had by 1942 dropped to $300. In the course of a thirteen-year career he worked with sympathetic directors like Howard Hawks, was friendly with celebrated actors like Clark Gable and Humphrey Bogart, acquired an attractive and attentive Hollywood mistress; but nothing that he wrote for the movies proved worth rescuing.

Worse than that: his screenwriting had a bad effect on his prose. During the war years Faulkner worked on a succession of scripts of a hortatory, uplifting, patriotic nature. It would be a mistake to load all the blame for the overblown rhetoric that mars his late prose onto these projects, but he himself came to recognise the harm Hollywood had done him. 'I have realised lately how much trash and junk writing for movies corrupted into my writing,' he admitted in 1947.[5]

There is nothing unusual in the story of Faulkner's struggles to balance his accounts. From the beginning he thought of himself as a *poète maudit*, and it is the lot of the *poète maudit* to be disregarded and underpaid. All that is surprising is that the burdens he took on – the high-spending wife, the impecunious relatives, the disadvantageous studio contracts – should have been borne so tenaciously (though with much griping on the side), even at the cost of his art. Loyalty is as strong a theme in Faulkner's life as in his writing, but there is such a thing as mad loyalty, mad fidelity (the Confederate South was full of it).

In effect, Faulkner spent his middle years as a migrant worker sending his pay packet home to Mississippi; the biographical record is largely a record of dollars and cents. In Faulkner's worryings over money Parini rightly discerns a deeper absorption. 'Money is rarely just money,' Parini writes. 'The obsession with money that seems to dog Faulkner throughout his life must, I think, be regarded as a measure of his waxing and waning feelings of stability, value, purchase on the world . . . a means of calculating his reputation, his power, his reality.' (pp. 295–6)

A position as writer in residence on some quiet Southern college campus might have been the salvation of William Faulkner, giving him a steady income and demanding not much in return, allowing him time for his own work. A canny Robert Frost had since 1917 been showing that one could trade on the bardic aura to secure oneself academic sinecures. But, lacking a high-school diploma, mistrustful of talk that sounded too 'literary' or 'intellectual', Faulkner made no return to the groves of academe until 1946, when he was persuaded to speak to students at the University of Mississippi. The experience was not as bad as he had feared; at the age of sixty, at a more or less nominal salary, he joined the University of Virginia as writer in residence, a position he retained until his death.

One of the ironies of the life of this academic laggard is that he had probably read more widely, if less systematically, than most college professors. In Hollywood, said the actor Anthony Quinn, even though he wasn't highly rated as a screenwriter he had 'a tremendous reputation as an intellectual.' Another irony is that

Faulkner was adopted by the New Critics as master of a kind of prose ideally suited to dissection in the college classroom. 'So much to unfold that had been carefully and ingeniously folded by the author,' enthused Cleanth Brooks, doyen of the New Criticism. Thus Faulkner became the darling of the New Haven formalists as he was already the darling of the French existentialists, without being quite sure what either formalism or existentialism was.[6]

The Nobel Prize for literature, awarded for 1949, presented in 1950, made Faulkner famous even in America. Tourists came from far and wide to gawp at his home in Oxford, to his vast irritation. Reluctantly he emerged from the shadows and began to behave like a public figure. From the State Department came invitations to travel abroad as a cultural ambassador, which he dubiously accepted. Nervous before the microphone, even more nervous fielding 'literary' questions, he prepared for sessions by drinking heavily. But, once he had developed a patter to cope with journalists, he grew more comfortable with the role. He was ill-informed about foreign affairs – he did not read newspapers – but that suited the State Department well enough. His visit to Japan was a striking public relations success; in France and Italy he received massive attention from the press. As he remarked sardonically, 'If they believed in my world in America the way they do abroad, I could probably run one of my characters for President . . . maybe Flem Snopes.'[7]

Less impressive were Faulkner's interventions back home. Pressure was building on the South and its segregated institutions. In letters to editors of newspapers, he began to speak out against abuses and to urge fellow white Southerners to accept the Negro as a social equal.

There was a backlash. 'Weeping Willie Faulkner' was denounced as a pawn of Northern liberals, as a Communist sympathiser. Though he was never in physical danger, he claimed (in a letter to a Swedish friend) to foresee a day when he would have to flee the country 'something as the Jew had to flee from Germany during Hitler'.[8]

He was of course overdramatising. His views on race were never radical and, as the political atmosphere grew more charged and developed states' rights overtones, descended into confusion. Segregation was an evil, he said; nevertheless, if integration were forced upon the South he would resist (in a rash moment he even said he would take up arms). By the late 1950s his position had become so out of date as to be positively quaint. The civil rights movement should adopt as watchwords, he said, decency, quietness, courtesy, and dignity; the Negro should learn to deserve equality.

It is easy enough to disparage Faulkner's forays into race relations. In his personal life his behaviour toward African-Americans seems to have been generous, kindly, but, unavoidably, patronising: he belonged, after all, to a *patron* class. In his political philosophy he was a Jeffersonian individualist; it was this, rather than any residue of racism in his blood, that made him suspicious of black mass movements. If his scruples and equivocations soon rendered him irrelevant to the civil rights struggle, he was courageous in taking any stand at all at the time when he did. His public statements made him somewhat of a pariah in his home town, and had more than a little to do with his decision, after his mother's death in 1960, to quit Mississippi and move to Virginia. (At the same time, it must be said, the prospect of riding to the hounds with the Albermarle County Hunt was a powerful drawcard: Faulkner in his last years regarded himself as pretty much written out, and foxhunting became the new passion of his life.)

★

Faulkner's interventions in public affairs were ineffectual not because he was stupid about politics but because the appropriate vehicle for his political insights was not the essay, much less the letter to the editor, but the novel, and in specific the kind of novel he invented, with its unequalled rhetorical resources for inter-weaving past and present, memory and desire.

The territory on which Faulkner the novelist deployed his best resources was a South that bears a strong resemblance to the real South of his day – or at least the South of his youth – but is not the whole of the South. Faulkner's South is a white South haunted by black presences. Even *Light in August*, the novel that is most clearly *about* race and racism, has at its centre not a black man but rather a man whose fate it is to confront or be confronted with blackness as an interpellation, an accusation from outside himself.

As historian of the modern South, Faulkner's abiding achieve-ment is the Snopes trilogy (*The Hamlet*, 1940; *The Town*, 1957; *The Mansion*, 1959), in which he tracks the takeover of political power by an ascendant poor white class in a revolution as quiet, implacable, and amoral as a termite invasion. His chronicle of the rise of the redneck entrepreneur is at the same time mordant and elegiac and despairing: mordant because he detests what he sees as much as he is fascinated by it; elegiac because he loves the old world that is being eaten up before his eyes; and despairing for many reasons, not least of which are, first, that the South he loves was built, as he knows better than anyone, on twin crimes of dispossession and slavery; second, that the Snopeses are just another avatar of the Falkners, thieves and rapists of the land in their day; and therefore, third, that as critic and judge he, William 'Faulkner', has no ground to stand on.

No ground unless he falls back on the eternal verities. 'Courage and honor and pride, and pity and love of justice and of liberty' is the litany of virtues recited in *Go Down, Moses* by Ike McCaslin, who is pretty much spokesman for Faulkner's wished-for, ideal self, a man who, having taken stock of his history and of the diminished and fast-diminishing world around him, renounces his patrimony, abjures fatherhood (thus putting an end to the procession of the generations), and becomes a simple carpenter.[9]

Courage and honour and pride: to his litany Ike might have added endurance, as he does elsewhere in the same story: 'Endurance . . . and pity and tolerance and forbearance and fidelity and love of children . . .' (p. 225) There is a strongly moralistic strain in Faulkner's later work, a stripped-down Christian humanism stubbornly held to in a world from which God has retired. When this moralism proves unconvincing, as it often is, that is usually because Faulkner has failed to find an adequate fictional vehicle for it. The frustrations he experienced in putting together *A Fable* (written 1944–53, published 1954), which he intended to be his magnum opus, were precisely in finding a way to embody his anti-war theme. The exemplary figure in *A Fable* is Jesus reincarnated in and re-sacrificed as the unknown soldier; elsewhere in the late work he is the simple, suffering black man or, more often, black woman, who by enduring an unendurable present keeps alive the germ of a future.

For a man who lived an uneventful and largely sedentary life, William Faulkner has evoked prodigious biographical energies. The first big biographical monument was erected in 1974 by Joseph Blotner, a younger colleague from the University of Virginia whom Faulkner clearly liked and trusted, and whose two-volume *Faulkner: A Biography* provides a full and fair treatment of his subject's outward life. Even Blotner's one-volume, 400,000-word condensation (1984) may, however, prove too rich in detail for most readers.

Frederick R. Karl's huge tome *William Faulkner: American Writer*

(1989) has as its stated aim 'to understand and interpret [Faulkner's] life psychologically, emotionally, and literarily.' (p. xv) There is much in Karl that is admirable, including dauntless ventures into the maze of Faulkner's compositional practices, which involved working on numbers of projects at the same time, shunting material from one to another.

As Karl justly observes, Faulkner is 'the most historical of [America's] important writers'; accordingly he treats Faulkner as an American responding creatively to the historical and social forces in which he is enmeshed. (p. 666) As *literary* biographer what he tries to comprehend is how a man so deeply suspicious of modernisation and what it was doing to the South could at the same time in his novelistic practice have been a radical modernist.

Karl's Faulkner emerges as a figure of grandeur as well as pathos, a man who, perhaps in thrall to a Romantic image of the doomed artist, was prepared to sacrifice himself to the project of living through a destiny from which any rational person would have walked away. But Karl's book is spoiled by continual reductive psychologising. For instance, Faulkner's neat handwriting – an editor's dream – is taken as evidence of an anal personality, his silly lies about his exploits with the RAF as a sign of a schizoid personality, his attention to detail as proof of obsessiveness, his affair with a young woman as revealing of incestuous desires for his daughter.

'Often a lesser novel can provide more incisive biographical insights than a great one,' says Karl. (p. 75) If this is so – and not many contemporary biographers would disagree – then we confront a general problem about literary biography and the status of so-called biographical insights. May it not be that if the minor work seems to reveal more than the major work, what it reveals is worth knowing only in a minor way? Perhaps Faulkner – to whom the odes of John Keats were a poetic touchstone – was indeed what he felt himself to be: a being of negative capability, one who disappeared into, lost himself in, his profoundest creations. 'It is my ambition to be a private individual, abolished and voided from history, leaving it markless,' he wrote to Cowley: 'It is my aim . . . that the sum and history of my life . . . shall be . . . : He made the books and he died.'[10]

Jay Parini is the author of biographies of John Steinbeck (1994) and Robert Frost (1999), and of two novels with a strong biographical content: *The Last Station* (1990), about the last days of Leo Tolstoy, and *Benjamin's Crossing* (1997), about the last days of Walter Benjamin.[11]

Parini's life of Steinbeck is solid but unremarkable. The Frost book is more self-reflective: biography, Parini muses, may be less like historiography than we like to think and more like novel-writing. Of his own biographical novels, the one on Tolstoy is the more successful, perhaps because there is such a multiplicity of accounts of life on Yasnaya Polyana to draw on. In the Benjamin book Parini has to spend too much time explaining who his self-absorbed hero is and why we should be interested in him.

In the case of Faulkner, Parini attempts what neither Blotner nor Karl offers: a critical biography, that is to say, a reasonably full account of Faulkner's life together with an assessment of his writings. There is a great deal to be said for what he has produced. Though he relies heavily on Blotner for the facts, he has gone further than Blotner by conducting interviews with the last generation of people to have known Faulkner personally, some of whom have interesting things to say. He has a fellow writer's appreciation for Faulkner's language, and expresses that appreciation vividly. Thus the prose of 'The Bear' proceeds 'with a kind of inexorable ferocity, as though Faulkner composed in excited reverie'. Though by no means hagiography, his book pays eloquent tribute to its subject: 'What most impresses about Faulkner as writer is the sheer persistence, the will-to-power that brought him back to the desk each day, year after year . . . [His] grit was . . . as much physical as mental; [he] pushed ahead like an ox through mud, dragging a whole world behind him.' (pp. 261, 429)

In a non-specialist book like this, one of the first decisions the writer has to make is whether it should reflect the critical consensus or take a strong individual line. By and large, Parini goes for a version of the consensus option. His scheme is to follow Faulkner's life chronologically, interrupting the narrative with short critical essays of an introductory nature on individual works. In the right hands such a scheme could result in exemplary specimens of the critic's art. But Parini's essays are not up to exemplary standard. Those on Faulkner's best-known books tend to be his best; of the rest, too many consist of not particularly deft synopsis plus summary of the critical debate, where what counts as debate tends to be rather humdrum academic inquiry.

As in Karl's book, there is also a degree of questionable psychologism. Thus Parini offers a rather wild reading of *As I Lay Dying* – a short novel built around the grotesque trip on which the Bundren children take their mother's corpse on the way to the grave – as a symbolic act of aggression by Faulkner against his own mother as well as a 'perverse' wedding present to his wife. 'Does Estelle supplant Miss Maud [his mother] in Faulkner's mind?' asks Parini. 'Such questions are beyond answers, but it's the province of biography to ask them, to allow them to play over the text and trouble it.' (p. 151) Perhaps it is indeed the province of the biographer to trouble the text with fancies plucked from the air; perhaps not. More to the point is whether either Faulkner's mother or his wife understood the novel as a personal attack on them. There is no record that either did.

Parini's explorations of Faulkner's mind entail much talk of parts of the self, or selves within the self. Does Faulkner disapprove of the adulterous lovers in *The Wild Palms*? Answer: while 'a part of his novelistic mind' condemns them, another part does not. Why does Faulkner in the late 1930s choose to focus on Flem Snopes, the beady-eyed, cold-hearted social climber of the trilogy? 'I suspect it has something to do with exploring his own aggressive self,' Parini writes. Having 'succeeded beyond his own dreams . . . [Faulkner] wanted to think on that success and to understand the impulses that might have led him to it.' (pp. 238, 232–3)

Was it really Faulkner's 'aggressive self' that produced the great novels of the 1930s, achievements at which Flem would have sneered, so little money did they make for their author? Does Flem's crooked genius really resemble Faulkner's baffled relationship with money, including his naiveté in signing a contract with Warner Brothers, the most stolidly unadventurous of the studios, that made him their slave for seven years?

All in all, Parini's book is a puzzling mixture: on the one hand it shows a real feel for Faulkner as a writer, on the other, a readiness to vulgarise him. The worst instance comes in his remarks on Rowan Oak, the four-acre property that Faulkner bought in run-down state in 1929 and lived on until his death. Faulkner was prepared to spend money he did not have on renovating Rowan Oak, Parini writes, because 'he had a vision of antebellum luxury and superiority that he wanted, above all else, to re-create in his daily life . . . The film *Gone with the Wind* . . . appeared [in 1939], taking the nation by storm. Faulkner didn't need to see it. It was his life's story.' (p. 250) Anyone who has read Blotner on daily life at Rowan Oak will know how far it was from the fantasy of Tara.

★

'A book is the writer's secret life, the dark twin of a man: you can't reconcile them,' says one of the characters in *Mosquitoes* (1927).[12]

Reconciling the writer with his books is a challenge that Blotner sensibly does not take on. Whether either Karl or Parini, in their different ways, brings together the man who signed his name 'William Faulkner' with his dark twin is an open question.

The acid test is what Faulkner's biographers have to say about his alcoholism. This is not a subject around which one should pussyfoot. The notation on the file at the psychiatric hospital in Memphis to which Faulkner was regularly taken in a stupor was, Blotner reports, 'An acute and chronic alcoholic.' (p. 574) Though Faulkner in his fifties looked handsome and spry, that was only a shell. A lifetime's drinking had begun to impair his mental functioning. 'This is more than a case of acute alcoholism,' wrote his editor Saxe Commins in 1952. 'The disintegration of the man is tragic to witness.' Parini adds the chilling testimony of Faulkner's daughter: when drunk, her father could be so violent that 'a couple of men' had to stand by to protect her and her mother.[13]

Blotner does not try to understand Faulkner's addiction, merely chronicles its ravages, describes its patterns, and quotes the hospital records. In Karl's reading, drinking was the form that rebellion took in Faulkner, the way in which he defended his art against the pressures of family and tradition. 'Take away the alcohol and, very probably, there would be no writer; and perhaps no defined person.' (pp. 130-2) Parini does not demur, but sees a therapeutic purpose to Faulkner's drinking as well. His binges were 'downtime for the creative mind,' he says. They were 'useful in some peculiar way. They cleared away cobwebs, reset the inner clock, allowed the unconscious, like a well, to slow fill [*sic*].' Emerging from a binge was 'as if he'd had a long and pleasant sleep'. (p. 281)

It is in the nature of addictions to be incomprehensible to those who stand outside them. Faulkner himself is of no help here: he does not write about his addiction, does not, as far as we know, write from inside it (he was mostly sober when he sat down at his desk). No biographer has yet succeeded in making sense of it; but perhaps making sense of an addiction, finding the words to account for it, giving it a place in the economy of the self, will always be a misconceived enterprise.

(2005)

16 Saul Bellow, the early novels

AMONG AMERICAN NOVELISTS of the latter half of the twentieth century, Saul Bellow stands out as one of the giants, perhaps *the* giant. His noontime stretches from the early 1950s (*The Adventures of Augie March*) to the late 1970s (*Humboldt's Gift*), though as late as 2000 he was still bringing out notable fiction (*Ravelstein*). In 2003, while he was still alive, the Library of America admitted him to its version of the classic canon by republishing his first three novels – *Dangling Man* (1944), *The Victim* (1947), *The Adventures of Augie March* (1953) – and promising the rest of the oeuvre.[1]

Dangling Man (1944) and *The Victim* (1947) brought Bellow favourable critical attention, but they were both rather literary efforts, European in their inspiration. It was the loud, sprawling *Augie March* that won Bellow a public.

The eponymous hero of *Augie March* is born into the world around 1915 – the year of Bellow's own birth – into a Jewish family in a Polish neighbourhood of Chicago. Augie's father makes no appearance, and his absence is barely commented on. His mother, a sad and shadowy figure, is nearly blind. He has two brothers, one of them mentally handicapped. The family subsists, somewhat fraudulently, on welfare and on the contributions of a Russian-born boarder, Grandma Lausch (no relation of theirs), for whom young Augie fetches books from the library ('How many times do I have to tell you if it doesn't say *roman* I don't want it? . . . *Bozhe moy!'*) and from whom he picks up a smattering of culture. (p. 392)

It is Grandma Lausch who in effect brings up the March boys. When her fondest hope is disappointed – that one of them will turn out to be a genius whose career she can manage – she sets her sights on turning them into good clerks. She is dismayed when they grow up rough and unmannerly. Worse, in fact: like other boys in the neighbourhood, Augie goes in for petty lawbreaking. But he has too much conscience for a life of crime. His first organised heist leaves him so miserable that he drops out of the gang.

Looking back on this childhood from the perspective of his mid-thirties, when he commits to paper the story we are reading, Augie wonders what effect it had on him to grow up not in the 'shepherd-Sicily' of the poets but in the midst of 'deep city vexation.' (p. 477) He need not trouble himself. The strongest parts of the book of his life come out of an intense reliving of an urban childhood rich in spectacle and social experience, of a kind that few American children today enjoy.

As a young man in the Depression years, Augie continues to hover on the fringes of criminality. From an expert he learns the art of stealing books, which he then sells to students at the University of Chicago. But he keeps his heart pure, more or less, rationalising the theft of books as a special case, a benign form of larceny.

There are also countervailing influences, among them a fatherly employer who presents Augie with a set, slightly spoiled, of the Harvard Classics. These Augie keeps in a crate under his bed, dipping into them when the mood takes him. Later he will act as a research assistant to a wealthy amateur scholar. Thus, though he never goes to college, by one means or another his adventures in reading continue. And the reading he does is serious, even by University of Chicago standards: Hegel, Nietzsche, Marx, Weber, de Tocqueville, Ranke, Burckhardt, to say nothing of the Greeks and Romans and the Church Fathers. No *romanciers*.

Augie's elder brother Simon is a man of appetite, larger than life. Though no philistine, Simon pinpoints Augie's reading as the chief obstacle to his plan that Augie should find himself a wealthy girl to marry, study law at night school, and become his partner in the coal business. In obedience to Simon, Augie for a while lives a double life, working in the coalyard all day, then dressing up to frequent the salons of the *nouveaux riches*.

Under Simon's tutelage Augie has his first chance to taste the good life, and in particular the silky warmth of expensive hotels. 'I didn't want to be just borne down by the grandeur of it,' he writes.

But . . . finally they [the appurtenances of the hotel] are what becomes great – the multitude of baths with never-failing hot water, the enormous air-conditioning units and the elaborate machinery. No opposing greatness is allowed, and the disturbing person is the one who won't serve by using or denies by not wishing to enjoy. (p. 656)

No opposing greatness is allowed. Augie is clearsighted enough and pragmatic enough to recognise that whoever denies the power manifested in the great American hotel runs the risk of marginalising himself, no matter what authority he may call on to back him from the Harvard Classics. On the grounds that what he is writing is not the summing-up of a life but a mid-term report, Augie declines to take a position for or against the hotels of Chicago, for or against the kind of future they represent. He also pleads what amounts to juridical incompetence. 'But then how does anybody form a decision to be against and persist against? When does he choose and when is he chosen instead?' (p. 656)

Augie's cautious stance is not dissimilar to the stance of Henry Adams before the 1893 Chicago Exposition; and Adams himself ironically evokes the ghost of Edward Gibbon confronting the ruins of Rome. 'Chicago asked in 1893 for the first time,' Adams writes, 'the question whether the American people knew where they were driving.' The answer, it seems to him, is that they do not. Nevertheless, they might still be 'driving or drifting unconsciously' toward a point when they can then articulate the goal of it all. The wisest position for an observer to take – particularly an observer who is himself an American – would be no position at all, simply watching and waiting.[2]

Another presence at Augie's elbow, signalled by rises in the quotient of portentous rumination and gaseous language, is Theodore Dreiser, Bellow's great predecessor as recorder of Chicago life. In such characters as Carrie Meeber (*Sister Carrie*) and Clyde Griffiths (*An American Tragedy*) Dreiser gave us uncomplicated, yearning Midwestern souls, neither good nor bad by nature, sucked like Augie into the orbit of big-city luxury, access to which, they quickly discover, requires no credentials, no ancient blood, no education, no password, nothing except money.

Clyde Griffiths is a drifter in the Dreiserian sense: he does not choose his fate, his American version of tragedy, but drifts into it. Augie is in danger of being a drifter too: a personable young man whose adventures in consumption wealthy women are all too eager to subsidise. If what little distinguishes an Augie from a Clyde – brushes with the Russian novel and the Harvard Classics – is no proof against the power of the great hotel, what makes Augie's story different from the story of any other child of his times?

To this question Bellow offers only a Proustian response: the young man who begins his story with the words 'I am an American,

Chicago born . . . and go at things as I have taught myself, free-style, and will make the record in my own way,' (p. 383) and ends it by recalling how he wrote those words and then comparing himself to Columbus – 'Columbus too thought he was a flop . . . Which don't prove there was no America' (p. 995) – is not a flop, even if he can excogitate no opposing power to the blind gigantism of America, for the achieved memoir itself constitutes such a power. Literature, Bellow asserts, interprets the chaos of life, gives it meaning. In his readiness first to be swept along by the forces of modern life and then to re-engage with them through the medium of his 'free-style' art, Augie, we are given to understand, is better equipped than he knows to oppose the seductions of the drifting lifestyle.

One element of Dreiser that Bellow does not take over is the deterministic machinery of fate. Clyde's fate is sombre, Augie's is not. One or two careless slips and Clyde ends up in the electric chair; whereas from all the perils that surround him Augie emerges safe and sound.

Once it becomes clear that its hero is to lead a charmed life, *Augie March* begins to pay for its lack of dramatic structure and indeed of intellectual organisation. The book becomes steadily less engaging as it proceeds. The scene-by-scene method of composition, each scene commencing with a tour de force of vivid scene-setting, begins to seem mechanical. The many pages devoted to Augie's spell in Mexico engaged in a harebrained scheme to train an eagle to catch iguanas add up to precious little, despite the compositional resources lavished on them. Augie's principal wartime escapade, torpedoed, trapped with a mad scientist in a lifeboat off the African coast, is simply comic-book stuff.

This is not to say that Augie himself is an intellectual cipher. By conviction he is a philosophical idealist, even a radical idealist, to whom the world is a complex of interlocking ideas-of-the-world, millions of them, as many as there are human minds. Each of us, he believes, tries to advance his or her unique idea by recruiting fellow human beings to play a role in it. Augie's rule, developed over the course of half a lifetime, is to refuse recruitment into other people's ideas.

His own world model grows out of the imperative to simplify. The modern world, in his view, overburdens us with its bad infinity. 'Too much of everything . . . too much history and culture . . . , too many details, too much news, too much example, too much influence . . . Which who is supposed to interpret? Me?' (p. 902) His response to too much of everything is, first, to 'become what I am'; (p. 937) second, to buy land, get married, settle down, teach school, do home carpentry, and learn to fix the car. As a friend comments, 'I wish you luck.' (p. 905)

By his own account, Bellow had a great time writing *Augie March*, and for the first few hundred pages his creative excitement is palpable and infectious. The reader is exhilarated by the daring, high-speed, racy prose, by the casual ease with which one *mot juste* ('Karas, in a sharkskin, double-breasted suit and presenting a look of difficulties in shaving and combing terrifically outwitted') after another is tossed off. (p. 498) Not since Mark Twain had an American writer handled the demotic with such verve. The book won its readers over with its variety, its restless energy, its impatience with the proprieties. Above all, it seemed to say a great *Yes!* to America.

Now, in retrospect, that *Yes!* can be seen to have come at a price: the price of critical consciousness. *Augie March* presents itself as, in some sense, the story of the coming to maturity of Bellow's generation. But how good a representative of that generation is Augie? He hangs around with left-wing students, he reads Nietzsche and Marx, he works as a union organiser, he even contemplates a job as bodyguard to Leon Trotsky in Mexico, yet the broader world picture barely registers on him. When war arrives, he is stunned. 'Wham! The war broke out . . . I went off my rocker, I hated the enemy, I couldn't wait to go and fight.' (p. 905) At what point does his absorption in the here and now turn into idiocy?

The Library of America compendium edition comes with fifteen pages of notes by James Wood. These notes are particularly useful in the case of *Augie March*, where names and allusions are strewn like confetti. Wood nails down many of Augie's glancing references, but there are plenty left over. Who was it, for example, who was set on a horse by his weeping sisters to go and study Greek in Bogotá? (p. 477) What ambassador from what country blew shellac through the water pipes of Lima to stop the rust? (p. 658)

Dangling Man, which Bellow wrote almost a decade earlier during the war years, is a short novel in the form of a journal. The journal-keeper is a young Chicagoan named Joseph, an unemployed history graduate supported by his working wife. Joseph uses his journal to explore how he has become what he is, and in particular to understand why, about a year ago, he abandoned the philosophical essays he was writing and began to 'dangle', a word which in the slang of the times meant waiting in limbo for word from one's draft board but to which Bellow gives a more existential sense.

So wide does the gap seem between himself as he is now and his earnest, innocent past self that at moments Joseph the journal-keeper thinks of himself as the double of the earlier Joseph, wearing his cast-off clothes. The earlier self had still been able to function in society, to strike a balance between his job in a travel agency and his scholarly pursuits. Yet even then there had been troubling premonitions, feelings of alienation from the world.

From his window he would survey the urban prospect – chimneys, warehouses, billboards, parked cars. Does such an environment not deform the soul, he would ask himself? 'Where was there a particle of what, elsewhere, or in the past, had spoken in man's favour? . . . What would Goethe say to the view from this window?' (p. 55)

It may seem comical that in the Chicago of 1941 someone should have been occupied in such grandiose musings, says Joseph the journal-keeper, yet in each of us there is an element of the fantastical. By mocking such philosophising as comical he is in effect denying his better self.

Though in the abstract the early Joseph is prepared to accept that man is aggressive by nature, when he looks into his own heart he can detect there nothing but gentleness. One of his idler ambitions is to found a utopian colony where spite and cruelty will be forbidden. Therefore one of the developments that most dismays the later Joseph is to find himself being overtaken by unpredictable fits of uncharacteristic violence. He loses his temper with his adolescent niece and spanks her, shocking her parents. He manhandles his landlord. He shouts at a bank employee. He feels that he is 'a sort of human grenade whose pin has been withdrawn'. (p. 107) What is happening to him?

An artist friend tries to persuade him that the monstrous city around them is not the real world: the real world is the world of art and thought. In the abstract Joseph is prepared to respect this position and see its beneficial effects: through sharing with others the products of his imagination, the artist allows an aggregate of lonely individuals to become a community of sorts. But he, Joseph, is not an artist. His potentiality is to be a good man. Yet living as he does 'separate, alienated, distrustful', he might as well be in jail. (p. 65) What is the point of being good in a jail cell? Goodness has to be practised in company; it has to be attended by love.

In a powerful passage, he blames his violent outbursts on the unbearable contradictions of modern life. Brainwashed into believing that each of us is an individual of inestimable value with an individual destiny, that there is no limit to what we can attain, we set off, each of us, in quest of individual greatness. Inevitably we fail to find it. Then we begin to 'hate immoderately and punish ourselves and one another immoderately. The fear of lagging [behind] pursues and maddens us . . . It makes an inner climate of darkness. And occasionally there is a storm of hate and wounding rain out of us.' (p. 63)

In other words, by enthroning Man at the centre of the universe, the Enlightenment, particularly in its Romantic phase, imposed impossible psychic demands on us, demands that work themselves out not just in petty fits of violence such as his own, or in such moral aberrations as the pursuit of greatness through crime (*vide* Dostoevsky's Raskolnikov), but also perhaps in the war that is consuming the world. This is why, in a paradoxical move, Joseph the journal writer terminates his reflections, lays down his pen, and enlists. Isolation redoubled – the isolation imposed by the ideology of individualism, and then the isolation of self-scrutiny – has brought him, he believes, to the brink of insanity. Perhaps war will teach him what he has been unable to learn from philosophy. He ends his journal with the cry:

> Hurray for regular hours!
> And for the supervision of the spirit!
> Long live regimentation! (p. 140)

Joseph draws a distinction between a mere self-obsessed individual like himself wrestling with his thoughts and the artist, who through the demiurgic faculty of the imagination turns his petty personal troubles into universal concerns. But the pretence that Joseph's private wrestlings are mere journal entries meant for his eyes alone is barely maintained. For among the entries are pages – renderings of city scenes for the most part, or sketches of people Joseph meets – whose heightened diction and metaphoric inventiveness betray them as productions of the poetic imagination that not only cry out for a reader but reach out to and create a reader. Joseph may pretend he wishes us to think of him as a failed scholar, but we know, as he must suspect, that he is a born writer.

Dangling Man is long on reflection, short on action. It occupies uneasy ground between the novella proper and the personal essay or confession. Various personages come onstage and exchange words with the protagonist, but beyond Joseph in his two sketchy manifestations there are no characters, properly speaking. Behind the figure of Joseph can be discerned the lonely, humiliated clerks of Gogol and Dostoevsky, brooding their revenge; the Roquentin of Sartre's *Nausea*, the scholar who undergoes a strange metaphysical crisis that estranges him from the world; and the lonely young poet of Rilke's *Notebooks of Malte Laurids Brigge*. In this slim first book Bellow has not yet developed a vehicle adequate to the kind of novel he is feeling his way towards, one that will offer the customary novelistic satisfactions, including involvement in what feels like real-life conflict in a real-life world, yet leave its author free to deploy his reading in European literature and thought in order to explore contemporary life and its discontents. For that step in Bellow's evolution we will have to wait for *Herzog* (1964).

Asa Leventhal, who may or may not be the victim in the short novel *The Victim*, is an editor on a small trade magazine in Manhattan. At work he has to endure the pricks of casual anti-Semitism. His wife, whom he loves dearly, is out of town.

One day, on the street, Leventhal gets the feeling he is being watched. A man approaches him, greets him. Dimly he recalls the man's name: Allbee. Why is he late, asks Allbee – does he not remember that they had a rendezvous? Leventhal can remember no such thing. Then why he is here, asks Allbee? (Time and again Allbee will throw Leventhal with such logical ju-jitsu.)

Having trapped Leventhal, Allbee embarks on a tedious story from the past in which Allbee had fixed Leventhal up with an interview with his (Allbee's) boss, during which Leventhal had (on purpose, Allbee says) behaved insultingly, as a result of which Allbee lost his job.

Leventhal dimly recalls the events but rejects the implication that the interview was part of a plot against Allbee. If he stormed out of the interview, he says, it was because Allbee's boss showed no interest in hiring him.

Nevertheless, says Allbee, he is now jobless and homeless and has to sleep in flophouses. So what is Leventhal going to do about it?

Thus commences Allbee's persecution of Leventhal – or so it feels to Leventhal. Doggedly Leventhal resists Allbee's claim that he has been wronged and is therefore owed. All of this resistance is presented from the inside: there is no helping hint from the author to tell us whose side to take, which of the two is the victim and which the persecutor. Nor are we issued with any authorial guidance in the moral area. Is Leventhal prudently resisting being taken for a ride, or is he refusing to accept that we are each our brother's keeper? *Why me?* – that is Leventhal's sole cry. Why does this stranger blame me, hate me, seek redress from me?

Leventhal claims his hands are clean, but the friends he consults are not so sure. Why did he become mixed up in the first place, they ask, with an unsavoury character like Allbee? Is he being entirely honest with himself about his motives?

Leventhal recalls his first meeting with Allbee, at a party. A Jewish girl had sung a ballad, and Allbee had told her she should try a psalm instead. 'If you're not born to them [American ballads], it's no use trying to sing them.' (p. 174) Did he, Leventhal, at that moment unconsciously mark down Allbee as an anti-Semite, and decide to pay him back?

With a heavy heart, Leventhal offers Allbee refuge in his apartment. Their cohabitation is a miserable failure. Allbee's personal habits are squalid. He pries into Leventhal's private papers. (Allbee: If you don't trust me, why leave your desk unlocked?) Leventhal loses his temper and strikes Allbee, but Allbee keeps bouncing back.

Allbee preaches a lesson that (he says) Leventhal ought to be able to understand *despite being a Jew*, namely that we have all to repent and become new men. Leventhal doubts Allbee's sincerity and says so. You doubt me because you are a Jew and I am not, replies Allbee. But why *me*? demands Leventhal again. 'Why?' replies Allbee. 'For good reasons; the best in the world . . . I'm giving you a chance to be fair, Leventhal, and to do what's right.' (p. 328)

Arriving home one evening, Leventhal finds the door locked against him and Allbee in bed with a prostitute – not just in bed, in Leventhal's bed. Leventhal's outrage amuses Allbee. 'Where else, if not in bed? . . . Maybe you have some other way, more refined, different. Don't you people claim that you are the same as everybody else?' (p. 362)

Who is Allbee? A madman? A prophet in deep disguise? A sadist who selects his victims at random?

Allbee has his own story. He is like the plains Indian, he says, who in the coming of the railroad foresees the end of his old way of life. He has decided to join the new dispensation. Leventhal the Jew, member of the new master race, must find him a job on the railroad of the future. 'I want to get off [my] pony and be a conductor on that train.' (p. 329)

With his wife about to return, Leventhal orders Allbee to find other accommodation. In the middle of the night he wakes up to find the apartment full of gas. Allbee has been trying unsuccessfully to gas himself in the kitchen.

Allbee disappears from Leventhal's life. Years pass. By degrees Leventhal sheds the feeling that he has 'got away with it'. (p. 372) There was never any need to feel guilty, he reflects. Allbee had no right to envy him his good job, his happy marriage. Envy like that rests on a false premise: that to each of us a promise has been made. No such promise has ever been made to any of us, neither by God nor by the state.

Then one evening he runs into Allbee in the theatre. Allbee is squiring a faded actress; he smells of drink. I have found my place on the train, Allbee informs him, but not as conductor, merely as a passenger. I have come to terms with 'whoever runs things'. 'What's your idea of who runs things?' asks Leventhal. (p. 379) But Allbee has disappeared into the crowd.

Bellow's Kirby Allbee is an inspired creation, comic, pathetic, repulsive, and menacing. Sometimes his anti-Semitism seems amiable in a bluff kind of way; sometimes he seems to have been taken over by his own caricature of the Jew, who now lives inside him, an anti-Jew speaking through his lips. You Jews are taking over the world, he whines. There is nothing for us poor Americans to do but seek out a humble corner for ourselves. Why do you victimise us so? What harm have we ever done you?

There is also a patrician-American twist to Allbee's anti-Semitism. 'Do you know, one of my ancestors was Governor Winthrop,' he says. 'Isn't it [i.e., isn't the present state of affairs] preposterous? It's really as if the children of Caliban were running everything.' (p. 259)

Above all Allbee is shameless, id-like, unclean. Even his moments of ingratiation are offensive. Let me touch your hair, he pleads with Leventhal – 'It's like an animal's hair.' (p. 323)

Leventhal is a good husband, a good uncle, a good brother, a good worker in trying circumstances. He is enlightened, he is not a troublemaker. He wants to be part of mainstream American society. His father did not care what gentiles thought of him as long as they paid what they owed. 'That was his father's view. But not his. He rejected and recoiled from it.' (p. 232) He has a social conscience. He is aware of how easily, in America in particular, one can fall among 'the lost, the outcast, the overcome, the effaced, the ruined.' (p. 158) He is even a good neighbour – after all, none of Allbee's gentile friends had been prepared to take him in. What more can be demanded of him?

The answer is: everything. *The Victim* is Bellow's most Dostoevskian book. The plot is adapted from Dostoevsky's *The Eternal Husband*, the story of a man accosted out of the blue by the husband of a woman he had an affair with years ago, someone whose insinuations and demands become more and more insufferably intimate. But it is not just the plot for which Bellow is indebted to Dostoevsky, and the motif of the detested double. The very spirit of *The Victim* is Dostoevskian. The supports for our neat, well-ordered lives can crumble at any minute; inhuman demands can without warning be made of us, and from the strangest quarters; it will be only natural to resist (*Why me?*); but if we want to be saved we have no choice, we must drop everything and follow. Yet this essentially religious message is put in the mouth of a repulsive anti-Semite. Is it any wonder that Leventhal baulks?

Leventhal's heart is not closed; his resistance is not complete. There is something in all of us, he recognises, that fights against the slumber of the quotidian. In Allbee's company, at stray moments, he feels on the point of escaping the confines of his old identity and seeing the world through fresh eyes. Something seems to be occurring in the area of his heart, some kind of premonition, whether of a heart attack or something more exalted he cannot say. At one moment he looks at Allbee and Allbee looks back and they might as well be the same person. At another – rendered in Bellow's most masterly understated prose – we are somehow convinced that Leventhal is teetering on the point of revelation. But then a great fatigue overtakes him. It is all too much.

Looking back over his career, Bellow has tended to disparage *The Victim*. If *Dangling Man* was his BA as a writer, he has said, *The Victim* was his PhD. 'I was still learning, establishing my credentials, proving that a young man from Chicago had a right to claim the world's attention.'[3] He is too modest. *The Victim* is within inches of joining *Billy Budd* in the first rank of American novellas. If it has a weakness, it is a weakness not of execution but of ambition. It was within Bellow's powers to make Leventhal enough of an intellectual heavyweight to dispute with Allbee (and with Dostoevsky behind him) the universality of the Christian model of the call to repentance. But he did not do so.

(2004)

17   Arthur Miller, *The Misfits*

THE MISFITS (1961) was put together by a notable set of creative people. The film is based on an original screenplay by Arthur Miller. It was directed by John Huston; and it starred Marilyn Monroe and Clark Gable in what turned out to be their last big roles. Though it was not a great box-office success, it continues to hang around on the fringes of critical attention, and deservedly so.

The plot is simple. A woman, Roslyn, visiting Reno, Nevada, for a quick divorce, gets friendly with a group of part-time cowboys and goes off with them into the desert on a jaunt to trap wild horses. There she discovers that the horses will end up not as riding mounts but as pet food. The discovery precipitates a breakdown of trust between her and the men, a breakdown that the film patches over only in the most uneasy and unconvincing of ways.

Aside from the ending, the script is a strong one. Miller is operating at the tail end of a long literary tradition of reflecting on the closing of America's western frontier, and the effects of that closing on the American psyche. Huckleberry Finn, at the end of the book about him by Mark Twain, still had the recourse of lighting out for the territories so as to escape civilisation (and Nevada, in the 1840s of Huck's childhood, was one of the territories in question).

Miller's cowboys, a century or so later, are trapped in the States with nowhere to go. One of them, Gaye (Clark Gable), has become a gigolo preying on divorcees. Another, Perce (Montgomery Clift) scrapes together a living as a rodeo performer. The third, Guido (Eli Wallach), exhibits the dark side of the male homosociality of the frontier, namely a vicious misogyny.

These are Miller's misfits, men who have either failed to make the transition to the modern world or are making that transition in an ignominious way. The three are presented with a rounded-ness that is rare in cinema, the result of Miller's deft professional stagecraft.

But of course Miller's title has a second, ironic meaning. If the cowboys are misfits in Eisenhower's America, the Nevada mustangs are even more deeply so. There used to be tens of thousands of them; now there are only pitiful troops up in the hills, barely worth being exploited. From being an embodiment of the freedom of the frontier, they have become an anachronism, creatures with no useful role in a mechanised civilisation. It is their lot to be herded and hunted from the air; if they are not actually being shot from the air, that is only because their flesh would spoil before the horse-butcher could arrive with his refrigerated truck.

And then, of course, Roslyn (Marilyn Monroe) is a misfit too, in ways less easy to put a finger on, ways that lead us to the creative heart of the film. Miller was married to Monroe at the time, though the marriage broke up during the course of the filming; one suspects that the character of Roslyn was shaped around Monroe, or around Miller's sense of who the inner Monroe was or could be. In some of the more impressive scenes, Miller and Huston do no more than create a space in which Monroe is allowed to act out herself, create herself on film.

Ironies run particularly deep here, since Monroe in part embodied, and in part struggled against, the dumb-blonde type that the Hollywood star system prescribed for her. A further complication: it is not always easy to distinguish the elusive charm of the character Roslyn from the slack, Nembutal-induced good humour of the troubled actress.

The key scene in this respect occurs about thirty minutes into the film. Roslyn has been dancing with Guido, while Gaye and Roslyn's older friend Isabelle look on. Roslyn is charming, full of vitality; but whatever further signals she is sending out, Guido misreads. To him the dance is sexual courtship; but Roslyn keeps evading him in a way that is beyond mere coyness. Eventually she dances out of the house into the evening sun ('Watch out!' calls Gaye – 'There's no step!') and continues her dance around the trunk of a tree, falling at last into a half-undressed coma.

Gaye understands what possesses Roslyn no better than Guido does, but he knows enough to hold Guido back. The two men, and Isabelle, stand and watch in bafflement while Roslyn – who at this point, one can recognise with historical hindsight, might as well be Monroe herself, or at least Arthur Miller's Monroe – does her thing.

What is Roslyn-Monroe's thing? In part it is Angst of a rather hand-me-down kind, for which Left Bank café existentialism must be blamed. But in part, too, it has to do with a resistance to the highly focused and even regimented models of sexuality purveyed not only by Hollywood and the media but by academic sexology. Roslyn is dancing out a diffuse and – in the light of the rest of the film – forlorn sensuality to which neither Guido's sexual preda-toriness nor Gaye's old-fashioned suave courtliness is an adequate response.

Another haunting scene comes toward the end of the film, when it is brought home to Roslyn with full force that the men have been lying to her, that finally they care more for the macho exploit in which they are involved – capturing the wretched horses

– than they care for her, that pleas and even bribery will get her nowhere. In despair and rage she tears herself away from the men; she screams and rants and weeps against their heartlessness. To a more conventional director, this high moment – the moment when all veils are torn from Roslyn's eyes and she realises that, as a woman and perhaps also as a human being, she is alone – would have seemed an opportunity for acting in an old-fashioned sense: for intense close-ups, for crosscutting from face to angry face. In fact Huston shoots the scene contrary to such conventions. The camera stays on the side of the men; Roslyn is so far away that she is almost swallowed up by the expanse of the desert; her voice cracks; her words are incoherent. The effect is disturbing.

But the scenes – the long sequence of scenes – that stay most indelibly in the mind are those involving the horses.

In the credit sequences to any film involving animal participants that is made nowadays, at least any film made in the West, cinemagoers are assured that no hardship was caused to the animals, that what may have appeared to be hardship was only filmic sleight of hand. One presumes that such assurances were brought about by pressure from animal rights organisations upon the film industry.

Not so in 1960. The horses used in the filming of *The Misfits* were wild horses; the exhaustion and pain and terror one sees on the screen are real exhaustion and pain and terror. The horses are not acting. The horses are the real thing, being exploited by Huston and the people behind Huston for their strength and beauty and endurance; for the spiritual integrity of their response to their enemy, man; for actually being what they seem to be and are held to be in the mythology of the West: creatures of the wild, untamed.

The point is worth stressing because it brings us close to the heart of film as a representational medium. Film, or at least the visual component of naturalistic film, does not work via intermediary symbols. When you read, in a book, 'His hand brushed hers,' it is not a real hand that brushes a real hand but the idea of a hand that brushes the idea of another hand. Whereas in a film, what you see is the visual record of something that once really happened: a real hand that came in contact with another real hand.

Part of the reason why the debate on pornography is still alive in respect of the photographic media when it has all but died out in the case of print is that the photograph is read, and justifiably so, as a record of something that really happened. What is represented on celluloid was actually done at some time in the past by actual people in front of a camera. The story in which the moment is embedded may be a fiction, but the event was a real one, it belongs to history, to a history that is relived every time the film is rolled.

Despite all the cleverness that has been exercised in film theory since the 1950s to bring film into line as just another system of signs, there remains something irreducibly different about the photographic image, namely that it bears in or with itself the trace of a real historical past. That is why the horse-capturing sequences of *The Misfits* are so disturbing: on the one side, out of the field of the camera lens, a gang of horse-wranglers and directors and writers and sound technicians united in trying to fit the horses into places that have been prescribed for them in a fictional construct called *The Misfits*; on the other side, in front of the lens, a handful of wild horses who make no distinction between actors and stuntmen and technicians, who don't know about and don't want to know about a screenplay by the famed Arthur Miller in which they are or are not, depending on one's point of view, the misfits, who have never heard of the closing of the Western frontier but are at this moment experiencing it in the flesh in the most traumatising way. The horses are real, the stuntmen are real, the actors are real; they are all, at this moment, involved in a

terrible fight in which the men want to subjugate the horses to
their purpose and the horses want to get away; every now and
again the blonde woman screams and shouts; it all really happened;
and here it is, to be relived for the ten thousandth time before
our eyes. Who would dare to say it is just a story?

(2000)

18   Philip Roth, *The Plot Against America*

In 1993, over the name 'Philip Roth', there appeared a book entitled *Operation Shylock: A Confession*, which besides being a dazzling raid into territory that had seemed to be staked out by John Barth and the metafictionists, was also about Israel and its relations with the Jewish Diaspora. *Operation Shylock* presents itself as the work of an American writer named Philip Roth (within the book, however, there are two such Philip Roths) who admits to a history of covertly assisting the Israeli intelligence services. We may choose to take this confession at face value. On the other hand, this confession may be part of a larger fiction: *Operation Shylock – A Confession: A Novel*. Which would be the truer reading? The 'Note to the Reader' with which the book concludes seems to promise an answer. The note commences, 'This book is a work of fiction,' and ends, 'This confession is false.' We are, in other words, in the sphere of the Cretan Liar.[1]

If Roth did and did not mean his book about Israel to be read as a lie, an invention, is his new book about America – which contains a similar Note commencing with the words '*The Plot Against America* is a work of fiction' – to be read in the same way, namely with its truth status held in suspension? In a sense, no, obviously not. The plot of *The Plot Against America* cannot be true since many of the events on which it hinges are universally known never to have occurred. For instance, there was no President Charles Lindbergh in the White House in the years 1941–42, putting into effect secret orders from Berlin. Just as obviously, however, Roth has not concocted this lengthy fantasy of an America in thrall to the Nazis simply as a literary exercise. So what is the relation of his story to the real world? What is his book 'about'?[2]

Roth's President Lindbergh favours an oratorical style based on the clipped declarative sentence. His administration runs sinister programmes with reassuring titles like 'Just Folks' and 'Homestead 42' (compare 'Homeland Security', 'Patriot Act'). Behind him lurks an ideologue of a vice-president impatient to get his hands on the levers of power. The similarities between the Lindbergh presidency and the presidency of George W. Bush are hard to brush over. Is Roth's novel of America under fascist rule then 'about' America under the younger Bush?

At the time the book was launched, Roth took steps to head off such a reading. 'Some readers are going to want to take this book as a *roman à clef* to the present moment in America,' he wrote in the *New York Times Book Review*. 'That would be a mistake . . . I am not pretending to be interested in [the years 1940–1942] – I *am* interested in those two years.'[3]

The disclaimer sounds unambiguous, and it is. Nevertheless, a novelist as seasoned as Roth knows that the stories we set about writing sometimes begin to write themselves, after which their truth or falsehood is out of our hands and declarations of authorial intent carry no weight. Furthermore, once a book is launched into the world it becomes the property of its readers, who, given half a chance, will twist its meaning in accord with their own preconceptions and desires. Again Roth is aware of this: in the same *New York Times* piece he reminds us that, though Franz Kafka did not write his novels as political allegories, East Europeans under Communist rule read them as such and put them to work for political ends.

Finally, we might note that this is not the first time Roth has invited us to think about a slide into fascism led from above. In *American Pastoral* (1997) the hero's father, watching the Watergate hearings on television, observes of the circle around Richard Nixon:

> These so-called patriots . . . would take this country and make Nazi Germany out of it. You know the book *It Can't Happen Here*? There's a wonderful book, I forget the author, but the idea couldn't be more up-to-the-moment. These people have taken us to the edge of something terrible.[4]

The book referred to is the now barely readable *It Can't Happen Here* (1935), in which Sinclair Lewis imagines a takeover of the American government by an unstable mix of far-right and populist forces. As a model for his fascist president Lewis uses not Lindbergh but Huey Long.

In any sensible reading, *The Plot Against America* can be 'about' the presidency of George W. Bush in only the most peripheral way. It needs a paranoid reader to turn it into a *roman à clef* for the early twenty-first century. However, one of the things that *The Plot Against America* is about is, precisely, paranoia. In Roth's story, the plot from above, which is immediately a plot against America's Jews but ultimately a plot against the American republic, works so insidiously that at first sensible people cannot see it. Those who talk about plots are dismissed as crazy.

Roth's fictive history begins in 1940 when, riding on the back of a campaign to keep America out of the newly erupted European war, the aviator Charles Lindbergh defeats Franklin Delano Roosevelt for the presidency. Plenty of folk are horrified by the election of a known Nazi sympathiser. But in the face of the new president's success in keeping America peaceful and prosperous, opposition dwindles. Roosevelt retires to lick his wounds. The first laws targeting Jews are passed, and evoke no outcry.

What resistance there is crystallises around an unlikely centre. Week after week the journalist Walter Winchell uses his radio programme to lambaste Lindbergh. Outside the Jewish community there is little support for Winchell. The *New York Times* criticises his tirades for their 'questionable taste' and applauds the advertisers who have him removed from the airwaves. Winchell responds by denouncing the proprietors of the *Times* as 'ultra-civilised Jewish Quislings'. Stripped of his only access to the media, Winchell announces himself as a candidate for the Democratic nomination in 1944. At a rally in the Lindbergh heartland, however, he is assassinated. At the memorial service Fiorello La Guardia delivers a Mark Antony-type oration, full of scorching irony, over the coffin. In response Lindbergh climbs into his plane, flies off into the blue, and is never heard from again. (pp. 240, 242)

After Lindbergh's disappearance, things get worse before they get better. His vice-president and successor, Burton K. Wheeler, is an extremist. Under Wheeler there is a brief reign of terror. Riots break out; Jews and Jewish businesses are targeted. Anne Morrow Lindbergh, of all people, raises her voice in protest, and is promptly whipped off into protective custody by the FBI. There is talk of a war against Canada, which has been giving shelter to Jews from its mighty southern neighbour.

Then the country pulls itself right. Resistance brings together political figures like La Guardia and Dorothy Thompson, wife of Sinclair Lewis and animating spirit behind *It Can't Happen Here*, with decent Americans from all walks of life. In an extraordinary presidential election in November 1942 Roosevelt is returned to office, and Japan promptly bombs Pearl Harbor. Thus, exactly one year late, the ship of history – American history, that is – resumes its wonted course.

The 1940s are conveyed to us through the eyes of one Philip Roth, born 1933, a youngster with a stable and happy disposition that comes from being 'an American child of American parents in an American school in an American city in an America at peace with the world'. As the Lindbergh programme unrolls, however, young Philip has to absorb, step by step, a lesson that may well be at the heart of his author's enterprise: that the history we learn from history books is a censored, domesticated version of the real thing. Real history is the unpredictable, 'the relentless unforeseen'. 'The terror of the unforeseen is what the science of history hides.' To the extent that it chronicles the irruption of the relentless unforeseen into the life of a child, *The Plot Against America* is a history book, but of a fantastic kind, with its own truth, the sort of truth Aristotle had in mind when he said that poetry is truer than history – truer because of its power to condense and represent the multifarious in the typical. (pp. 7, 113, 114)

Philip's father, Herman Roth – whose real-life avatar has already been eulogised by his son in *Patrimony* (1991) – is a man of sterling qualities with a more intense, or perhaps more romantic, loyalty to the ideals of American democracy than anyone else in the book. Herman does his best to shield his family from the gathering storm; but in order to keep them from relocation from their native Newark to the hinterland (this is what Homestead 42 is all about – isolating Jews), he has to quit his job selling insurance and take night work lugging crates in the produce market; and even there he is not safe from the threats of Agent McCorkle of the FBI.

The spectacle of his father's powerlessness against the state sets off a psychic breakdown in Philip. This begins with petty delinquency, proceeds through alienation ('She's somebody else,' he thinks to himself, watching his mother – '*everybody* is'), and ends with him fleeing home to seek sanctuary in a Catholic orphanage. He is quite clear about the meaning of running away from home. 'I wanted nothing to do with history. I wanted to be a boy on the smallest scale possible.' (pp. 194, 232)

Philip's breakdown is treated with a light hand – despite the menace in the air, the tone of the book is comic. His flight expresses panic more than rejection of family and heritage. One of Roth's alter egos, Nathan Zuckerman, has in the past insinuated that Roth the obedient, dutiful son is an impostor, and – worse – a boring impostor, that the true Roth is the sly, scabrous rebel who first stuck out his head in *Portnoy's Complaint* (1969). *The Plot Against America* in effect speaks back to Zuckerman, offering a pedigree for the more filial, 'citizenly' Roth.[5]

Nevertheless, Lindbergh, and what Lindbergh represents – licence for everything that is ugliest in the American psyche to emerge and run riot – forces Philip to grow up too fast, lose his childhood illusions too early. In the longer term, what effect does this abrupt awakening from childhood have on Philip? In a sense the question is illegitimate. Since Roth's novel ends in 1942, we do not get to see Philip after nine. But if the author Philip Roth had meant to write about a fictive child whose sole existence is between the pages of a novel, he would not have called that child Philip Roth, born in the same year as himself and of parents with the same names as his. *In some sense* the young Philip Roth about whose childhood we read continues his life in the life of the Philip Roth who six decades later not only narrates the child's story but writes it too.

In some sense, then, we are reading not just the story of a representative Jewish-American child of the generation that came to awareness in the 1940s – albeit here in a perverted version of the

1940s – but also the story of the real, historical Philip Roth. Puzzling out in what sense the real Philip Roth can be said to bear the marks of the child Philip's ravaged childhood may help us to answer the question, what is this book, this work of fiction, really about?

Whatever marks are borne by Philip seem all the stranger as one scrutinises them. Oskar Matzerath, in Günter Grass's *The Tin Drum*, bears in or on himself more obviously than Philip the proof that he wanted nothing to do with history. Oskar asserts his right to childhood not by hiding from history, which cannot be done, not even in an orphanage, but by ceasing to grow, which – in a sense – can be done. But the history with which Oskar collides, the history of the Third Reich, is not some abstract 'unforeseen': it really happened, as attested in common memory and recorded in thousands of books and millions of photographs. The history that scars Philip, on the other hand, happened only in Philip Roth's head and is recorded only in *The Plot Against America*. Making sense of *The Plot* and its imaginary world is therefore nowhere near as straightforward as making sense of *The Tin Drum*.

Just how imaginary, however, is the world recorded in Roth's book? A Lindbergh presidency may be imaginary, but the anti-Semitism of the real Lindbergh was not. And Lindbergh was not alone. He gave voice to a native anti-Semitism with a long pre-history in Catholic and Protestant Christianity, fostered in numbers of European immigrant communities, and drawing strength from the anti-black bigotry with which it was, by the irrational logic of racism, tightly entwined (of all America's 'historic undesirables', suggests Roth, none could be more unlike than blacks and Jews).[6] A volatile and fickle voting public captivated by surface rather than substance – Tocqueville foresaw the danger long ago – might in 1940 as easily have fallen for the aviator hero with the simple message as for the incumbent with the proven record. In this sense, the fantasy of a Lindbergh presidency is only a concretisation, a realisation for poetic ends, of a certain potential in American political life.

With this reading of Lindbergh in mind, we may return to the question of the scar carried into the future by the child of the 1940s. And here, rather than searching into the life and character of the real Philip Roth, a questionable enterprise under any circumstances, it may help to turn to the other Roth boy, Philip's elder brother Sandy, the one who did not run away from history (and did not write a book about his childhood either). Philip, passionately patriotic, collects icons (postage stamps) of exemplary Americans. Sandy, artistically gifted, prefers to draw his heroes. Both own treasured images of Lindbergh the aviator; as Jews, both face a crisis when Lindbergh reveals his true political colours. Philip does not want to give up his Lindbergh stamps; Sandy hides his Lindbergh portraits under his bed.

Under the influence of a collaborationist rabbi to whom their mother's sister is married, but against his parents' wishes, Sandy enrols voluntarily in the Just Folks programme, which takes Jewish children away from the cities for the summer and quarters them with typical (i.e., Lindbergh-inclined) non-Jewish families in rural areas. He spends a summer on a farm in Kentucky and comes back husky and tanned, unable to understand why his parents, whom he sneers at as 'ghetto Jews' suffering from a 'persecution complex', get excited about Hitler. It takes Sandy a full year to appreciate that what he calls a persecution complex may really be a survival mechanism. (p. 193)

By any objective standard, Sandy emerges from the Lindbergh years as scarred as his younger brother, perhaps more so, since he has to live like an alien in a disapproving parental household. If those years had really occurred, the historical Philip Roth's elder brother – who is just as real as Philip, and lived through the same history – would bear the marks too. But there were no Lindbergh years, and therefore there are no Lindbergh marks as such. What then is the nature of the scar that *both* brothers, the writer and the non-writer, bear, as a result of a history that is *poetically* (in Aristotle's sense) called the Lindbergh presidency; or is it only the writer brother who bears the scar; or is there in fact no scar at all?

Though young Philip will of course grow up to become a famous writer, *The Plot* is not a book about the incubation of the writer's soul. Nowhere does Roth invoke the trope of the artist as a being wounded by life whose wound becomes the source of his art. The only answer that seems to make sense of the Lindbergh scar is that the scar is Jewishness itself – Jewishness, however, of a particular etiology: Jewishness as an outsider's idea – and a hostile outsider's at that – of what it is to be a Jew, an idea forced upon the growing child too early, and by means that, while they might not be extreme in themselves, might easily – the 1940s, the quint-essential time of the unforeseen, provide proof aplenty – become extreme.

What the plot against America does to young Philip between the ages of seven and nine is terrible. It forces upon him – though less, it must be noted, at first hand than through the medium of newsreels and radio programmes and from eavesdropping on his parents' worried conversations – a vision of a world based on hatred and suspicion, a world of them and us. It turns him from a Jewish American into an American Jew, or in the eyes of his enemies just a Jew in America. In waking him up to 'reality' too early, it strips him of his childhood. Or rather, the Zionists would say, it strips him of his illusions. A Jew can expect no home on earth but in the Jewish homeland.

What is it to be a Jew in America? Does a Jew belong in America? Can America be a Jew's true home? Herman and Bess Roth,

Philip's parents, were born in the United States in the early twentieth century, into immigrant families. They love their native country and work hard to make their way in it. Philip offers a tribute to their generation that is not without overtones of elegy:

> It was work that identified and distinguished our neighbours for me far more than religion. Nobody . . . had a beard or dressed in the antiquated Old World style or wore a skullcap . . . The adults were no longer observant in the outward, recognizable ways . . . [The one] stranger who did wear a beard . . . [and] appeared every few months after dark to ask in broken English for a contribution toward the establishment of a Jewish national homeland in Palestine . . . seemed unable to get it through his head that we'd already had a homeland for three generations . . . (pp. 3–4)
>
> These were Jews who needed no large terms of reference, no profession of faith or doctrinal creed, in order to be Jews, and they certainly needed no other language – they had one, their native tongue, whose vernacular expressiveness they wielded effortlessly . . . What they were was what they couldn't get rid of – what they couldn't even begin to want to get rid of. Their being Jews issued from their being themselves, as did their being American. (p. 220)

The account Roth gives here of the Judaism of people like his parents is wholly affirmative. There is no hint of what he suggests elsewhere: that for some Jews a religion reduced to an ethical code plus some social practices may prove too barren, that to give a fuller meaning to their lives they may plunge hysterically into cults (Mickey Sabbath's wife in *Sabbath's Theater*) or revolutionary violence (Meredith Levov in *American Pastoral*).

The Jewishness of Herman Roth and his kind may be devoid

of a metaphysical dimension but it does embody a chemistry that neither the Zionists nor the architects of Homestead 42 are able to grasp. Jewish-Americanness is a compound, not a simple mixture. One cannot simply subtract one element ('Jewishness' or 'Americanness') and be left with the other. To be American – to speak the American language, participate in the American way of life, be absorbed in American culture – does not require that one cease being a Jew or entail a loss of Jewishness; conversely, being relocated by fiat from a Jewish to an 'American' (i.e., gentile) community will not make one more of an American. The same holds or held true for the Jews of Europe. Roth quotes with approval Aharon Appelfeld's mordant observation: 'I have always loved assimilated Jews, because that was where the Jewish character, and also, perhaps, Jewish fate, was concentrated with greatest force.'[7]

After the election of Lindbergh, Herman takes his family on a trip to Washington, DC, where he hopes that contact with the enduring monuments of American democracy will wash away the bad taste. Instead the family is given a taste of what public life in the wider America is becoming. They are turned out of their hotel room on a pretext and subjected to anti-Semitic menaces by fellow tourists. Lindbergh's triumph has clearly been read by middle Americans as a signal that the hunting season can commence.

A strange man attaches himself to the Roths. He claims to be a professional guide and will not be shaken off. Who is he really? In their new, paranoid state, the Roth parents suspect he is an FBI agent, and test him out. He passes every test. The simple truth is that he is what he says, a tour guide, and a good one too. But in the new America, nothing is any longer simple. A trip that had been intended to reassure the boys about their common heritage turns into a lesson in exclusion. Philip: 'A patriotic paradise, the American Garden of Eden spread before us, and we stood huddled together there, the family expelled.' In the starkest terms, that is what the plot in Roth's title is meant to achieve and, at the level of the imaginary, does achieve: to expel Jews from America. *Juden raus*. That is what Philip cannot forget. (p. 66)

To put all talk of metaphorical scarring in perspective, finally, we ought not to forget the third boy in the Roth household: Alvin, their twenty-one-year-old ward, an orphan in the true sense of the word, who runs off to join the Canadian army and fight the Nazis, loses a leg ingloriously, and returns to Newark in a wheelchair with a medal and a seething rage against all and sundry. With grim purposefulness Alvin descends into a life of crime, his anti-fascist past dismissed as a foolish juvenile escapade. Scarred more deeply than either of the brothers, Alvin is in the book to give a sobering reminder of what real history can do in the way of destroying lives.

Although the mind through which the events of 1940–42 are mediated is that of a child, the account we get is not a *faux-naïf* one. The voice speaking to us is that of the child grown up, yet subjecting himself to the vision of his younger self, and in return lending to the younger self a concentrated self-awareness that no child possesses.

There are no particular signs that the grown-up voice reaches us from the first decade of the twenty-first century (there is hardly any forward perspective beyond 1945), but given the autobiographical traces we may take it as belonging to the historical Philip Roth or his fictional alter ego 'Philip Roth', from whose repertoire the wisdom of hindsight has been deliberately excluded, and who passes over every opportunity to be smart at the expense of the child. If one may speak of the affection of a grown man for his childhood self, then the affection and respect of the writer for young Philip is one of the most appealing aspects of the book.

The modulation between youthful freshness of vision and adult insight is brought off with such skill that we lose awareness of who is speaking in our ear at any given moment, child or man. Only rarely does Roth's hand fail, as for example when the child Philip sees his aunt Evelyn for who she is: 'Her pretty face, with its large features and thickly applied makeup, suddenly looked to me preposterous – the carnal face of [a] ravenous mania.' (p. 217)

Subjecting himself to a child's world-view means that Roth has to eschew a range of stylistic resources, in particular the harsher reaches of irony and the wails and tirades of desperate eloquence that distinguish such novels as *The Dying Animal* (2001) and the great *Sabbath's Theater* (1995), an eloquence sparked by the brute resistance of the world to the human will or by the prospect of approaching extinction. On the other hand, it does place Roth out of range of William Faulkner, the influence of whose heady prose has sometimes overwhelmed him of late, particularly in *The Human Stain* (2000).

Roth has grown in stature as a writer as he has grown older. At his best he is now a novelist of authentically tragic scope; at his very best he can reach Shakespearean heights. By the standard set by *Sabbath's Theater*, *The Plot Against America* is not a major work. What it offers in place of tragedy is pathos of a heart-wrenching kind saved from sentimentality by a sharp humour, a risky, knife-edge performance that Roth brings off without a slip.

The subject of the keenest pathos is not young Philip – though, clutching his stamp album, heading off into the night, determined to be just a boy again, Philip is pathetic enough – but Philip's neighbour and shadow self, Seldon Wishnow. Like Philip, Seldon is a clever, impressionable, obedient little boy. He is also fatally unlucky, a born victim, and Philip wants nothing to do with him (Seldon of course adores Philip). In his efforts to shake off the curse of Seldon, Philip suggests to Aunt Evelyn, who works in the relocation bureau, that the Wishnows, widow and son, be packed off to Kentucky. To his dismay she acts on his suggestion. Within months of arriving in the town of Danville, Seldon's mother has been set upon and murdered by anti-Semitic vigilantes, and Seldon has to be brought back to Newark an orphan. Philip thus has to bear not only the guilt of sending Mrs Wishnow to her death but the punishment of having Seldon quartered upon him.

The night of his mother's disappearance, Seldon telephones Newark (he knows no one in Kentucky), and Mrs Roth, calling on all her resources of motherly firmness, confronts no less a task than keeping the excitable child sane. Their long-distance conversation contains some of the most heart-rending (we know Seldon's mother is dead but Seldon and Mrs Roth do not, though she suspects the worst) yet funniest dialogue Roth has written.

An historical novel is, by definition, set in a real historical past. The past in which *The Plot Against America* is set is not real. *The Plot* is thus, generically speaking, not an historical but a dystopian novel, though an unusual one, since the dystopian novel is usually set in the future, a future toward which the present seems to be tending. George Orwell's *1984* is an exemplary dystopian novel. It looks forward to 1984 from the perspective of a 1948 in which the threat of total control seems ominously strong.

In the typical dystopian novel there is a convenient gap between present and future – convenient because it frees the author from having to demonstrate step by step how present turns into future. Roth's task is more difficult. He needs to provide two lines of suturing: the imaginary Lindbergh years have to be sutured at one end to the real history from which they diverge in mid-1940, and at the other end to the real history that they rejoin in late 1942. By strict standards, Roth's surgery fails and has to fail. Even under a resolutely isolationist administration, American history cannot proceed independently of world history. The absence of America from the international stage for two years would inevitably have affected the course of the war and thereby changed the world.

If, by its nature, Roth's alternative history cannot pass the test of the real, can it pass the lesser test of the plausible? Is it plausible, for example, that Congress should not have been disquieted by the spectacle of Japanese forces sweeping through Indonesia, India, and Australia, thereby laying the foundations for a vast Co-Prosperity Sphere run from Tokyo? Is it plausible that what the US armed forces took four years of real history (1942–45) to achieve could be achieved in three years of revised history (1943–45)?

Questions like these would be less relevant if Roth were indulging in a fable of the 'what if?' kind. But the challenge he has set himself is more rigorous. Roth is writing a realistic novel about imagined events. From the premise of the election of a fascist to the White House all else ought to follow by a logic of plausibility. That is why, in order to explain American inaction, Roth has to go to the trouble of creating a network of secret agreements between Nazi Germany and imperial Japan on the one hand, and their puppet in the White House on the other. That is why he has to revise the chronology of the war. But by the standard of plausibility to which he subjects himself, this historical framework is more than a little rickety.

In real life, Charles Lindbergh responded to Pearl Harbor by joining the war effort and flying bombing runs against the Japanese. He died in 1974. What happens to the fictional Lindbergh after October 1942, when he takes off, flying solo, and is never seen again?

We get no solid answer, only rumours. According to one rumour Lindbergh was forced down on Canadian soil by British planes.

According to the Germans he has been kidnapped by the international Jewish conspiracy. The British say that he ditched his plane in the Atlantic and was taken by U-boat to Germany. Anne Morrow Lindbergh puts out a story that the Lindbergh child was not murdered in 1932 but spirited away to Germany, where he has been held as a hostage to ensure that his parents carry out the will of their German masters; and that Charles Lindbergh himself was shot out of the skies by German agents because he was no longer deemed trustworthy. In the face of these competing versions, all that we as readers of this fictional history can say is that we do not know what happened to Lindbergh, and, more seriously, that we do not know why the Lindbergh presidency or plot had to end when it did, given that resistance to it had not got beyond the stage of speechmaking.

The spirit that reigns rather distantly over the last, hurried-sounding pages of *The Plot Against America* is that of Jorge Luis Borges. But Borges would have made better use of the layer of solid historical research on which Roth has built his book. As Lindbergh himself disappears into thin air, leaving nothing behind, so his presidency disappears, leaving its trace only on the mind of the boy who will grow into Philip Roth the writer. Save for the book we hold in our hands, there is no Lindbergh legacy. The two ghostly, parallel years in the American story – and, since the world is indivisible, in the story of the world – might as well not have occurred.

What Borges knew is that the ways of history are more complex and more mysterious than that. If there had been a President Lindbergh, our lives would be different today, probably worse, though exactly how we cannot be sure.

(2004)

IN A STORY by Nadine Gordimer dating to the 1980s, a working-class British couple take in as lodger a quiet, studious young man from the Middle East. He becomes intimate with their daughter, gets her pregnant, and proposes marriage. The parents give their dubious consent. Before he can marry the girl, however, announces the lodger, she must travel unescorted to his home country to meet his family. As he says goodbye to her at the airport, he slips explosives into her suitcase. The plane is blown up; all the passengers die, including his duped bride-to-be and their unborn child.[1]

In the story there is no indication that Gordimer has any interest in why the lodger should perform so inhuman, indeed so diabolical an act, and more generally in what forces act upon young Muslim men to drive them to acts of terror. A decade later, as if to make amends for that incuriosity, she revisits the kernel situation – the Arab who for ulterior motives woos and marries a Western woman – and finds in it the seeds of a far more original and interesting line of development. The novel *The Pickup* (2001) is the fruit of that re-exploration.[2]

Julie Summers is a white South African from a wealthy family. She is young, she has a good job, all is well in her life. One day her car breaks down in the centre of the city. The mechanic who fixes it is handsome, dark-eyed, foreign. She befriends him; eventually they have an affair.

Abdu, as he calls himself, turns out to be an 'illegal', one of the hundreds of thousands of foreigners in South Africa without papers working on the fringes of the formal economy. Most of these illegals are from other African countries, but Abdu is from an unnamed Middle Eastern country, a country without oil or other natural assets. South Africa is one of several escape routes from poverty and backwardness that Abdu has tried: he has already had spells in Britain and Germany doing jobs the locals turn up their noses at.

For the land of his birth Abdu has only contempt. It is not even a proper country, he says, just a patch of desert demarcated by lines some long-dead European drew on a map. His burning ambition is to become a legal immigrant, preferably to a wealthy Western democracy.

Sex between Abdu and Julie is wonderful; for the rest they have little in common. She reads Dostoevsky; he reads newspapers. She sees people through a template of race and class; he sees them as either legals or illegals. He dislikes her circle of friends, disaffected members of the new post-apartheid intelligentsia, black and white, of whose lifestyle he disapproves and whom he considers naïve, ignorant of the real world. He prefers her father and her father's banker colleagues, of whose crass values and moral vacuity Julie is ashamed, and who in turn want nothing to do with the penniless foreigner she has picked up.

Abdu presses Julie to enlist her family on his side in his battle to become legal. But he has left it too late: from the immigration authorities he receives notice that he is to be deported.

At this point he expects Julie to drop him, as he would drop anyone whose usefulness to him had expired. Instead she goes out and buys two air tickets, which she displays to him wordlessly. The gesture shakes him. For a moment he sees her in all her mystery, an autonomous being with hopes and desires of her own. Then the old barriers go up again: if the woman cleaves to him, it must either be because she is in thrall to him sexually or because she is playing a complicated moral game of a kind that only the idle rich have time for.

Julie's decision to accompany him home creates one practical problem. He cannot introduce to his family a woman who is no better than a whore. He will have to marry her first. So hastily they are married in a registry office.

Why has Julie taken the momentous and apparently foolish step of abandoning a not unsatisfactory life in not uninteresting surroundings to run away to a benighted corner of the world with a man who, she must know, does not love her, who switches his very smile on and off as a way of controlling her?

One reason is sex, with the meaning that Julie, with Gordimer behind her, gives to sex. Words may lie, but sex always tells the truth. Since sex with Abdu continues to be profoundly satisfying, there must be some deeply hidden potential to the relationship. Furthermore, in Julie's feelings for Abdu there is something maternal and protective. Beneath the surface of his hard male contempt she finds him touchingly boyish and vulnerable. She cannot abandon him.

Most of all, however, Julie is tired of South Africa in a way that, while it may be hard to find credible in someone so young, is all too easy to believe in someone of Gordimer's generation – tired of the daily demands that a country with a centuries-long history of exploitation and violence and disheartening contrasts of poverty and affluence makes upon the moral conscience. Wistfully Julie quotes to Abdu (who is indifferent to poetry) lines by William Plomer: 'Let us go to another country / Not yours or mine / And start again.' (p. 88) Had James Baldwin not already annexed it, *Another Country* would be a fitting title for Gordimer's book, capturing the animating concern of her duo – how to make a new life – better than *The Pickup*.

So Julie and Abdu land in Abdu's disdained country of origin, and the true name of Julie's abductor is revealed: Ibrahim ibn Musa, whose three brothers are respectively a butcher's assistant, a waiter, and a domestic servant. Ibrahim arrives not full of glory as the son who has built a successful life abroad, but as a deportee, a reject.

Having settled his wife under his mother's eye in the bleak provincial town where they live, Ibrahim repairs to the capital, where he spends his time haunting embassies, pursuing contacts, in quest of the elusive visa to the West.

For Hamlet, having to kowtow to bureaucrats is one of the insults of daily life that poisons the will to live. No one in modern times has to endure more of the insolence of office than a Third World visa petitioner. Ibrahim, however, will swallow any amount of insolence as long as the beacon of Permanent Residence continues to glow. Permanent Residence is a blessed state. Permanent Residents are the masters of the world. With their magical papers in their wallets, all doors are open to them.

What Ibrahim has to offer in return for a new life is somewhat paltry: a dubious degree from an obscure Arab university, a halting command of English, a deep thirst to shed the identity he was born into, a strategic readiness to accept the West at its own valuation, and, now, a trophy wife, 'the right kind of foreigner'. (p. 140)

While he waits for word from on high, Ibrahim sits in coffee shops with his friends talking politics. His friends are representative young Arab nationalists. They want the modern world and its appurtenances but they do not want to be taken over by it. They want to rid themselves of corrupt governments, by revolution if necessary, as long as revolution accommodates traditional morality and religion.

Ibrahim is quietly sceptical. Getting involved in the politics of the Middle East will, in his eyes, doom him to permanent residence in poverty and backwardness. His longings are of another kind; they arouse him in ways he cannot articulate, setting him apart from his fellows.

Australia turns him down, then Canada and Sweden. But after a year of petitioning the United States comes through with two visas. Ibrahim is jubilant. He and Julie will live in California ('Everyone wishes to live there'); he will go into information technology or else, with the help of Julie's stepfather, into the casino business. (p. 238) He cannot believe his ears when Julie announces she is not coming with him. She will remain with his family, she says; she has found another country, and it is not America, it is here.

Ibrahim's friends want a new, better Islam incorporating selected aspects of the West. Ibrahim's family has the same vision, though in a more down-to-earth form. They want big cars, soap operas, cell phones, household gadgets. As for the rest of the West, they prefer to have nothing to do with it. The West is a 'world of false gods'. (p. 189) They cannot understand why Ibrahim wants to go there.

One of the more plausible explanations for why, despite a century of democratic movements and uprisings, Western-type democracy has failed to take root in the Middle East is that Arab nationalists have wanted to pick and choose from the Western cornucopia, taking over science and technology and/or educational systems and/or institutions of government without being ready to absorb their philosophical underpinnings as well, the false gods of rationalism, scepticism, and materialism. If, in this account, Ibrahim's friends are in the process of falling into the same trap as their fathers and grandfathers, while Ibrahim is simply in the grip of a delusion, where does Julie stand?

Plunged into a Middle Eastern family, Julie is at first dismayed by her lowly position as a woman as well as by the absence of the comforts she is used to. But she soon knuckles under and becomes a good daughter-in-law, doing the humbler household chores, contributing to the community by offering English lessons, commencing a study of the Koran, and generally adapting to a new rhythm of life.

This is no mere show, nor is it an exercise in cultural tourism. We are unambiguously given to understand that in the course of the year she spends in Ibrahim's home Julie undergoes a funda-mental change of a spiritual if not religious nature. She begins to understand what being part of a family can mean; she also begins to understand how life can be so deeply infused with the Islamic code that everyday behaviour and religious observance can hardly be distinguished.

None of this comes about because Ibrahim's family is particu-larly exemplary. Though Ibrahim's mother, who becomes Julie's model and who gradually warms to his foreign bride, lives a deeply spiritual life, the other members of the family are unexceptional people of their place and time. Nor does the change occur because she gives herself over to Islam. Her spiritual development is effected instead by what one can only call the spirit of the place. A few blocks away from the family home starts the desert. It becomes Julie's habit to rise before dawn and sit at the edge of the desert, allowing the desert to enter her.

Ibrahim dismisses his wife's engagement with the desert as a silly romantic game. Julie herself is well aware of Western roman-ticisation of the desert, of what she calls the 'charades' of people like T. E. Lawrence and Hester Stanhope. For her the desert has another meaning, one that she can pin down only by saying that it 'is there always'. It is hard not to infer that in her lone daily confrontation with the desert, this young woman, who has already turned her back in most ways that matter on the allure of the materialistic West, is learning to face her own death. (pp. 198, 229)

In Gordimer's novel *July's People* (1981), set in a future which by good fortune did not come to pass, South Africa is plunged into civil war. A white couple, their world turned upside down, seek refuge in the back country under the wing of a former black servant. Their world picture undergoes a chastening revision. As in *The Pickup*, it is the woman rather than the man who is sensitive and pliant enough to grow from the experience.

The Pickup has an inward, spiritual dimension absent from *July's People*. But it has a comparable political thrust, not only in its exploration of the mind of the economic migrant, or one type of economic migrant, but in its critique and ultimately its dismissal of the false gods of the West, presided over by the god of market capital, to whose whims Julie's South Africa has abandoned itself so unreservedly and who has extended his sway even into Ibrahim's despised patch of sand (Ibrahim's father draws a small salary as a straw man in an international money-laundering operation).

In its inspiration *The Pickup* is clearly indebted to Albert Camus's story 'The Adulterous Woman', in which the main character, a French-Algerian woman, steals away from her husband in the night in order to expose herself to the desert and experience the mystical ecstasy, physical as much as spiritual, that it induces.[3] Despite its length, *The Pickup* is more a novella than a novel, narrower in its range than such products of Gordimer's major phase as *The Conservationist* (1974) and *Burger's Daughter* (1979). Its genre becomes clearer once a subplot concerning a gynaecologist uncle of Julie's falsely accused of unprofessional conduct – a subplot only tenuously connected with the story of Julie and Ibrahim – is stripped away.

There are other ways in which *The Pickup* is less than perfect in its narrative art. The main plot, for instance, rests on an implausibility. There is no objective need for Ibrahim to humiliate himself in quest of a visa. His wife, with an expensive education and some business experience behind her, a trust fund in her name, and a mother married to a wealthy American, could in the blink of an eyelid attain the blessed state of residence in the United States, bringing Ibrahim along under her spousal wing. If Gordimer chooses to follow an implausible plot-line, it can only be because it is imperative that her heroine end up in the Arab Middle East, not in California.

Despite such flaws, however, *The Pickup* remains a deeply interesting book, interesting as much for what it suggests about the trajectory that Gordimer's oeuvre is following as for the two types she explores in it: the confused and conflicted young man, incurious about and even blind to the history and culture that have formed him, bound to his mother in his deeper psychic life, despising the desires of his own body, imagining he can remake himself by relocating to another continent; and the unexceptional young woman who trusts her impulses and finds herself by humbling herself. Not just an interesting book, in fact, but an astonishing one: it is hard to conceive of a more sympathetic, more intimate introduction to the lives of ordinary Muslims than we are given here, and from the hand of a Jewish writer too.

If there has been a single principle that has animated Gordimer's writings from the 1960s to the democratisation of South Africa in the 1990s, it has been the quest for justice. Her good people are people unable to live in or profit by a state of injustice; the people she subjects to her coldest interrogation are those who find ways of stilling their conscience, of accommodating themselves to the world as it is.

The justice for which Gordimer hankers is broader than a just social order and a just political dispensation. In a less easily definable way, she also longs for just relations in the private realm. Gordimer's justice may thus be said to have an ideal quality. What it cannot be said to have is a spiritual dimension. The inward turn of Julie Summers, her communion with the inhuman desert, thus marks a new departure in Gordimer.

Two years after *The Pickup* Gordimer published a collection of short pieces, *Loot*, in which the spiritual turn in her thought is carried further, though not, it must be said, deeper. Pride of place in the collection belongs to a ninety-page cycle of stories called 'Karma', in which, with a more than glancing nod to Italo Calvino, Gordimer follows the adventures of a soul as it achieves or fails to achieve reincarnation in various individual human lives.

The most powerful of these stories tells of a Moscow hotel chambermaid who falls for a visiting Italian businessman and lets herself be taken to Milan. There, tiring of her, the businessman marries her off to a cousin of his, a butcher and cattle-breeder. On a visit to the enterprise where the cattle are raised, she recognises for the first time what she represents to these Western Europeans: an animal, a breeder, a female unit with a functioning reproductive system. Unwilling to play such a role, she deliberately aborts the child she is carrying, a child that might have housed the homeless soul.

In another of the 'Karma' stories a lesbian couple, liberal white South Africans with a bruising history of anti-apartheid activism behind them, decide to have a child. But then it occurs to them that they can never be sure the sperm they get from the bank will not have come from an apartheid torturer. Fearful that the being they bring into the world may reincarnate the spirit of the old South Africa, they retreat from their resolution.

In these two stories the soul has knocked at the gate but been barred from entry: for its own sake, the women who guard the gate have decided not to admit it into the world as the world presently is. In another story in the series, however, the puzzled soul is granted not just incarnation but a double incarnation in a South African trapped in limbo by the race classification laws of the old apartheid state, with a genetic identity that makes her 'white' and a social identity that makes her 'Coloured'.

The 'Karma' series blends historical critique, mainly of the new world order, with wry observations, some of them cosmic in perspective (*And this too shall pass*, Gordimer seems to be saying), some metafictional: participating in one life after another, reflects the soul, is much like being a novelist inhabiting one character after another.

The other substantial piece in *Loot* is in more familiar Gordimer vein: a report to the world on the state of Africa in the form of a story entitled 'Mission Statement'.

Roberta Blayne is British, in her forties, divorced, a cool and sensible woman. She works for an international aid agency that would, by most standards, count as enlightened: in its estimation, Africa is not 'ontologically incurable,' though the cure has not yet been found. Roberta, who in this respect embodies the subdued pessimism about earthly improvement that pervades *Loot*, shares this view.[4]

In the unnamed Anglophone African country to which she is sent, Roberta meets and has an extended affair with a senior civil servant, Gladstone Shadrack Chabruma, a married man, similarly cool and reserved. They become, in effect, a couple.

With the end of her tour of duty nearing, Chabruma proposes to Roberta that she stay behind. He will marry her: as his second

wife, the wife for official occasions, she will further his career
while at the same time she can pursue her own. It is a solution
of an African kind; his first wife, an uneducated woman characterised by a colleague of Roberta's as a 'homebody of the new
kind, [a] city peasant', will adapt. (p. 53)

As so often with Gordimer, this story operates at the inter-
section of the private and the public. Although Roberta has been
born and bred in England, she turns out to have an African skeleton
in her closet. In fact, no one in England, we are given to understand – at least no one of a certain social class – can escape the
shadow of that country's imperial entanglement with Africa. In
Roberta's case, there was a grandfather who ran a mine in this
very province, a grandfather whom she dimly recollects telling a
story of how once a week he would dispatch an African servant
to fetch a box of whisky from the store, a trip that took several
days on foot. The servant would bear the box back on his head.
'What heads they [Africans] have . . . thick as a log,' the grandfather would say, and his friends would laugh. (p. 42)

In a moving moment, Roberta lies weeping in Chabruma's
arms, owning up to this legacy of racist contempt, resisting an
urge to cradle and caress her lover's abused and insulted head. As
a writer, Gordimer is at her most powerful in such epiphanies:
gestures or configurations of bodies in which the truth of a situation emerges starkly and completely.

Chabruma tries to comfort the sorrowing Roberta. Racist talk
was 'their tradition', he says; she does not have to carry the blame
for it. (p. 65) But this puts her in a quandary: if she is to be relieved
of the burden of the past on the grounds that history is just history,
how can she reject Chabruma's argument that custom is just
custom, that his own tradition entitles him to two wives? The
story ends with Roberta in deep unease. If she were to accept
Chabruma's proposal, might it not merely be out of a wish to

atone for the past; and if she were to refuse, might that not merely be out of a Western woman's pride in what is owed to her?

Loot contains too many slight, forgettable pieces to measure up to the standard of such earlier collections as *Livingstone's Companions* (1972), *Something Out There* (1980), or *A Soldier's Embrace* (1984). One of the shorter pieces, 'The Diamond Mine', ought however to be singled out. It is a marvellously deft and confident treatment of a girl's sexual awakening, and a reminder of how well Gordimer has always written of sex.

Since early in her career Gordimer has been exercised by the question of her own place, present and future, in history. The question has two forks: What will the verdict of history be on Europe's project of colonising sub-Saharan Africa, of which she has willynilly been part; and what historical role is available to a writer like her born into a late colonial community?

The ethical framework for her own life's work was laid in the 1950s, as the iron curtain of apartheid was descending, when she first read Jean-Paul Sartre and the Algerian-born Albert Camus. Under the influence of that reading she adopted the role of witness to the fate of South Africa. 'The function of the writer,' wrote Sartre, 'is to act in such a way that nobody can be ignorant of the world and that nobody may say that he is innocent of what it is all about.'[5] The stories and novels Gordimer wrote in the next three decades are populated with characters, mainly white South Africans, living in Sartrean bad faith, pretending to themselves that they do not know what it is all about; her self-ordained task was to bring to bear on them the evidence of the real in order to crack their lie.

At the heart of the novel of realism is the theme of disillusionment. At the end of *Don Quixote*, Alonso Quixana, who had set out to right the wrongs of the world, comes home sadly aware not only that he is no hero but that in the world as it has become there can be no more heroes. As stripper-away of convenient illusions and unmasker of colonial bad faith, Gordimer is an heir of the tradition of realism that Cervantes inaugurates. Within that tradition she was able to work quite satisfactorily until the late 1970s, when she was made to realise that to black South Africans, the people to whose struggle she bore historical witness, the name Zola, to say nothing of the name Proust, carried no resonance – that she was too European to matter to the people who mattered most to her. Her essays of the period show her struggling inconclusively in the toils of the question of what it means to write *for* a people – to write for their sake and on their behalf, as well as to be read by them.[6]

With the end of apartheid and the relaxation of the ideological imperatives that under apartheid had overshadowed all cultural affairs, Gordimer was liberated from such self-laceration. The fiction she has published in the new century shows a welcome readiness to pursue new avenues and a new sense of the world. If the writing tends to be somewhat bodiless, somewhat sketchy by comparison with the writing of her major period, if the devotion to the texture of the real that characterises her best work is now only intermittent, if she is sometimes content to gesture toward what she means rather than pinning it down exactly in words, that is, one senses, because she feels she has already proved herself, does not need to perform those Herculean labours anew.

(2003)

20 Gabriel García Márquez, *Memories of My Melancholy Whores*

GABRIEL GARCÍA MÁRQUEZ's novel *Love in the Time of Cholera* (1985) ends with Florentino Ariza, at last united with the woman he has loved from afar all his life, cruising up and down the Magdalena River in a steamboat flying the yellow flag of cholera. The couple are seventy-six and seventy-two respectively.

In order to give unfettered attention to his beloved Fermina, Florentino has had to break off his current affair, a liaison with a fourteen-year-old ward of his, whom he has initiated into the mysteries of sex during Sunday-afternoon trysts in his bachelor apartment (she proves a quick learner). He gives her the brush-off over a sundae in an ice-cream parlour. Bewildered and in despair, the girl commits unobtrusive suicide, taking her secret with her to the grave. Florentino sheds a private tear and feels intermittent pangs of grief over her loss, but that is all.

América Vicuña, the child seduced and abandoned by an older man, is a character straight out of Dostoevsky. The moral frame of *Love in the Time of Cholera*, a work of considerable emotional range but a comedy nonetheless, of an autumnal variety, is simply not large enough to contain her. In his determination to treat América as a minor character, one in the line of Florentino's many mistresses, and to leave unexplored the consequences for Florentino of his offence against her, García Márquez drifts into morally unsettling territory. Indeed, there are signs that he is unsure of how to handle her story. Usually his verbal style is brisk, energetic, inventive, and uniquely his own, yet in the Sunday-afternoon scenes between Florentino and América we pick up arch echoes of Vladimir Nabokov's *Lolita*: Florentino undresses the girl 'one article of clothing at a time, with little baby games: first these little shoes for the little baby bear . . . next these little flow-ered panties for the little bunny rabbit, and a little kiss on her papa's delicious little dickey-bird'.[1]

Florentino is a lifelong bachelor, an amateur poet, a writer of love letters on behalf of the verbally challenged, a devoted concert-goer, somewhat miserly in his habits, and timid with women. Yet despite his timidity and physical unattractiveness, he has during half a century of surreptitious womanising brought off 622 conquests, on which he keeps aides-memoires in a set of notebooks.

In all of these respects Florentino resembles the unnamed narrator of García Márquez's new novella. Like his predecessor, this man keeps a list of his conquests as an aid to a book he plans to write. In fact he has a title ready in advance: *Memoria de mis putas tristes,* memoir (or memorial) of my sad whores, rendered by Edith Grossman as *Memories of My Melancholy Whores*. His list reaches 514 before he gives up counting. Then, at an advanced age, he finds true love, in the person not of woman of his own generation but of a fourteen-year-old girl.[2]

The parallels between the books, published two decades apart, are too striking to ignore. They suggest that in *Memories of My Melancholy Whores* García Márquez may be having another go at the artistically and morally unsatisfactory story of Florentino and América in *Love in the Time of Cholera*.

The hero, narrator, and putative author of *Memories of My Melancholy Whores* is born in the port city of Barranquilla,

Colombia, around 1870. His parents belong to the cultivated bourgeoisie; nearly a century later he still lives in the decaying parental
home. He used to make a living as a journalist and teacher of
Spanish and Latin; now he subsists on his pension and the weekly
column he writes for a newspaper.

The record he bequeaths us, covering the stormy ninety-first
year of his life, belongs to a specific subspecies of memoir: the
confession. As typified in the *Confessions* of Saint Augustine, the
confession tells the story of a squandered life culminating in an
inner crisis and a conversion experience, followed by spiritual
rebirth into a new and richer existence. In the Christian tradition
the confession has a strongly didactic purpose. Behold my example,
it says: behold how through the mysterious agency of the Holy
Spirit even so worthless a being as I can be saved.

The first ninety years of our hero's life have certainly been
squandered. Not only has he wasted his inheritance and his talents,
but his emotional life has been remarkably arid too. He has never
married (he was engaged long ago, but walked out on his bride
at the last minute). He has never been to bed with a woman
whom he has not paid: even when the woman has not wanted
money he has forced it on her, turning her into another of his
whores. The only enduring relationship he has had has been with
his house servant, whom he mounts ritually once a month while
she does the laundry, always *en sentido contrario*, a euphemism
which Grossman translates as 'from the back', thus making it
possible for her to claim, as an old woman, that she is still *virgo
intacta*. (p. 13)

For his ninetieth birthday, he promises himself a treat: sex with
a young virgin. A procuress named Rosa, with whom he has long
had dealings, ushers him into a room in her brothel where a
fourteen-year-old girl lies ready for him, naked and drugged.

She was dark and warm. She had been subjected to a regimen of hygiene and beautification that did not overlook even the incipient down on her pubis. Her hair had been curled, and she wore natural polish on the nails of her fingers and toes, but her molasses-colored skin looked rough and mistreated. Her newborn breasts still seemed like a boy's, but they appeared full to bursting with a secret energy that was ready to explode. The best part of her body were her large, silent-stepping feet with toes as long and sensitive as fingers. She was drenched in phosphorescent perspiration despite the fan . . . It was impossible to imagine what her face was like under the paint . . . but the adornments and cosmetics could not hide her character: the haughty nose, heavy eyebrows, intense lips. I thought: A tender young fighting bull. (pp. 25–6)

The first response of the experienced roué to the sight of the girl is unexpected: terror and confusion, an urge to run away. However, he joins her in bed and halfheartedly tries to explore between her legs. She moves away in her sleep. Drained of lust, he begins to sing to her: 'Angels surround the bed of Delgadina.' Soon he finds himself praying for her too. Then he falls asleep. When he awakes at five in the morning, the girl is lying with her arms opened in the form of a cross, 'absolute mistress of her virginity'. God bless you, he thinks, and takes his leave. (pp. 28, 29–30)

The procuress telephones to jeer at him for his pusillanimity and offer him a second chance to prove his manhood. He declines. 'I can't anymore,' he says, and at once feels relieved, 'free at last of a servitude' – servitude to sex, narrowly understood – 'that had kept me enslaved since the age of thirteen.' (p. 45)

But Rosa persists until he gives in and revisits the brothel. Again the girl is sleeping, again he does no more than wipe the perspiration off her body and sing: 'Delgadina, Delgadina, you will be

Gabriel García Márquez

my darling love.' (His song is not without dark undertones: in the fairy story Delgadina is a princess who has to flee the amorous advances of her father.) (p. 56)

He makes his way home in the midst of a mighty storm. A newly acquired cat seems to have turned into a satanic presence in the house. Rain pours through holes in the roof, a steam pipe bursts, the wind smashes the window panes. As he struggles to save his beloved books, he becomes aware of the ghostly figure of Delgadina beside him, helping him. He is certain now that he has found true love, 'the first love of my life at the age of ninety'. (p. 60) A moral revolution takes place within him. He confronts the shabbiness, meanness, and obsessiveness of his past life and repudiates it. He becomes, he says, 'another man'. It is love that moves the world, he begins to realise – not love consummated so much as love in its multiple unrequited forms. His column in the newspaper becomes a paean to the powers of love, and the reading public responds with adulation. (p. 65)

By day – though we never witness it – Delgadina, like a true fairy-tale heroine, goes off to the factory to sew buttonholes. Nightly she returns to her room in the brothel, now adorned by her lover with paintings and books (he has vague ambitions to improve her mind), to sleep chastely beside him. He reads stories to her aloud; now and again she utters words in her sleep. But on the whole he does not like her voice, which sounds like the voice of a stranger speaking from within her. He prefers her unconscious.

On the night of her birthday an erotic consummation sans penetration takes place between them.

I kissed her all over her body until I was breathless . . . As I kissed her the heat of her body increased, and it exhaled a wild, untamed fragrance. She responded with new vibrations along every inch of her skin, and on each one I found a

distinctive heat, a unique taste, a different moan, and her
entire body resonated inside with an arpeggio, and her nipples
opened and flowered without being touched. (pp. 72–3)

Then misfortune strikes. One of the clients in the brothel is
stabbed, the police pay a visit, scandal threatens, Delgadina has to
be spirited away. Though her lover scours the city for her, she
cannot be found. When at last she re-emerges in the brothel, she
seems years older and has lost her look of innocence. He flies into
a jealous rage and storms off.

Months pass, his rage dwindles. An old girlfriend offers wise
advice: 'Don't let yourself die without knowing the wonder of
fucking with love.' His ninety-first birthday comes and goes. He
makes peace with Rosa. The two agree they will jointly bequeath
their worldly goods to the girl, who, Rosa claims, has in the mean-
time fallen head over heels in love with him. Joy in his heart, the
sprightly swain looks forward to 'at last, real life'. (pp. 100, 115)

The confessions of this reborn soul may indeed have been
penned, as he says, to ease his conscience, but the message they
preach is by no means that we should abjure fleshly desires. The
god whom he has ignored all his life is indeed the god by whose
grace the wicked are saved, but he is at the same time a god of
love, one who can send an old sinner out in quest for 'wild love'
(*amor loco*, literally 'crazy love') with a virgin – 'my desire that day
was so urgent that it seemed like a message from God' – then
breathe awe and terror into his heart when he first lays eyes on
his prey. Through his divine agency the old man is turned in no
time at all from a frequenter of whores into a virgin-worshipper
venerating the girl's dormant body much as a simple believer might
venerate a statue or icon, tending it, bringing it flowers, laying
tribute before it, singing to it, praying before it. (pp. 3, 11)

★

There is always something unmotivated about conversion experiences: it is of their essence that the sinner should be so blinded by lust or greed or pride that the psychic logic leading to the turning point in his life becomes visible to him only in retrospect, when his eyes have been opened. So there is a degree of inbuilt incompatibility between the conversion narrative and the modern novel, as perfected in the eighteenth century, with its emphasis on character rather than on soul and its brief to show step by step, without wild leaps and supernatural interventions, how the one who used to be called the hero or heroine but is now more appropriately called the central character travels his or her road from beginning to end.

Despite having the tag 'magic realist' attached to him, García Márquez works very much in the tradition of psychological realism, with its premise that the operations of the individual psyche have a logic that is capable of being tracked. He himself has remarked that his so-called magic realism is simply a matter of telling hard-to-believe stories with a straight face, a trick he learned from his grandmother in Cartegena; furthermore that what outsiders find hard to believe in his stories is often commonplace Latin American reality. Whether we find this plea disingenuous or not, the fact is that the mixing of the fantastical and the real − or, to be more precise, the elision of the *either-or* holding 'fantasy' and 'reality' apart − that caused such a stir when *One Hundred Years of Solitude* came out in 1967 has become commonplace in the novel well beyond the borders of Latin America. Is the cat in *Memories of My Melancholy Whores* just a cat or is it a visitor from the underworld? Does Delgadina come to her lover's aid on the night of the storm, or does he, under the spell of love, merely imagine her visit? Is this sleeping beauty just a working-class girl earning a few pesos on the side, or is she a creature from another realm where princesses dance all night and fairy helpers perform superhuman labours and maidens are put to sleep by enchantresses? To demand unequivo-cal answers to questions like these is to mistake the nature of the storyteller's art. Roman Jakobson liked to remind us of the formula used by traditional storytellers in Majorca as a preamble to their performances: *It was and it was not so.*[3]

What is harder to accept for readers of a secular bent, since it has no apparent psychological basis, is that the mere spectacle of a naked girl can cause a spiritual somersault in a depraved old man. The old man's ripeness for conversion may make better psychological sense if we take it that he has an existence stretching back beyond the beginning of his memoir, into the body of García Márquez's earlier fiction, and specifically into *Love in the Time of Cholera*.

Measured by the highest standards, *Memories of My Melancholy Whores* is not a major achievement. Nor is its slightness just a conse-quence of its brevity. *Chronicle of a Death Foretold* (1981), for instance, though of much the same length, is a significant addition to the García Márquez canon: a tightly knit, enthralling narrative and at the same time a dizzying masterclass in how multiple histories – multiple truths – can be constructed to cover the same events. Yet the goal of *Memories* is a brave one: to speak on behalf of the desire of older men for underage girls, that is, to speak on behalf of paedophilia, or at least show that paedophilia need not be a dead end for either lover or beloved. The conceptual strategy García Márquez employs toward this end is to break down the wall between erotic passion and the passion of veneration, as manifested particu-larly in the cults of the virgin that are such a force in southern Europe and Latin America, with their strong archaic underlay, pre-Christian in the first case, pre-Columbian in the second. (As her lover's description of her makes clear, Delgadina has something of the fierce quality of an archaic virgin goddess about her: 'the haughty nose, heavy eyebrows, intense lips . . . a tender young fighting bull.')

Once we accept a continuity between the passion of sexual desire and the passion of veneration, then what originates as 'bad' desire of the kind practised by Florentino Ariza upon his ward can without changing its essence mutate into 'good' desire of the kind felt by Delgadina's lover, and thus constitute the germ of a new life for him. *Memories of My Melancholy Whores* makes most sense, in other words, as a kind of supplement to *Love in the Time of Cholera* in which the violator of the trust of the virgin child becomes her faithful worshipper.

When Rosa hears her fourteen-year-old employee referred to as Delgadina (from *la delgadez*, delicacy, shapeliness) she is taken aback and tries to tell her client the girl's humdrum real name. But he does not want to listen, just as he prefers that the girl herself should not speak. When, after her long absence from the brothel, Delgadina reappears wearing unfamiliar make-up and jewellery, he is outraged: she has betrayed not only him but her own nature. In both incidents we see him willing upon the girl an unchanging identity, the identity of a virgin princess.

The old man's inflexibility, his insistence that his beloved adhere to the form in which he has idealised her, has a looming precedent in Hispanic literature. Obeying the rule that every knight errant must have a lady to whom to dedicate his feats of arms, the old man who calls himself Don Quixote declares himself servitor to the Lady Dulcinea of Toboso. The Lady Dulcinea has some tenuous relation to a peasant girl from the village of Toboso on whom Quixote has had an eye in the past, but essentially she is a fantasy figure he has invented, as he has invented himself.

Cervantes' book begins as a send-up of the chivalric romance but turns into something more interesting: an exploration of the mysterious power of the ideal to resist disillusioning confrontations with the real. Quixote's return to sanity at the end of the book, his abandonment of the ideal world he has tried so valiantly to inhabit in favour of the real world of his detractors, strikes everyone around him, and the reader too, with dismay. Is this what we really want: to give up the world of the imagination and settle back into the tedium of life in a rural backwater in Castile?

The reader of *Don Quixote* can never be sure whether Cervantes' hero is a madman under the spell of a delusion, whether on the contrary he is consciously playing out a role – living his life as fiction – or whether his mind flickers unpredictably between states of delusion and self-awareness. There are certainly moments when Quixote seems to claim that dedicating oneself to a life of service can make one a better person, regardless of whether that service is to an illusion. 'Since I became a knight errant,' he says, 'I have been valiant, well-mannered, liberal, polite, generous, courteous, bold, gentle, patient, [and] long-suffering.' While one may have reservations about whether he has been quite as valiant, well-mannered, etc., as he claims, one cannot ignore the quite sophisticated assertion he makes about the power a dream may have to anchor our moral life, or deny that since the day Alonso Quixana took on his chivalric identity the world has been a better place; or, if not better, then at least more interesting, more lively.[4]

Quixote seems a bizarre fellow at first acquaintance, but most of those who come into contact with him end up half converted to his way of thinking, and therefore half quixotic themselves. If there is any lesson he teaches, it is that in the interest of a better, more lively world it might not be a bad idea to cultivate in oneself a capacity for dissociation, not necessarily under conscious control, even though this might lead outsiders to conclude that one suffers from intermittent delusions.

The exchanges between Quixote and the Duke and Duchess in the second half of Cervantes' book explore in depth what it means to pour one's energies into living an ideal and therefore perhaps unreal (fantastic, fictive) life. The Duchess poses the key question politely but firmly: Is it not true that Dulcinea 'does not exist in the world but is an imaginary lady and that your grace [i.e. Quixote] engendered and gave birth to her in your mind?'

'God knows if Dulcinea exists in the world or not,' replies Quixote, 'or if she is imaginary or not imaginary; these are not the kinds of things whose verification can be carried through to the end. [But] I neither engendered nor gave birth to my lady . . .' (*Don Quixote*, p. 672)

The exemplary cautiousness of Quixote's reply is evidence of a more than passing acquaintance on his part with the long debate on the nature of being from the pre-Socratics through to Thomas Aquinas. Even allowing the possibility of authorial irony, Quixote does seem to be suggesting that if we accept the ethical superiority of a world in which people act in the name of ideals over a world in which people act in the name of interests, then uncomfortable ontological questions such as the Duchess's might well be postponed or even brushed under the carpet.

The spirit of Cervantes runs deep in Spanish literature. It is not hard to see in the transformation of the nameless young factory hand into the virgin Delgadina the same process of idealisation by which the peasant girl of Toboso is transformed into the Lady Dulcinea; or, in the preference of García Márquez's hero that the object of his love remain unconscious and wordless, the same distaste for the real world in all its stubborn complexity that keeps Quixote at a safe distance from his mistress. As Quixote can claim to have become a better person through serving a woman who is unaware of his existence, so the old man of the *Memories* can claim to have arrived on the doorstep of 'at last, real life' by learning to love a girl whom he does not in any real sense know and who certainly does not know him. (The most quintessentially Cervantean moment of the memoir occurs when its author gets to see the bicycle on which his beloved rides – or is claimed to ride – to work, and in the fact of a real-life bicycle finds 'tangible proof' that the girl with the fairy-tale name – whose bed he has shared night after night – 'existed in real life'.) (pp. 115, 71)

In his autobiography *Living to Tell the Tale*, García Márquez tells the story of the composition of his first extended fiction, the novella 'Leaf Storm' (1955). Having – as he thought – finalised the manuscript, he showed it to his friend Gustavo Ibarra, who to his dismay pointed out that the dramatic situation – the struggle to get a man buried against the resistance of the authorities, civic and clerical – was lifted from Sophocles' *Antigone*. García Márquez reread *Antigone* 'with a strange mixture of pride at having coincided in good faith with so great a writer, and sorrow at the public embarrassment of plagiarism'. Before publishing, he revised the manuscript drastically and added an epigraph from Sophocles to signal his debt.[5]

Sophocles is not the only writer to have left a mark on García Márquez. His earlier fiction bears the imprint of William Faulkner to such an extent that he can justly be called Faulkner's most devoted disciple.

In the case of *Memories*, the debt to Yasunari Kawabata is conspicuous. In 1982 García Márquez wrote a story, 'Sleeping Beauty and the Airplane', in which Kawabata is specifically alluded to. Seated in the first-class cabin of a jet crossing the Atlantic beside a young woman of extraordinary beauty who sleeps throughout the flight, García Márquez's narrator is reminded of a novel by Kawabata about ageing men who pay money to spend nights with drugged, sleeping girls. As a work of fiction the 'Sleeping Beauty' story is undeveloped, no more than a sketch. Perhaps for this reason, García Márquez feels free to re-use its basic situation – the no longer young admirer side by side with the sleeping girl – in *Memories of My Melancholy Whores*.[6]

In Kawabata's 'House of the Sleeping Beauties' (1961) a man on the brink of old age, Yoshio Eguchi, resorts to a procuress who supplies drugged girls for men with specialised tastes. Over a period of time he spends nights with several of these girls. The house rules forbidding sexual penetration are mainly superfluous, since most of the clientele is old and impotent. But Eguchi – as he keeps telling himself – is neither. He flirts with the idea of breaking the rules, of raping one of the girls, impregnating her, even asphyxiating her, as a way of showing his manhood and his defiance of a world that treats old men like children. At the same time he is attracted by the thought of overdosing and dying in the arms of a virgin.

Kawabata's novella is a study of the activities of eros in the mind of a sensualist of an intensive and self-aware kind, acutely – perhaps morbidly – sensitive to odours and fragrances and nuances of touch, absorbed by the physical uniqueness of the women he is intimate with, prone to brood on images from his sexual past, not afraid to confront the possibility that his attraction toward young women may screen desire for his own daughters, or that his obsession with women's breasts may originate in infantile memories.

Above all, the isolated room containing only a bed and a living body to be handled or mishandled, within limits, as he pleases, unwitnessed and therefore at no risk of being shamed, constitutes a theatre in which Eguchi can confront himself as he really is, old and ugly and soon to die. His nights with the nameless girls are filled with melancholy rather than joy, with regret and anguish rather than physical pleasure.

The ugly senility of the sad men who came to this house was not many years away for Eguchi himself. The immeasurable expanse of sex, its bottomless depth – what part of it had Eguchi known in his sixty-seven years? And around the old men, new flesh, young flesh, beautiful flesh was forever being born. Were not the longing of the sad old men for the unfinished dream, the regret for days lost without ever being had, concealed in the secret of this house?[7]

García Márquez does not so much imitate Kawabata as respond to him. His hero is very different in temperament from Eguchi, less complex in his sensualism, less inward-looking, less of an explorer, less of a poet too. But it is in what goes on in bed in the respective secret houses that the true distance between García Márquez and Kawabata must be measured. In bed with Delgadina, García Márquez's old man finds a new and elevating joy. To Eguchi, on the other hand, it remains an endlessly frustrating mystery that unconscious female bodies, whose use can be bought by the hour and whose floppy, mannequin-like limbs can be disposed as the client wishes, should have such power over him that they bring him back to the house again and again.

The question regarding all sleeping beauties is of course what will happen when they awake. In Kawabata's book there is, symbolically speaking, no awakening: the sixth and last of Eguchi's girls dies at his side, poisoned by the drug that sent her to sleep. In García Márquez, on the other hand, Delgadina seems to have absorbed through her skin all the attentions that have been poured on her, and to be on the point of waking, ready to love her worshipper in return.

García Márquez's version of the tale of the sleeping beauty is thus much sunnier than Kawabata's. Indeed, in the abruptness of its ending it seems deliberately to close its eyes to the question of the future of any old man with a young love, once the beloved is permitted to step off her goddess pedestal. Cervantes has his hero visit the village of Toboso and present himself on his knees to a girl chosen almost at random to be the embodiment of

Dulcinea. For his pains he is rewarded with an earful of pungent peasant abuse flavoured with raw onion, and quits the scene confused and discomfited.

It is not clear that García Márquez's little fable of redemption would be sturdy enough to bear a conclusion of this kind. García Márquez might take a look too at the Merchant's tale, the sardonic story of cross-generational marriage in Chaucer's *Canterbury Tales*, and in particular at its snapshot of the couple caught in the clear dawn light after the exertions of their bridal night, the old husband sitting up in bed in his nightcap, the slack skin of his neck quivering, the young wife beside him consumed in irritation and distaste.

(2005)

21   V. S. Naipaul: *Half a Life*

DURING THE 1930S the English writer W. Somerset Maugham (1874–1965) developed an interest in Indian spirituality. He visited Madras and was taken to an ashram to meet a man who, born Venkataraman, had retreated into a life of silence, self-mortification, and prayer, and was now known simply as the Maharshi. While waiting for his audience, Maugham fainted, perhaps because of the heat. When he came to, he found he could not speak (it must be mentioned that Maugham was a lifelong stammerer). The Maharshi comforted him by pronouncing that 'Silence is also conversation.'[1]

News of his fainting fit, according to Maugham, spread across India. Through the powers of the Maharshi, the rumour went, a pilgrim from the West had briefly been translated into the realm of the infinite. Though Maugham had no recollection of any visit to the infinite, the encounter clearly left a mark on him: he describes it in *A Writer's Notebook* (1949) and again in an essay in *Points of View* (1958); he also works it into *The Razor's Edge* (1944), the novel with which he made his name in the United States.

The Razor's Edge has as its hero an American who, having prepared himself by acquiring a deep tan and adopting Indian garb, visits the guru Shri Ganesha and under his guidance has an ecstatic spiritual experience, 'an experience of the same order as the mystics have had all over the world through the centuries'. With Shri Ganesha's blessing, this proto-hippie returns to Illinois, where he plans to practise 'calmness, forbearance, compassion, self-lessness and continence' while making a living as a taxi-driver. 'It's a mistake to think that those holy men of India lead useless lives,' he says. 'They are a shining light in the darkness.'[2]

The story of the meeting between Venkataraman the holy man and Maugham the writer, and their happy collaboration, Venkataraman providing Maugham with a marketable version of Indian spirituality, Maugham providing Venkataraman with publicity and floods of business, is the germ of V. S. Naipaul's 2001 novel *Half a Life*.[3]

In the novel Naipaul is concerned less with the question of whether Venkataraman and similar dispensers of gnomic wisdom are fakes – he takes that as read – than with the more general phenomenon of religious practice that centres on self-denial. Why do people – in India in particular – choose to pursue lives of fasting, celibacy, and silence? Why are they revered for it? What human consequences follow from their example of sanctity?

To understand the prestige of self-denial, Naipaul suggests, we need to see Indian asceticism historically. Once upon a time Hindu temples supported an entire priestly caste. Then, as a consequence of foreign invasions, first Muslim, later British, the temples lost their revenues. Temple priests became trapped in a vicious cycle: poverty led to loss of energy and desire, which led to passivity, which led to deeper poverty. The caste seemed to be in terminal decline. Instead of quitting the temples and finding some other source of support, however, priests came up with an ingenious transvaluation of values: going without food, and denial of the appetites in general, was propagated as admirable in itself, worthy of veneration and hence of tribute.

This, in summary, is Naipaul's briskly materialist account of how a Brahmin ethos of self-denial and fatalism, an ethos that scorns individual enterprise and hard work, gained the high ground in India.

In Naipaul's rewriting of the Venkataraman story, a nineteenth-century Brahmin named Chandran has the gumption to break out of the temple system. He saves his pennies, journeys to the nearest big town – the capital of one of the nominally independent back-water states in British India – and finds a job as a clerk in the maharajah's palace. After him his son continues the climb of the family through the ranks of the civil service. All seems well: the Chandrans have found a safe niche for themselves where they can quietly prosper without any longer having to mortify their bodies.

But the grandson (we are now in the 1930s) is a rebel of a kind. Rumours of Gandhi and his nationalist movement abound. The Mahatma calls for a boycott of universities. The grandson (henceforth called simply Chandran) obeys the call by burning his Shelley and Hardy in the college yard (he does not like literature anyway) and waiting for a storm to break over his head. But no one, it appears, has noticed.

Gandhi proclaims that the caste system is wrong. How does a Brahmin fight the caste system? Answer: by marrying down. Chandran picks out an ugly, dark-skinned girl in his class belonging to a so-called backward caste – in everyday parlance, a 'backward' – and pays court to her in clumsy fashion. In no time at all, using lies and threats, the girl has compelled him to make good on his promises and marry her.

In disgrace with his family, Chandran is put to work in the maharajah's tax office. There he indulges in surreptitious acts of what he tells himself is civil disobedience, though his true motives are simply idle and malicious. When his mischief-making is exposed and he is threatened with the law, he has a stroke of genius: he takes sanctuary in one of the temples, and there protects himself from what he chooses to call persecution by taking a vow of silence. His vow turns him into a local hero. People come to watch him being silent and to bring offerings.

It is into this morass of deceit and hypocrisy that the gullible Westerner William Somerset Maugham treads, come to find out the deeper truth that only India can tell. 'Are you happy?' Maugham asks the holy man Chandran. Using pencil and pad, Chandran replies: 'Within my silence I feel quite free. That is happiness.' (p. 30) *What wisdom!* thinks Maugham. The comedy is rich: the principal freedom Chandran enjoys is freedom from prosecution.

Maugham publishes a book about his visit, and Chandran is suddenly famous at home – famous for having been written about by a foreigner. (Chandran is not just famous in India: he joins a growing list of minor characters – one thinks of Rosencrantz and Guildenstern or of Rochester's wife in *Jane Eyre* – who find themselves whipped out of their original literary environment and given grander roles in other books.) Visitors from abroad follow in Maugham's footsteps. To them Chandran repeats his story of a glittering career in the civil service sacrificed for a life of prayer and self-sacrifice. Soon he comes to believe his own lies. Following in the footsteps of his Brahmin ancestors, he has found a way of repudiating the world yet prospering. He sees no irony in this. Instead he feels awe: a higher power must be guiding him.

Like Kafka's hunger artist, Chandran makes a living doing what he secretly finds easy: denying his appetites (though his appetites are not so exiguous that he cannot father two children on his backward wife). In Kafka's story, despite the hunger artist's protest-ations to the contrary, there is a certain heroism in self-starving, a minimal heroism befitting post-heroic times. In Chandran there is no heroism at all: it is authentic poverty of spirit that allows him to be content with so little.

In his first and most critical book about India, *An Area of Darkness* (1964), Naipaul describes Gandhi as a man deeply influenced by Christian ethics, capable, after twenty years spent in South Africa, of seeing India with the critical eye of an outsider, and in this sense 'the least Indian of Indian leaders'. But India turned the tables on Gandhi, says Naipaul: by transforming him into a mahatma, an icon, it enabled itself to ignore his social message.[4]

Chandran likes to think of himself as a follower of Gandhi. But, Naipaul suggests implicitly, the question Chandran continually asks of himself is not the Gandhian 'How shall I act?' but the Hindu 'What shall I give up?' He prefers giving up to acting in the world because giving up costs him nothing.

In honour of his British patron, Chandran names his first-born William Somerset Chandran. Since young Willie comes from a mixed (that is, mixed-caste) marriage, it is thought prudent to send him to a Christian school. Predictably, Willie learns from his Canadian missionary teachers to aspire to be a missionary and a Canadian too. In his English compositions he fantasises himself as a regular Canadian boy with a 'Mom' and a 'Pop' and a family car. His teachers reward him with high marks, though his father is hurt to find himself written out of his son's life.

In due course, however, Willie finds out what the missionaries are really up to: making converts to Christianity, destroying heathen religion. Feeling fooled, he stops going to school.

Calling in old debts, Chandran writes to Maugham asking him to pull strings on the boy's behalf. He gets a typewritten letter back: 'Dear Chandran, It was very nice getting your letter. I have nice memories of the country, and it is nice hearing from Indian friends. Yours very sincerely . . .' (p. 47) Other foreign friends prove equally evasive. Then someone in the British House of Lords waves a wand and Willie, at the age of twenty, is whisked across the seas on a scholarship.

The year is 1956. London is bursting at the seams with immigrants from the Caribbean. Before long race riots have broken out: young whites in mock Edwardian clothes roam the streets looking for blacks to beat up. Willie hides in his college rooms. Hiding out is a not unfamiliar experience: it is what he did at home when there were caste riots.

What Willie learns about in London is, principally, sex. The girlfriend of a Jamaican fellow student takes pity on him and relieves him of his virginity. She then gives him a useful little cross-cultural lecture. Because marriages in India are arranged, she says, Indian men don't feel they need to satisfy a woman sexually. But things are different in England. He should try harder.

Willie consults a paperback called *The Physiology of Sex* and learns that the average man can maintain an erection for ten or fifteen minutes. Dismayed, he puts the book down and refuses to read further. How is he, an incompetent and a late starter, coming from a country where sex is not spoken about and there is no such thing as an art of seduction, going to acquire a girlfriend?

How can I find out more about sex, he asks his Jamaican friend? Sex is a brutal business, the friend replies; you have to start young. In Jamaica we get our experience by forcing ourselves on little girls.

Willie plucks up enough courage to approach a streetwalker. Their intercourse is joyless and humiliating. 'Fuck like an Englishman,' she commands when he takes too long. (p. 113)

Chandran the charlatan *sadhu* and his son the inept lover: they might seem the stuff of comedy, but not in Naipaul's hands. Naipaul has always been a master of analytical prose, and the prose of *Half a Life* is as clean and cold as a knife. The male Chandrans are defective human beings whose incompleteness chills rather than amuses; the backward wife and the sister, who grows into a smug left-wing fellow-traveller, are little better.

Both father and son believe they see through other people. But if they detect lies and self-deception all around them, that is only because they are incapable of imagining anyone unlike themselves. Their shrewdness of insight is grounded in nothing but a self-protective reflex of suspicion. Their rule of thumb is always to give the least charitable interpretation. Self-absorption, minginess of spirit, rather than inexperience, is at the root of Willie's failures in love.

As for Willie's father, a measure of his constitutional meanness is his response to books. As a student he finds he does not 'understand' the courses he is taking, and in particular does not 'understand' literature. (p. 10) The education he is subjected to, principally English literature taught by rote, is certainly irrelevant to his daily life. Nevertheless, there is in him a deep impulse *not* to understand, *not* to learn. He is, strictly speaking, ineducable. His bonfire of the classics is not a healthily critical response to a deadening colonial education. It does not free him for another, better kind of education, for he has no idea of what a good education might be. In fact, he has no ideas at all.

Willie is similarly blank-minded. Arriving in Britain, he is soon made aware of how ignorant he is. But in a typical reflex action he finds someone else to blame, in this case his mother: he is incurious about the world because he is the child of a backward. Inheritance is character is fate.

College life reveals to him that Indian etiquette and British etiquette are equally quaint and irrational. But this insight does not spell the beginning of self-knowledge. *I know about both India and England*, he reasons, *whereas the English know only about England, therefore I am free to say what I like about my country and my background.* He invents a new and less shameful past for himself, turning his mother into a member of an ancient Christian community and his father into the son of a courtier. The act of refashioning himself excites him, gives him a feeling of power.

Why are this unappealing father and son the way they are? What do they reveal – what, in Naipaul's hands, are they intended to reveal – about the society that produced them? The key word here is *sacrifice*. Willie has been quick to identify the joylessness at the heart of his father's brand of Gandhianism because he knows at first hand what it is like to be given up. One of the stories Willie writes as a schoolboy is about a Brahmin who ritually sacrifices 'backward' children for the sake of riches, and ends up sacrificing his own two children. It is this story, titled 'A Life of Sacrifice', with its not so covert accusation against him, that determines Chandran the father – a man who makes a living out of what he calls self-sacrifice – to send his son away to a foreign country: 'The boy will poison what remains of my life. I must get him far away from here.' (p. 42)

What Willie has detected is that sacrificing your desires means, in practice, not loving the people you ought to love. Chandran reacts to detection by pushing the loveless sacrifice of his son one step further. Behind Chandran's fiction that he has sacrificed a career for the sake of a life of self-mortification lies a Hindu tradition embodied, if not in Gandhi himself (whom Willie and his mother despise), then in what Indians like Chandran have made of Gandhi in turning him into the national holy man; embodied more generally in a fatalistic philosophy that teaches that best is least, that striving toward self-improvement is ultimately pointless.

Though bored by his studies, Willie clearly has gifts as a writer. At the prompting of an English friend to whom he shows the stories he wrote at school, he reads Hemingway. Using 'The Killers' as his prime model, translating situations from Hollywood movies into vaguely conceived Indian settings, splicing stories from London onto stories he remembers from home, he throws himself into a fury of composition. To his surprise he finds that he can be truer to his own feelings when he uses situations from far outside his own experience and characters who are quite unlike him than in putting together 'cautious, half-hidden parables' of the type he had written at school. (p. 82)

Naipaul has often in the past mined his own life story for his fiction. In certain respects the apprentice writer W. S. Chandran is based on the apprentice writer V. S. Naipaul. Chandran may be less widely read than Naipaul at the same age (Naipaul could call on as literary models Evelyn Waugh, Aldous Huxley, and, for his characteristically English tone, 'aloof everywhere, unsurprised, immensely knowing', Somerset Maugham).[5] On the other hand, both find literary inspiration in Hollywood; and in Willie's discovery that he is truest to himself when he seems most remote it is hard not to hear his author responding anachronistically to the orthodoxy that the writer should write from the position of his or her nationality, race, and gender.

For weeks on end Willie is absorbed in composing his fictions. But as his writing leads him inexorably to questions he does not want to face, he begins to falter, then quits. Never again in his life – at least in the life we read of in *Half a Life* – does he take up the pen.

He emerges from the creative storm with a manuscript of twenty-six stories, which he offers to a sympathetic publisher. The book, when it comes out, is barely noticed, and by that time he is anyhow ashamed of it. But he does get a fan letter from a girl with a Portuguese name. 'In your stories for the first time I find moments that are like moments in my own life,' she writes. (p. 116) Knowing how his stories were put together, Willie finds this hard to believe. Nevertheless the two arrange to meet, and they fall in love. Her name is Ana; she is heiress to an estate in Mozambique. On an impulse, Willie follows Ana to Africa and spends eighteen years there as her kept man. The second half of *Half a Life* is taken up with the story of those years. Deeply interesting though it is, this second half provides nothing to match, in depth of analysis, the story of the Chandrans, father and son.

Naipaul's India is abstract and his London sketchy, but his Mozambique is convincingly realised. Mozambique of colonial times produced no writers of stature. The best-known Mozambiquan writer today, Mia Couto, belongs to the post-independence generation, and is anyhow too much under the sway of magic realism to be relied on as a chronicler of his country's past. Thus Naipaul would seem to be free to invent a fantasy antebellum Mozambique of his own. But he does not do so. His allegiance is to the real, to real history as borne by real people; the second part of *Half a Life* has a strongly journalistic flavour, with Willie Chandran used as medium for representative vignettes of colonial life. This part of the novel adheres in fact to a mode of writing that Naipaul has perfected over the years, in which historical reportage and social analysis flow into and out of autobiographically coloured fiction and travel memoir – a mixed mode that may turn out to be his principal legacy to English letters.

The picture we get of Mozambique in its last years under Portuguese rule (Willie spends the years 1959–77 there) is fresh and surprising. Ana is a Creole, an Africanised Portuguese. On the social scale, this ranks her below European-born Portuguese but above *mestizos*, who are in turn above blacks. To Willie, coming from caste-bound India, minute social gradations based on parentage are of course far from strange.

The circle in which Ana and Willie move is made up of plantation owners and farm managers; social life consists of visits with neighbours and trips to town for supplies. Willie (who is in this respect indistinguishable from his author) explores this settler way of life without the condescension one might expect of a *bien-pensant* Western liberal. In fact he approves of Creole society, notably of the opportunities it allows for sexual variety. Even when the guerrillas close in and the end grows nigh, his settler friends go on 'enjoying the moment, filling the old room with talk and laughter, like people who didn't mind, like people who knew how to live with history'. 'I never admired the Portuguese as much as I admired them then,' he reflects afterwards. 'I wished it was possible for me to live as easily with the past.' (pp. 187–8)

The freedom to swim against the stream evinced here is consistent with Naipaul's attitude toward his own colonial past, namely that descent from indentured Indian plantation workers need not be allowed to slot one into lifelong psychic victimage. When Naipaul looks back with an historian's eye over imperialism, colonialism, and slavery, he takes in more than just the Western varieties. Thus he sees India as more deeply marked by its subjection to the rule of the Muslim Moghuls than of the British. Europeans are not the only foreigners to have settled in Africa. The East African littoral has absorbed Arabs and Indians as well as Europeans, and Africanised them.

One strand of Naipaul's complex self-conception and self-creation is as participant in the reconquest of Britain by former subject peoples. 'In 1950 in London,' he writes in *The Enigma of Arrival*, 'I was at the beginning of that great movement of peoples that was to take place in the second half of the twentieth century – a movement and a cultural mixing greater than the peopling of the United

States.' (p. 141) *The Enigma of Arrival* itself is the story of a man arriving in England from the ex-Empire to explore and finally settle in rural Wiltshire, one of the so-called home counties.

Migrants of the kind that Naipaul writes about had received a colonial education that was comically old-fashioned by metropolitan standards. That very education, however, made of them trustees of a culture that had decayed in the 'mother' country. 'Indians are the only surviving Englishmen,' said Malcolm Muggeridge famously.[6] The often magisterial stance that Naipaul adopts in his books is more Victorian that any indigenous Briton would dare to command.

The adventures Willie Chandran has in Africa turn out to be mainly sexual. His relations with Ana are not passionate for long. Soon he begins to visit African prostitutes, many of them, by Western standards, children. From child prostitutes he graduates to an affair with a friend of Ana's named Graca, and Graca shows him how brutal sex can be. 'How terrible it would have been,' he thinks afterwards, 'if . . . I had died without knowing this depth of satisfaction, this other person that I had just discovered within myself.' With uncharacteristic sympathy his thoughts go to his parents in benighted India, to 'my poor father and mother who had known nothing like this moment'. (pp. 190, 191)

Willie has one more step to climb in his sexual ascent. With delicate obliqueness, Ana gives him to understand that Graca is mentally unstable. And indeed, as the Portuguese troops pull out and the guerrillas move in, Graca falls into a mania of self-abasement. Willie begins to see why religions condemn sexual extremism. Anyhow, he has grown tired of his colonial adventure. He is forty-one; half his life is over; he takes leave of Ana, retreats to his sister in the snows of Germany; the book ends.

Half a Life is the story of the progress of a man from a loveless beginning to a solitary end that may turn out to be not an end, just a plateau of rest and recuperation. The experiences that bring about his progress are sexual in nature. The women with whom he has them figure as objects of desire, repugnance, or fascination – sometimes all three – reported on with a mercilessly unclouded eye.

In the London part of the book we visit, for the third or fourth time in Naipaul's oeuvre, since *The Mimic Men* of 1967, the upstairs room with the naked electric bulb and the mattress on newspapers on the floor where the young man first has sex. Each time the scene is reworked; progressively it has become more bestial and more desperate. It is as though Naipaul will not let go of the scene until he has wrung a last meaning from it that it will not yield.

In Africa, as he embraces his first child prostitute, the ghosts of the women from his London past rise up before him. But just as he is about to falter, 'an extraordinary look of command and aggression and need filled [the girl's] eyes, her body became all tension, and I was squeezed by her strong hands and legs. In a split-second – like the split-second of decision when I looked down a gun-sight – I thought, "This is what Alvaro [the friend who has brought him to the brothel] lives for," and I revived.' After that experience 'I began to live with a new idea of sex . . . It was like being given a new idea of myself.' (p. 175)

The moment with the girl evokes the unlikely other passion Willie has discovered in Africa: guns. Aiming and pulling the trigger becomes, for him, an existential testing of the truth of the will, at a level beyond the reach of rational control. The African women he sleeps with test the truth of his desire in an equally naked way.

It is in identifying the sexual embrace as the ultimate testing-place of the truth of the self that Naipaul comes closest to articulating the nature of the spiritual journey Willie Chandran is engaged on, and to measuring his distance from a way of life – represented, if only parodically, by his father – that treats denial of desire as the road to enlightenment. Impersonal though they may be, it is through his intimate encounters with African women that Willie is able to exorcise the ghosts of London. Yet what is so different about these African women? Watching a covey of girls dancing provocatively before their clients, he glimpses the answer: they embody something beyond their individual selves, some inscrutable 'deeper spirit'. 'I began to have an idea that there was something in the African heart that was shut away from the rest of us, and beyond politics.' (p. 173)

Naipaul knows Africa well. He has lived and worked in East Africa: 'Home Again,' in *A Way with the World* (1994), is based on his time there. *In a Free State* (1971) and *A Bend in the River* (1979) are both 'about' Africa. Overall, Naipaul's vision of Africa has remained remarkably constant, one might even say rigid. Africa is a dreamlike and threatening place that resists understanding, that eats away at reason and the technological products of reason. Joseph Conrad, the man from the fringes of the West who became a classic of English literature, has been one of Naipaul's lifelong masters. For good or ill, Naipaul's Africa, with its images of rusting industrial machinery overgrown with forest vines, comes out of *Heart of Darkness*.

Half a Life does not give the impression of having been carefully worked on, and the technical weaknesses that result are not negligible. Naipaul's plan is to present the whole story as if recounted by Willie. Even the story of Chandran *père* is to be based on what Willie heard from his lips. But the plan is carried out only halfheartedly. Despite the coldness between father and son, Willie is given access to his father's most secret feelings, including his physical repugnance at his wife. At moments the pretence that Willie is guiding the story line is dropped in favour of interventions from an old-fashioned omniscient narrator.

There are other weaknesses too. Scenes of literary life in London read as if from a satirical *roman à clef* to which most readers will lack the key. The youthful Willie's love for Ana comes close to falling into cliché. Most strikingly of all, Willie's story ends not only without a resolution but without any glimpse of what such a resolution might be. *Half a Life* reads like the cut-off first half of a book that might be called *A Full Life*.

Strictures such as these will not trouble Naipaul. In his view the novel as a vehicle for creative energies reached its high point in the nineteenth century; to write impeccably crafted novels in our day is to indulge in antiquarianism. Given his own achievements in pioneering an alternative, fluid, semifictional form, this is a view worth taking seriously.

Nevertheless one is left at the end of *Half a Life* with the feeling that not only Willie Chandran but Naipaul himself does not know what will happen next. And what indeed does a forty-one-year-old refugee do who has never worked for a living and has only one accomplishment to his name, a book of stories published decades ago? Who is Willie Chandran anyway? Why is Naipaul, a prolific and famous writer, pouring his energies into an anti-self whose distinguishing mark is that he has turned his back on what might have become a literary career?

One of the more consistent strains in the story Naipaul tells of his own life is that it was by a pure effort of will that he became a writer. He was not gifted with fantasy; he had only his childhood in paltry Port of Spain to call on, no larger historical memory (this was where Trinidad failed him, and, behind Trinidad, India); he seemed to have no subject. Only after a decades-long labour of writing did he finally come to the Proustian realisation that he had known his true subject all along, and his subject was himself – himself and his efforts, as a colonial raised in a culture that did not (he was told) belong to him and without (he was told) a history, to find a way in the world.

Willie is not Naipaul, and the outline of Willie's life only intermittently corresponds with his creator's. Nevertheless, when it explores self-denial and what an ingrained heritage of self-denial turns into when it is itself denied, *Half a Life* carries the urgent and unmistakable accents of personal truth.[7] Is it possible that the immense feat of self-construction that Naipaul undertook during his third and fourth decades seems in retrospect to have exacted too high a price in denial of the body and its appetites, a price amounting to no less than half of a human life?

In the person of Chandran senior, Naipaul has diagnosed self-denial as the road of weakness taken by loveless spirits, an essentially magic way of winning victories in the natural dialectic between a desiring self and a resistant real world by suppressing desire itself. In the life-story of Chandran junior, Naipaul has tracked the unhappy consequences of being nurtured in such a culture of self-denial.

It is instructive to read the story of Willie Chandran side by side with the story that Anita Desai tells in her novel *Fasting, Feasting* (2000) of a young man similarly transported from his Indian home to a land where appetite reigns.[8]

Like Willie, Desai's Arun has been brought up under the rule of a father to whose standards he can never quite measure up. Like Willie, Arun wins a scholarship and finds himself more or less rudderless in a foreign city, in this case Boston, where he finds lodgings off campus in the home of an American family named Patton. His host-father, he discovers, is a hearty carni-

vore who likes to barbecue steaks on the patio. Mealtimes become
rituals of embarrassment: his caste rules forbid the eating of meat,
and though the taboo was not observed in his home, Arun finds
meat distasteful. His dietary habits soon become a pretext for a
feud between the Pattons. Mrs Patton declares herself a convert
to vegetarianism and produces for Arun her version of a meat-
less diet: lettuce and tomato sandwiches, cereal and milk.
Enveloped in woe, he dutifully eats: 'How was he to tell [her]
. . . that his digestive system did not know how to turn [this
food] into nourishment?' She even persuades him to cook, and
with feigned enjoyment swallows down the unappetising messes
that the morose boy – who in India never saw the inside of a
kitchen, having been waited on by servants and sisters – dishes
up. (p. 185)

Mr Patton and his son Rod retreat in bafflement to the barbecue,
while the daughter of the family hides out in her bedroom,
devouring chocolate bars and vomiting them up, loathing herself
all the time. In the bulimic girl Arun sees an uncanny resemblance
to his epileptic elder sister, who, unable to find words for her
protest against having 'her unique and singular being and its
hungers' ignored, resorts to frothing at the mouth. How strange,
he thinks, to encounter the same sort of hunger in America, 'where
so much is given, where there is both licence and plenty'. When
he had first arrived, he had exulted in anonymity: 'no past, no
family . . . no country.' But he has not escaped family after all, just
found a 'plastic representation' of it. What he had in India was
'plain, unbeautiful, misshapen, fraught and compromised'. What he
has found in its stead in America is 'clean, bright, gleaming, without
taste, savour or nourishment,' and equally loveless. (pp. 214, 172,
185)

The gross excess of food that Arun encounters in America, and
the dysfunctional dietary habits of the Patton household, clearly

bear a relation, albeit a skewed relation, to the feasting of Desai's title. What of fasting?

Arun is too young and unsure of himself to repudiate the way of life exemplified by the Pattons. Dutifully he tries to emulate the athletic exploits of Rod Patton. But it soon becomes clear to him that 'a small, underdeveloped and asthmatic boy from the Gangetic plains, nourished on curried vegetables and stewed lentils', can never hope to compete with a specimen of well-nourished American manhood. One way of remedying this state of affairs would be to switch from an Indian to an American diet, to cease being a faster and become a feaster too. But this is not a step he finds himself capable of taking. Arun remains vegetarian for reasons that are neither religious nor ethical and are certainly not social. By temperament or perhaps simply by physiological make-up he is not a carnivore. Flesh and (when Mrs Patton dons her swimsuit) fleshiness repel him, not because his dietary taboos have been insulted or because he is a moral puritan but because in his being he is an ascetic, just as in her being his epileptic sister is a religious devotee. The pathos of the boy – it is hard to call it tragedy, since Desai works with so determinedly muted a palette – is that he is barely able to find words for his misery, much less articulate its wider significance, namely that the modern world, including India in its modern aspect, offers less and less of a home to the fasting temperament. (p. 191)

Even at home in India, Arun's vegetarianism has been a source of strife. His father wants him to play manly sports and more generally be a success in life, by which he means that he should be less fatalistic and more enterprising, less passive and more active, less feminine and more masculine, less of an Indian and more of a Westerner. Having tried and failed to build up Arun's strength by feeding him beef, he interprets the boy's distaste for meat as a reprehensible atavism, a turning back to 'the ways of the forefathers, meek and puny men who had got nowhere in life'. (p. 33)

Consciously or not, Arun and his father thus embody the two sides, traditional and progressive, of a debate on national character that goes back to the mid-nineteenth century, a debate set going by the Hindu reformers Swami Dayanand Saraswati (1824–1883) and Swami Vivekananda (1863–1902). Both Saraswati and Vivekananda saw the Hindus of their day as having lost touch with the masculine, martial values of their ancestors; both advocated a return to 'Aryan' values, a return that would, if necessary, have to be accomplished by incorporating those features of the culture of their colonial overlords that most evidently gave the British their power. In the sphere of religion, Hinduism would have to be organised like a Christian church, with clear lines of internal governance. At a philosophical level, it might have to be accepted that history is linear rather than cyclical, and therefore that progress is not an illusion. At a more mundane level, dietary taboos might have to be relaxed: in a moment of what the historian Ashis Nandy brands as 'terrible defeatism', Vivekananda advocated that Hindus look to the three B's for salvation: Bhagvad-Gita, biceps, and beef.[9]

The tussle between Arun and his father over the Brahmanic taboo on beef is thus more than a simple family quarrel. The two stand for opposed views on what price the Hindu – and the Indian – should be prepared to pay – what he is required to give up – to become an actor in the modern world. In his confused and utterly unheroic refusal of the beef that Mr Patton slaps down on his plate, his reluctance to deny what looks to the strangers like self-denial, and more generally in his failure to find in the New World feast the kind of food that will nourish him, Arun not only preserves a minimal personal integrity but complicates and casts doubt over prescriptions like Willie Chandran's for getting on in the world. At a precultural level, the level of the body itself, he resists the pressures of assimilation: this 'under-developed' Indian body is not an American body and will never become one.

(2001)

Notes and References

1 Italo Svevo

1 Livia Veneziani Svevo, *A Memoir of Italo Svevo*, translated by Isabel Quigly (Evanston: Northwestern University Press, 2001).

2 *Italo Svevo: The Man and the Writer* (London: Secker, 1966), p. 172.

3 Italo Svevo, *Zeno's Conscience*, translated and with an introduction by William Weaver (New York: Knopf, 2001; London: Penguin, 2002), p. 404. I amend Weaver's translation slightly.

4 Italo Svevo, *As a Man Grows Older*, translated by Beryl de Zoete (New York: New York Review Books, 2001), p. 102.

5 Italo Svevo, *Emilio's Carnival*, translated by Beth Archer Brombert (New Haven: Yale University Press, 2001), pp. 16, 117, 170.

6 Quoted in John Gatt-Rutter, *Italo Svevo* (Oxford: Oxford University Press, 1988), p. 163.

7 Gatt-Rutter, pp. 281, 297.

8 'The Story of the Nice Old Man and the Pretty Girl', trans. L. Collison-Morley, in Italo Svevo, *Short Sentimental Journey and Other Stories* (London: Secker & Warburg, 1967; volume 4 of the Uniform Edition), p. 81.

9 Quoted in Gatt-Rutter, p. 307.

10 In Weaver's translation the passage reads: 'Unlike other sicknesses, life . . . doesn't tolerate therapies.' (p. 435) Weaver consistently uses 'therapy' for Svevo's *cura*, which can mean either the process of being under cure or the end result, being cured. But sometimes 'cure' gets Svevo's meaning more exactly than 'therapy,' as here, or

in Zeno's vow to himself that he will recover from Dr S's *cura*.
11 Gatt-Rutter, p. 328.

2 Robert Walser

1 For instance, a police photograph is reproduced in Elio Fröhlich and Peter Hamm, eds., *Robert Walser: Leben und Werk* (Frankfurt a/Main: Insel Verlag, 1980).

2 Quoted in Katharina Kerr, ed., *Über Robert Walser* (Frankfurt a/Main: Suhrkamp, 1978), vol. 2, p. 13.

3 George C. Avery, *Inquiry and Testament* (Philadelphia: University of Pennsylvania Press, 1968), p. 6.

4 *Jakob von Gunten*, trans. Christopher Middleton (New York: New York Review Books, 1999), p. 3.

5 'Robert Walser', in *Selected Writings*, vol. 2, ed. Michael W. Jennings, Howard Eiland, and Gary Smith; trans. Rodney Livingstone et al. (Cambridge, Mass.: Harvard University Press, 1999), p. 259.

6 Quoted in Avery, *Inquiry and Testament*, p. 11.

7 Quoted in K.-M. Hinz and T. Horst, eds., *Robert Walser* (Frankfurt a/Main: Suhrkamp, 1991), p. 57.

8 Quoted in Werner Morlang, 'The Singular Bliss of the Pencil Method', *Review of Contemporary Fiction* 12/1 (1992), p. 96.

9 Quoted in Mark Harman (ed.), *Robert Walser Rediscovered* (Hanover and London: University Press of New England, 1985), p. 206.

10 Quoted in Idris Parry, *Hand to Mouth* (Manchester: Carcanet, 1981), p. 35.

11 Quoted in Peter Utz, ed., *Wärmende Fremde* (Bern: Peter Lang, 1994), p. 64; in Kerr, ed., *Über Robert Walser*, bd. 2, p. 22.

12 Quoted in Utz, ed., *Wärmende Fremde*, p. 74.

13 Quoted in Agnes Cardinal, *The Figure of Paradox in the Work of Robert Walser* (Stuttgart: Heinz, 1982), p. 39.

14 Quoted in Morlang, 'The Singular Bliss of the Pencil Method', p. 96.

15 *The Robber*, trans. Susan Bernofsky (University of Nebraska Press, 2000); *Jakob von Gunten*, trans. Christopher Middleton (see note 4 above).

16 Susan Bernowsky, 'Gelungene Einfälle', in Utz, ed., *Wärmende Fremde*, pp. 123–4.

17 Bernofsky, 'Gelungene Einfälle', p. 117.

18 Walser, *Gesammelte Werke*, ed. Jochen Greven (Frankfurt a/Main: Suhrkamp, 1978), bd. X, p. 323.

19 Kerr (ed.), *Über Robert Walser*, bd. 2, p. 12.

20 The original is in Fröhlic and Hamm, eds., *Robert Walser: Leben und Werk*, p. 279.

3 Robert Musil, *The Confusions of Young Törless*

1 Musil, *Diaries 1899–1941*, ed. Mark Mirsky, trans. Philip Payne (New York: Basic Books, 1998), p. 209.

2 Brecht quoted in Werner Mittenzwei, *Exil in der Schweiz* (Leipzig: Reclam, 1978), p. 19; Musil quoted in Ignazio Silone, 'Begegnungen mit Musil', in *Robert Musil: Studien zu seinem Werk*, ed. Karl Dinklage (Reinbek: Rowohlt, 1970), p. 355.

3 Quoted in Karl Dinklage, 'Musil's Definition des Mannes ohne Eigenschaften', in *Robert Musil: Studien zu seinem Werk*, p. 114.

4 Quoted in David S. Luft, *Robert Musil and the Crisis of European Culture 1880–1942* (Berkeley: University of California Press, 1980), p. 108.

5 *Diaries 1899–1941*, p. 465.

6 *The Confusions of Young Törless*, trans. Shaun Whiteside (London: Penguin, 2001), p. 157.

7 *The Man without Qualities*, trans. Sophie Wilkins (New York: Knopf, 1996; London: Picador, 1997), vol. 2, p. 826.

8 *Diaries 1899–1941*, p. 384.

4 Walter Benjamin, the Arcades Project

1 Walter Benjamin, *The Arcades Project*, trans. Howard Eiland and Kevin McLaughlin (Cambridge, Mass.: Harvard University Press, 1999), p. 948. Hereafter referred to as *AP*.

2 Walter Benjamin, *Selected Writings. Volume 1: 1913–1926*, ed. Marcus Bullock and Michael W. Jennings, trans. Rodney Livingstone, Stanley

Corngold, Edmund Jephcott, Harry Zohn (Cambridge, Mass.: Harvard University Press, 1996), p. 446. Hereafter referred to as *V1*.

3 Walter Benjamin, *Selected Writings. Volume 2: 1927–1934*, ed. Michael W. Jennings, Howard Eiland, and Gary Smith, trans. Rodney Livingstone et al. (Cambridge, Mass.: Harvard University Press, 1999), p. 473. Hereafter referred to as *V2*.

4 Quoted in Susan Buck-Morss, *The Dialectics of Seeing: Walter Benjamin and the Arcades Project* (Cambridge, Mass.: MIT Press, 1997), p. 21.

5 Letter to Martin Buber, in Walter Benjamin, *Correspondence 1910–1940*, ed. Gershom Scholem and Theodor W. Adorno, trans. Manfred Jacobson and Evelyn Jacobson (Chicago: University of Chicago Press, 1994), p. 313.

6 Quoted in Buck-Morss, p. 383.

7 Walter Benjamin, *Gesammelte Schriften*, 7 volumes, ed. Rolf Tiedemann and Hermann Schweppenhäuser (Frankfurt: Suhrkamp, 1972–89), vol. 3, p. 52; *V2*, p. 559.

8 'The Work of Art . . . ,' in *Illuminations*, ed. Hannah Arendt, trans. Harry Zohn (New York: Schocken, 1969; London; Jonathan Cape, 1970), p. 238.

9 'On Some Motifs in Baudelaire,' in *Illuminations*, p. 190.

10 Quoted in Momme Brodersen, *Walter Benjamin: A Biography*, trans. Malcolm R. Green and Ingrida Ligers (London and New York: Verso, 1996), p. 239.

11 Quoted in Buck-Morss, p. 220.

12 Letter of 1931, quoted in Gerhard Richter, *Walter Benjamin and the Corpus of Autobiography* (Detroit: Wayne State University Press, 2000), p. 31.

13 Quoted in Rainer Rochlitz, *The Disenchantment of Art: The Philosophy of Walter Benjamin*, trans. Jane Marie Todd (New York: Guilford Press, 1996), p. 133.

14 *AP*, p. 460; *The Origin of German Tragic Drama*, trans. John Osborne (London: New Left Books, 1998), p. 34.

15 Quoted in Buck-Morss, p. 228.

16 Quoted in Buck-Morss, p. 291.

17 See *VI*, p. 360, note 38.

18 *Illuminations*, p. 3.

5 Bruno Schulz

1 Bruno Schulz, letter to Andrzej Pleśniewicz, quoted in Czeslaw Z. Prokopcyk, ed., *Bruno Schulz: New Documents and Interpretations* (New York: Peter Lang, 1999), p. 101.

2 Jerzy Ficowski, *Regions of the Great Heresy: Bruno Schulz, A Biographical Portrait*, translated and edited by Theodosia Robertson (New York: W. W. Norton, 2002), p. 105.

3 Letter to Romana Halpern, August 1938, in *Collected Works of Bruno Schulz*, ed. Jerzy Ficowski (London: Picador, 1998), p. 442. Hereafter referred to as *CW*.

4 *Drohobycz, Drohobycz and Other Stories*, trans. Alicia Nitecki (New York: Penguin, 2002).

5 *The Street of Crocodiles*, trans. Celina Wieniewska, introduction by Jerzy Ficowski (New York: Penguin, 1977).

6 Bruno Schulz, *Drawings and Documents from the Collection of the Adam Mickiewicz Literary Museum* (Warsaw, 1992).

6 Joseph Roth, the stories

1 Quoted in William M. Johnston, *The Austrian Mind: An Intellectual and Social History, 1848–1938* (Berkeley and Los Angeles: University of California Press, 1972), p. 238.

2 Quoted in Sidney Rosenfeld, *Joseph Roth* (University of South Carolina Press, 2001), p. 45.

3 Quoted in Helmuth Nürnberger, *Joseph Roth* (Hamburg: Rowohlt, 1981), p. 38.

4 Quoted in Nürnberger, p. 15.

5 Quoted in Nürnberger, p. 104.

6 Quoted in Nürnberger, pp. 70, 74.

7 Quoted in Nürnberger, p. 119.

8 *The Collected Stories of Joseph Roth*, trans. Michael Hofmann (New York: W. W. Norton, 2001). Published in the UK as *Collected Shorter*

Fiction of Joseph Roth (London: Granta, 2001).

9 Quoted in David Bronsen, ed., *Joseph Roth und die Tradition* (Agora Verlag, 1975), p. 128.

7 Sándor Márai

1 Sándor Márai, *Embers*, English translation from the German of Christina Viragh by Carol Brown Janeway (New York: Knopf, 2001; London: Penguin, 2003), p. 42.

2 *Land, Land! . . . : Erinnerungen*, German translation from the Hungarian by Hans Skirecki (Munich: Piper, 2001), p. 114.

3 *Bekenntnisse eines Bürgers: Erinnerungen*, German translation from the Hungarian by Hans Skirecki (Munich: Piper, 2001), p. 310.

4 *Das Vermächtnis der Eszter*, German translation from the Hungarian by Christina Viragh (Munich: Piper, 2000).

5 Quoted in László Rónay, 'Biographische Chronologie', in Sándor Márai, *Land, Land! . . .* (Berlin: Oberbaum, 2000), vol. 2, p. 161.

6 *Der Wind kommt vom Westen: Amerikanische Reisebilder*, German translation from the Hungarian by Artur Saternus (Langen Müller, 1964).

7 Diary 1968–75, in *Tagebücher: Auszüge* (Berlin: Oberbaum, 2001), pp. 25–6.

8 *Bekenntnisse eines Bürgers*, pp. 323, 350.

9 English translation from the Hungarian by Albert Tezla (Budapest: Corvina / Central European University Press, 1996).

10 *Die Zeit*, 14 September 2000.

11 *Conversations in Bolzano* (London: Viking, 2004), *Casanova in Bolzano* (New York: Knopf, 2004). English translation from the Hungarian by George Szirtes.

8 Paul Celan and his translators

1 *Paul Celan, Nelly Sachs: Correspondence*, trans. Christopher Clark (Riverdale-on-Hudson: Sheep Meadow Press, 1995), p. 17.

2 John Felstiner, *Paul Celan: Poet, Survivor, Jew* (New York: W. W. Norton, 1995), pp. 253, 181.

3 *Selected Poems and Prose of Paul Celan*, trans. John Felstiner (New York:

W. W. Norton, 2000), p. 329. Hereafter referred to as *SPP*.

4 Hans-Georg Gadamer, 'Epilogue', in *Gadamer on Celan*, translated and edited by Richard Heinemann and Bruce Krajewski (Albany: State University of New York Press, 1997), p. 142.

5 Introduction, *Poems of Paul Celan* (London: Anvil Press, 1988), p. 18.

6 Hans Egon Holthusen, quoted in Felstiner, p. 79.

7 Paul Celan, *Collected Prose*, trans. Rosemary Waldrop (Riverdale: Sheep Meadow Press, 1986), p. 16.

8 Theodor Adorno, 'Cultural Criticism and Society', in *Prisms*, trans. Samuel and Shierry Weber (London: Spearman, 1967), p. 34.

9 Felstiner, p. 161. A word of caution is called for. We have only Celan's account of the meeting. What Celan reports does not square with what Buber had written seven years earlier: 'They [our persecutors] have so radically removed themselves from the human sphere . . . that not even hatred, much less an overcoming of hatred, was able to arise in me. And what am I that I could presume to "forgive"!' Quoted in Maurice Friedman, 'Paul Celan and Martin Buber', *Religion and Literature* 29/1 (1997), p. 46.

10 *SPP*, p. 245; *Glottal Stop: 101 Poems*, trans. Nikolai Popov & Heather McHugh (Hanover and London: Wesleyan University Press, 2000), p. 19.

11 Quoted in Felstiner, p. 287.

12 *Poetry as Experience*, trans. Andrea Tarnowski (Stanford: Stanford University Press, 1999), pp. 38, 122. Lacoue-Labarthe's book was first published in 1986.

13 Paul Celan, *Breathturn* (Los Angeles: Sun & Moon Press, 1995), *Threadsuns* (Los Angeles: Sun & Moon Press, 2000), both trans. Pierre Joris.

9 Günter Grass and the *Wilhelm Gustloff*

1 Günter Grass, *Crabwalk*, trans. Krishna Winston (New York: Harcourt, 2003), p. 25.

2 *Cat and Mouse and Other Writings*, ed. A. Leslie Willson, trans. Ralph Manheim (New York: Continuum, 1994), p. 23.

3 *The Rat*, trans. Ralph Manheim (London: Secker, 1987), p. 63.

4 *The Call of the Toad*, trans. Ralph Manheim (New York: Harcourt Brace, 1992).

10 W. G. Sebald, *After Nature*

1 *The Emigrants*, trans. Michael Hulse (New York: New Directions, 1996; London: Vintage, 2002).

2 *Vertigo*, trans. Michael Hulse (New York: New Directions, 2000; London: Vintage, 2002).

3 *Unheimliche Heimat: Essays zur österreichischen Literatur* (Salzburg & Wien: Residenz, 1991).

4 *The Rings of Saturn*, trans. Michael Hulse (New York: New Directions, 1998; London: Vintage, 2002), p. 5.

5 *Austerlitz*, trans. Anthea Bell (New York: Random House, 2001; London: Penguin, 2002).

6 *For Years Now* (London: Short Books, 2001).

7 *After Nature*, trans. Michael Hamburger (New York: Random House, 2002; London: Penguin, 2004).

8 *On the Natural History of Destruction*, trans. Anthea Bell (New York: Random House, 2003).

11 Hugo Claus, poet

1 'Interview', in Hugo Claus, *Gedichten 1948–2004* (Amsterdam: Besige Bij, 2004), vol. 2, pp. 501-3.

2 'Chicago', in *Gedichten 1948–2004*, vol. 1, p. 269.

12 Graham Greene, *Brighton Rock*

1 *Brighton Rock* (New York: Penguin, 2004; London: Vintage, 2004), p. 261.

2 Marie-Françoise Allain, *The Other Man: Conversations with Graham Greene* (New York: Simon and Schuster, 1983), p. 125.

3 'Henry James: The Private Universe' (1936), in *Collected Essays* (Harmondsworth: Penguin, 1970), p. 34.

4 'François Mauriac' (1945), in *Collected Essays*, p. 91.

5 In 1926 'I became convinced of the probable existence of something

we call God,' wrote Greene. *A Sort of Life* (London: Bodley Head, 1971), p. 165.

6 Review of *The Heart of the Matter*, in *Collected Essays*, vol. 4 (London: Secker and Warburg, 1968), p. 441.

13 Samuel Beckett, the short fiction

1 I pass over the early short fiction: the stories making up *More Pricks than Kicks*, written between 1931 and 1933, and the handful of other pieces of short fiction from the same period. Of these one can fairly say that they would not be worth preserving had they not been written by Beckett. Their interest lies in the hints they give or fail to give of the work that is to follow.

2 Quoted in James Knowlson, *Damned to Fame: The Life of Samuel Beckett* (New York: Simon & Schuster, 1996; London: Bloomsbury, 1996), p. 601.

14 Walt Whitman

1 Walt Whitman, *Memoranda During the War*, ed. Peter Coviello (Oxford University Press, 2004), pp. 167–8.

2 Quoted in Paul Zweig, *Walt Whitman: The Making of the Poet* (New York: Basic Books, 1984), p. 339.

3 *Memoranda*, p. xxxviii.

4 *Leaves of Grass: Reader's Edition*, ed. Harold W. Blodgett and Sculley Bradley (New York: New York University Press, 1965), p. 751. Hereafter referred to as *LoG*.

5 Justin Kaplan, *Walt Whitman: A Life* (New York: Simon & Schuster, 1980), pp. 313, 316.

6 Quoted in Kaplan, p. 47.

7 *Leaves of Grass: 150th Anniversary Edition*, ed. and with an afterword by David S. Reynolds (New York: Oxford University Press, 2005), p. 101.

8 David S. Reynolds, *Walt Whitman* (New York: Oxford University Press, 2005), p. 118.

9 Jerome Loving, *Walt Whitman: The Song of Himself* (Berkeley and Los

Angeles: University of California, 1999), pp. 297, 299, 376.

10 Reynolds, *Walt Whitman*, p. 101.

11 Introduction to *Memoranda*, pp. xxxvi–xxxvii.

12 Jonathan Ned Katz, *The Invention of Heterosexuality* (New York: Dutton, 1995), pp. 43–47.

13 Quoted in Kaplan, p. 133.

14 *Memoranda*, p. 126.

15 Whitman, quoted in Kaplan, p. 337.

16 Loving, p. 259; Kaplan, p. 329.

17 Zweig, p. 343.

18 Reynolds, ed., p. 17; *LoG*, p. 52.

19 Reynolds, *Walt Whitman*, p. 117.

15 William Faulkner and his biographers

1 Quoted in Joseph Blotner, *Faulkner: A Biography*, one-volume edition (New York: Random House, 1984), p. 570.

2 Frederick R. Karl, *William Faulkner: American Writer* (London: Faber, 1989), p. 523.

3 Jay Parini, *One Matchless Time: A Life of William Faulkner* (New York: HarperCollins, 2004), pp. 20, 79, 141, 145. See also Karl, p. 213.

4 Quoted in Blotner, p. 106.

5 Quoted in Karl, p. 757.

6 Quinn quoted in Parini, p. 271; Brooks quoted in Parini, p. 292.

7 Quoted in Blotner, p. 611.

8 Quoted in Blotner, p. 599.

9 *Go Down, Moses* (Harmondsworth: Penguin, 1960), p. 227.

10 Quoted in Blotner, p. 501.

11 *John Steinbeck: A Biography* (London: Heinemann, 1994); *Robert Frost: A Life* (New York: Holt, 1999); *The Last Station: A Novel of Tolstoy's Last Year* (New York: Holt, 1990); *Benjamin's Crossing: A Novel* (New York: Holt, 1997).

12 *Mosquitoes* (London: Chatto & Windus, 1964), p. 209.

13 Commins quoted in Karl, p. 844; June Faulkner quoted in Parini, p. 251.

16 Saul Bellow, the early novels

1 Saul Bellow, *Novels 1944–53* (New York: Library of America, 2003).
2 *The Education of Henry Adams* (New York: Modern Library, 1931), p. 343.
3 1979 interview, in *Conversations with Saul Bellow*, ed. Gloria L. Cronin and Ben Siegel (Jackson: University of Mississippi Press, 1994), p. 161.

18 Philip Roth, *The Plot Against America*

1 Philip Roth, *Operation Shylock: A Confession* (London: Cape, 1993), p. 399.
2 Philip Roth, *The Plot Against America* (New York: Houghton Mifflin, 2004), p. 365.
3 Issue dated September 19, 2004, p. 11.
4 Philip Roth, *American Pastoral* (New York: Houghton Mifflin, 1997), p. 287.
5 Philip Roth, *The Facts: A Novelist's Autobiography* (1988) (London: Cape, 1989), p. 169.
6 Philip Roth, *The Human Stain* (2000) (New York: Vintage, 2001), p. 132.
7 *Operation Shylock*, p. 113.

19 Nadine Gordimer

1 'Some are Born to Sweet Delight', in *Jump and Other Stories* (London: Bloomsbury, 1991), pp. 67–88.
2 *The Pickup* (New York: Penguin, 2001).
3 Albert Camus, 'The Adulterous Woman', in *Exile and the Kingdom* (1957), trans. Justin O'Brien (Harmondsworth: Penguin 1962), pp. 9–29.
4 *Loot and Other Stories* (New York: Farrar, Straus, Giroux, 2003), p. 32.
5 *What is Literature?*, trans. Bernard Frechtman (London: Methuen, 1967), p.14.
6 Cf. 'A Writer's Freedom' (1975), 'Living in the Interregnum' (1982), and 'The Essential Gesture' (1984) in *The Essential Gesture*, ed. Stephen Clingman (Cape Town: David Philip, 1988); 'References: The Codes

of Culture' (1989) in *Living in Hope and History: Notes from Our Century* (London: Bloomsbury, 1999).

20 Gabriel García Márquez, *Memories of My Melancholy Whores*

1 Gabriel García Márquez, *Love in the Time of Cholera*, translated Edith Grossman (New York: Penguin, 1988), p. 295.

2 Gabriel García Márquez, *Memories of My Melancholy Whores*, trans. Edith Grossman (New York: Knopf, 2005).

3 Roman Jakobson, 'Linguistics and Poetics', in *Essays on the Language of Literature*, ed. Seymour Chatman and Samuel R. Levin (Boston: Houghton Mifflin, 1967), p. 316.

4 Miguel Cervantes, *Don Quixote*, trans. Edith Grossman (London: Secker & Warburg, 2004), p. 430.

5 Gabriel García Márquez, *Living to Tell the Tale*, trans. Edith Grossman (New York: Knopf, 2003), p. 395.

6 Gabriel García Márquez, *Strange Pilgrims: Twelve Stories*, trans. Edith Grossman (London: Cape, 1993), pp. 54–61.

7 Yasunari Kawabata, *The House of the Sleeping Beauties and Other Stories*, translated Edward G. Seidensticker (London: Quadriga Press, 1969), p. 39.

21 V. S. Naipaul, *Half a Life*

1 W. Somerset Maugham, *Points of View* (London: Heinemann, 1958), p. 58.

2 *The Razor's Edge* (London: Heinemann, 1944), pp. 267, 271, 272.

3 *Half a Life: A Novel* (New York: Knopf, 2001; London: Picador, 2002).

4 *An Area of Darkness* (London: Deutsch, 1964), p. 77.

5 Naipaul, *The Enigma of Arrival* (New York: Vintage, 1987; London: Picador, 2002), p. 135.

6 Quoted in Ashis Nandy, *The Intimate Enemy* (Delhi: Oxford University Press, 1983), p. 74.

7 The remarkably frank interviews collected in *Conversations with V. S. Naipaul*, edited by Feroza Jussawalla (Jackson: University of Mississippi Press, 1997), suggest that the story of Willie Chandran in London

has a strong autobiographical component. See particularly the 1994 interview with Stephen Schiff.

8 Anita Desai, *Fasting, Feasting* (Boston: Houghton Mifflin, 2000; London: Vintage, 2000).

9 Nandy, *The Intimate Enemy*, p. 47.

Life & Times of Michael K
In a South Africa that is collapsing under the pressures of civil strife, Michael K. sets out to take his ailing mother back to her rural home. A life-affirming novel that goes to the center of human experience—the need for an interior, spiritual life; for some connections to the world in which we live; and for purity of vision. "A major work of crystalline intensity."

—*Los Angeles Times*
ISBN 978-0-14-007448-2

The Master of Petersburg
"A fascinating study of the dark mysteries of creativity, grief, relationships between fathers and sons, and of the great Russian themes of love and death." —*The Wall Street Journal*
ISBN 978-0-14-023810-5

Slow Man
When photographer Paul Rayment loses his leg in a bicycle accident, he is forced to reexamine how he has lived his life. Through Paul's story, Coetzee addresses questions that define us all: What does it mean to do good? What in our lives is ultimately meaningful? How do we define the place we call "home"? In his clear and uncompromising voice, Coetzee struggles with these issues and offers a story that will dazzle the reader on every page.
ISBN 978-0-14-303789-7

Waiting for the Barbarians
For decades the Magistrate has been a loyal servant of the Empire, running the affairs of a tiny frontier settlement and ignoring the impending war with the barbarians. When interrogation experts arrive, however, he witnesses the Empire's cruel and unjust treatment of prisoners of war. Jolted into sympathy for their victims, he commits a quixotic act of rebellion that brands him an enemy of the state. "A real literary event."

—Irving Howe, *The New York Times Book Review*
ISBN 978-0-14-006110-9
ISBN 978-0-14-028335-8 (Great Books of the 20th Century Edition)

Youth
Scenes from Provincial Life II
J. M. Coetzee tells of his artistic and sexual coming of age in a remarkable portrait of a consciousness, isolated and adrift, turning in on itself. "A delight to read: it will make you angry, amused, scornful and sympathetic by turns."

—*San Francisco Chronicle*
ISBN 978-0-14-200200-1

Available in Hardcover from Viking

Diary of a Bad Year
In this ingenious work of fiction, J. M. Coetzee takes on the world of politics and explores the role of the writer in our times. Aging author "Señor C" is writing a book on his thoughts about the world, encompassing everything from George W. Bush to the current state of music. But when he hires a beautiful young woman to type his manuscript, the relationship that develops has a profound effect on both their lives. ISBN 978-0-670-01875-8